Innovative Design Thinking Approaches in Software Engineering

José Alfonso Aguilar-Calderón
Universidad Autónoma de Sinaloa, Mexico

Carolina Tripp-Barba
Universidad Autónoma de Sinaloa, Mexico

IGI Global
Scientific Publishing
Publishing Tomorrow's Research Today

Vice President of Editorial	Melissa Wagner
Director of Acquisitions	Mikaela Felty
Director of Book Development	Jocelynn Hessler
Production Manager	Mike Brehm
Cover Design	Jose Rosado

Published in the United States of America by
IGI Global Scientific Publishing
701 East Chocolate Avenue
Hershey, PA, 17033, USA
Tel: 717-533-8845
Fax: 717-533-7115
Website: https://www.igi-global.com E-mail: cust@igi-global.com

Library of Congress Cataloging-in-Publication Data

Names: Aguilar-Calderón, Jose Alfonso, 1983- editor | Tripp-Barba, Carolina, 1984- editor
Title: Innovative design thinking approaches in software engineering / edited by José Alfonso Aguilar-Calderón, Carolina Tripp-Barba.
Description: Hershey, PA : IGI Global Scientific Publishing, [2025] | Includes bibliographical references and index. | Summary: "The objective of the book is to clarify how design thinking can be effectively integrated into the software engineering process to enhance innovation, user satisfaction, and overall project success"-- Provided by publisher.

Identifiers: LCCN 2025000171 (print) | LCCN 2025000172 (ebook) | ISBN 9798369395318 h/c | ISBN 9798369395325 s/c | ISBN 9798369395332 ebook
Subjects: LCSH: Software engineering--Design | Software engineering--Technological innovations
Classification: LCC QA76.758 .I56 2025 (print) | LCC QA76.758 (ebook)
LC record available at https://lccn.loc.gov/2025000171
LC ebook record available at https://lccn.loc.gov/2025000172

British Cataloguing in Publication Data
A Cataloguing in Publication record for this book is available from the British Library.

Editorial Advisory Board

Table of Contents

Detailed Table of Contents

This chapter examines how Design Thinking is revolutionizing software engineering by shifting the focus from purely technical execution to human-centered innovation. It presents Design Thinking as a methodology grounded in empathy, creativity, iterative prototyping, and interdisciplinary collaboration. The chapter traces its evolution from design and architecture to its current role in software development, highlighting its integration with Agile, UX, and HCI practices. Through practical principles and real-world case studies in sectors like e-commerce, healthcare, and EdTech, it demonstrates that the creation of software that is not only functional but also intuitive, inclusive, and impactful. Ethical considerations such as accessibility, privacy, and sustainability are also addressed, emphasizing the responsibility of software engineers to design with purpose. Challenges related to implementation, such as resistance to change, resource constraints, and scaling, are critically analyzed

This chapter explores the integration of AI techniques into design thinking tools for software engineering, aiming to enhance problem-solving, innovation, and user-centered development processes. The study focuses on software engineers, designers, and technology-driven organizations seeking to optimize software development workflows through AI-powered design thinking. The methodological approach includes a comprehensive review of existing AI applications in design thinking, an analysis of AI-enhanced prototyping and ideation tools, and case studies

The ongoing democratization of software development, fueled by the proliferation of low-code/no-code platforms and AI-assisted tools, is fundamentally transforming the technological landscape by enabling non-technical citizen developers to create functional applications with minimal coding expertise. As organizations increasingly adopt these accessible development approaches to accelerate digital transformation, critical questions emerge regarding the potential erosion of established design principles, including user-centered methodologies and rigorous usability testing. This chapter systematically examines both the opportunities and challenges presented by this democratization movement, analyzing its impact on software quality, maintainability, and user experience. The discussion culminates in practical recommendations for balancing accessibility with excellence, ensuring that democratized software ecosystems produce solutions that are not only rapidly deployable but also robust, scalable, and genuinely user-centric in an increasingly competitive digital economy

The integration of Legal Design Thinking into software engineering represents a transformative shift in the development of legal technology. By applying user-centered design principles, this approach enhances legal accessibility, operational efficiency, and client satisfaction. This chapter systematically reviews the core tenets of Legal

Preface

In an era marked by rapid technological evolution and an ever-expanding digital landscape, software engineering faces unprecedented challenges and opportunities. This book, *Innovative Design Thinking Approaches in Software Engineering*, emerges as a timely response to the urgent need for methodologies that prioritize creativity, empathy, and user-centered design. Rooted in the Design Thinking paradigm, this collection explores how software engineering can evolve into a more inclusive, intuitive, and innovative discipline.

OVERVIEW OF THE SUBJECT MATTER

Design Thinking (DT) is a human-centered methodology for creative problem-solving. It empowers interdisciplinary teams to generate ideas, prototype solutions, and iteratively refine innovations based on user feedback. While traditionally associated with product and industrial design, DT has found fertile ground in software engineering, where user needs often intersect with complex technical requirements. This book assembles pioneering research and practice-based insights to show how DT can reshape the software development life cycle, from requirements elicitation to deployment and maintenance.

Where the Topic Fits in the World Today

The global software industry is shifting toward agile, adaptive, and user-focused approaches. With users expecting more seamless, accessible, and aesthetically pleasing digital experiences, developers and engineers are compelled to adopt methodologies that emphasize empathy and iterative refinement. Design Thinking meets this need by providing a framework that bridges technical expertise with deep user insight. As digital products become more integral to legal systems, education, health, entertainment, and civic life, the importance of human-centered engineering cannot be overstated. This book contributes to that mission.

Description of the Target Audience

This book is intended for a diverse yet specialized audience. It caters to:

- **Software Engineers and Developers** seeking innovative methods to enhance their practice
- **Researchers and Academics** exploring interdisciplinary applications of Design Thinking
- **Educators and Trainers** aiming to instill creativity and empathy in technical education
- **LegalTech and CivicTech Innovators** applying user-centered design in domain-specific software
- **Graduate and Postgraduate Students** studying software engineering, interaction design, or innovation methodologies

CHAPTER DESCRIPTIONS

Chapter 1: Revolutionizing Software Engineering - Innovative Design Thinking Approaches

The chapter titled "Revolutionizing Software Engineering: Innovative Design Thinking Approaches" provides a comprehensive exploration of how Design Thinking is reshaping the landscape of software engineering by emphasizing empathy, creativity, and human-centered problem-solving. The book positions Design Thinking as a transformative methodology that shifts software development from rigid, specification-driven practices to dynamic, user-focused innovation. It begins by redefining software engineering through empathy-driven development, highlighting how understanding users' needs and iteratively testing solutions lead to meaningful software experiences. The historical evolution of Design Thinking in the industry is traced from function-first software in the 1970s to today's collaborative, inclusive, and AI-enhanced design ecosystems, emphasizing a growing commitment to usability and user inclusion.

The key principles of Design Thinking in software are detailed, including empathy for users, clear problem definition, collaborative ideation, rapid prototyping, and continuous testing. These practices foster solutions that are not only functional but resonate with users emotionally and practically. The book explains how Design

Thinking integrates seamlessly with User-Centered Design (UCD) and Human-Computer Interaction (HCI), enhancing usability, accessibility, and iterative development through tools like journey maps, personas, and prototyping. Case studies from diverse sectors—e-commerce, healthcare, renewable energy, education, and DevOps—illustrate Design Thinking's tangible benefits, from improving checkout flows and scheduling systems to making platforms more accessible and intuitive.

The chapter also confronts the practical and organizational challenges of adopting Design Thinking. It outlines obstacles such as cultural resistance, resource constraints, methodological conflicts, stakeholder skepticism, and scalability issues. A comparative analysis is offered between Design Thinking and other methodologies like Agile, Lean, and Waterfall, highlighting how these can be blended to create hybrid approaches that suit varied project contexts. Ethical considerations form a core theme, with the text advocating for inclusive design, privacy protection, bias mitigation, and responsible innovation. Design Thinking is portrayed not just as a creative process, but as an ethical framework for developing technology that prioritizes human values.

A chapter on deep analysis emphasizes the importance of rigorous user research and synthesis, combining qualitative insights with data to define core problems and prototype solutions that truly address user pain points. The book's vision of the future of Design Thinking involves AI as a co-creator, cross-functional collaboration as standard practice, ethical foresight, inclusive design, and emerging tools like digital twins and sustainable development models. In conclusion, the text asserts that Design Thinking is not just a methodology but a mindset shift. It empowers software engineers to become architects of digital experiences that are ethical, inclusive, and deeply responsive to human needs—offering a path forward for building impactful technology in an increasingly complex world.

Chapter 2: Leveraging Artificial Intelligence Techniques in Design Thinking Tools for Software Engineering

This chapter, titled "Leveraging Artificial Intelligence Techniques in Design Thinking Tools for Software Engineering", provides an in-depth exploration of how artificial intelligence (AI) is reshaping design thinking within the realm of modern software engineering. It begins by framing the necessity of integrating user-centric methodologies like design thinking into increasingly complex and fast-paced development environments. Traditional methods such as Waterfall and even Agile often fail to address rapidly evolving user requirements with the same degree of adaptability and empathy that design thinking offers. However, the chapter acknowledges the limitations of traditional design thinking, particularly in terms of scalability and reliance on subjective feedback. This sets the stage for AI as a crucial enabler, helping overcome these challenges by automating repetitive tasks, enhancing collaboration, and delivering data-driven insights.

This text emphasizes the synergy between design thinking and AI, introducing tools such as Tabnine, Cody, Stepsize, Mintify, Bugasura, Mutable, Codeium, and Grit. These tools improve everything from code generation and debugging to tracking technical debt and supporting distributed teams. Real-world case studies illustrate these benefits: one company increased delivery speed and reduced bugs by integrating Tabnine, while another used Stepsize to identify and resolve technical debt efficiently. The integration of AI into the design process allows for more rapid prototyping, faster iteration, and better-informed decision-making, helping teams create innovative and high-quality software solutions. Despite the advantages, the chapter also discusses the challenges of AI adoption. Key concerns include over-automation, ethical risks such as bias and privacy issues, and resistance from teams wary of changing established workflows. The text stresses the importance of maintaining a balance between automation and human creativity. AI should enhance, not replace, the intuitive and empathetic elements central to design thinking. Best practices recommended include ongoing training, careful selection of AI tools tailored to team needs, and clear boundaries between automated tasks and human oversight.

Looking ahead, the chapter outlines emerging trends in AI-enhanced design thinking, such as generative design, VR-based prototyping, predictive UX, and self-learning systems. It calls for further research into scaling AI-augmented design thinking across large teams and ensuring ethical, inclusive design outcomes. In conclusion, the chapter argues that AI is a transformative force that can amplify the strengths of design thinking, provided it is implemented with strategic intent, ethical mindfulness, and a commitment to preserving the human-centered foundations of software innovation.

Chapter 3: FusionFlow: A Software Development Approach in the Era of Design Thinking and AI

The chapter titled "FusionFlow: A Software Development Approach in the Era of Design Thinking and Artificial Intelligence" introduces an innovative and modern methodology called FusionFlow, which integrates traditional software development practices with DT and AI to meet the evolving demands of digital transformation. It begins with a historical overview of software development methodologies—from the early days of manual coding to modern paradigms like Agile and DevOps—and identifies limitations in traditional approaches, such as rigid requirements, limited user engagement, siloed teams, and slow iteration cycles. These shortcomings highlight the need for a more adaptive, user-centric, and innovative methodology.

Design Thinking is introduced as a problem-solving methodology that emphasizes empathy, creativity, and iterative testing. The chapter details the evolution of DT and its application in software development, identifying its strengths in fostering innovation, improving user experience, and supporting rapid prototyping. In parallel, the text discusses how AI technologies—such as machine learning, natural language processing, and code generation tools—are revolutionizing software development by enhancing automation, reducing errors, and enabling faster decision-making.

The core contribution of the chapter is the introduction of the FusionFlow model. FusionFlow represents a fusion of traditional software processes, DT principles, and AI technologies, offering a flexible and iterative framework for building user-centric software efficiently. The model is structured into phases: discovery and requirements gathering, prototyping, development, testing, deployment, and continuous improvement. Each phase is designed to be adaptive, collaborative, and driven by user feedback. Notably, the model promotes the use of AI tools to automate repetitive tasks and enhance productivity, while leveraging DT to ensure solutions are deeply aligned with user needs. Key characteristics of FusionFlow include a focus on innovation, user-centered design, iterative development, automation, and cross-functional collaboration. The model supports real-time feedback loops, facilitates seamless integration of AI and DT, and encourages continuous improvement. A comparative analysis between DT and traditional Software Development Life Cycle (SDLC) methodologies is also provided, highlighting the enhanced flexibility, speed, and user engagement offered by FusionFlow.

The chapter concludes with a discussion of the benefits of FusionFlow, including reduced development time, cost savings, improved user satisfaction, and enhanced business value. It references empirical studies and industry reports—such as IBM's Design Thinking impact analysis—to substantiate claims of efficiency and profitability. Future research directions are proposed, including the development of metrics to evaluate FusionFlow and its application across various domains.

Chapter 4: Empathy-Driven Development: Integrating Design Thinking into Next-Gen Software Engineering

The chapter titled "Empathy-Driven Development: Integrating Design Thinking into Next-Gen Software Engineering" presents a comprehensive and transformative approach to software engineering, emphasizing empathy as a foundational principle throughout the software development lifecycle. It advocates for a shift from traditional development—focused mainly on functionality and efficiency—to a more human-centric methodology that deeply considers users' emotional, cognitive, and experiential needs. The chapter argues that design thinking, which prioritizes user empathy, creativity, and iterative development, is critical in building software that is not only technically robust but also engaging, inclusive, and ethically responsible.

The chapter begins by defining empathy-driven development and its benefits, such as improved user trust and satisfaction. It discusses practical techniques including collaborative prototyping, feedback loops, and user testing that bring empathy into real software workflows. Specific emphasis is placed on adapting these methods to emerging technologies like AI and Internet of Things, where understanding diverse user experiences becomes more critical. Through real-world examples from healthcare, education, and finance, the chapter demonstrates how empathetic design decisions lead to better user outcomes and competitive advantages.

A key section examines the integration of empathy into requirements engineering through tools like empathy mapping, user personas, and direct user interaction. These methods help uncover not just functional requirements, but also psychological and emotional needs, ultimately resulting in more personalized and effective software. Case studies from companies like Airbnb and Slack illustrate how addressing users' deeper motivations led to game-changing innovations and loyal user bases. The chapter also delves into ideation and innovation, highlighting tools such as mind mapping and collaborative brainstorming as means to unlock creativity. These techniques are illustrated with success stories from Spotify and Trello, showing how user-centered brainstorming sessions led to standout features. Rapid prototyping is presented as a crucial complement, enabling quick testing, refinement, and user validation through tools like Figma and InVision. Case studies from Uber and Instagram reinforce the importance of iterative feedback in delivering polished, user-aligned products. Empathetic user testing is explored as a strategy for integrating user feedback at every stage of development—from early concept to post-launch updates. Examples from Airbnb and Intuit show how continuous feedback loops improve product relevance and drive innovation. Challenges such as scope creep and feedback synthesis are acknowledged, with proposed solutions like structured analysis and inclusive user sampling.

Balancing creativity with engineering rigor is addressed, particularly the challenges of blending design thinking with structured engineering methodologies. The chapter suggests that agile frameworks are ideal for this integration, and provides examples like Google's Material Design to demonstrate successful collaboration between creative and technical teams. The text also explores the relevance of empathy in AI and IoT development, advocating for user-focused interfaces, ethical transparency, and contextual understanding. Examples include autonomous vehicles and smart thermostats that adapt to user needs while promoting trust and simplicity.

Empathy is further positioned as a key success factor in agile and lean methodologies. It enhances responsiveness to change, minimizes unnecessary features, and improves team collaboration. The evolution of products like Slack and Spotify is cited to show how empathy enables agile responsiveness and lean efficiency without compromising user value.

Finally, the chapter presents empathy-driven software development as essential for the future of technology. It ensures that software is not only functionally effective but also meaningful, ethical, and responsive to human diversity. With the rise of AI, IoT, and immersive technologies, empathy is no longer optional but a strategic imperative for innovation and social impact in software engineering.

Chapter 5: The Democratization of Software Development and Design Thinking: Governing Design Quality in Citizen Software Development

This chapter investigates how the rise of citizen development—enabled by low-code/no-code platforms and artificial intelligence—is reshaping the software development landscape. As software creation becomes accessible to individuals without formal training, known as citizen developers, organizations are witnessing a shift in roles, methodologies, and expectations. While this democratization empowers a broader audience to develop solutions rapidly and at reduced cost, it also introduces challenges in maintaining design quality, user empathy, and ethical oversight. The chapter emphasizes that as development becomes faster and more agile, critical phases of Design Thinking—such as empathizing with users, defining the problem, ideating, prototyping, and testing—are often overlooked or poorly executed. This results in products that may fail to meet user needs, suffer from usability issues, or reflect poorly considered design decisions.

The chapter also discusses organizational opportunities and risks associated with citizen development. Businesses, governments, startups, and research institutes can benefit from faster innovation and broader participation. However, without clear governance, design literacy, and oversight, there is a risk of fragmented systems, reduced usability, and inconsistency in software quality. Embedding Design Thinking effectively in citizen development requires cultural changes, stakeholder buy-in, and the development of centralized resources that support inclusive, user-focused innovation. Furthermore, the chapter explores the transformative potential of artificial intelligence in this context. AI can enhance every stage of Design Thinking—from generating user personas and ideating solutions to prototyping and testing—by offering intelligent suggestions, automating design tasks, and analyzing user feedback. However, the integration of AI brings ethical concerns, such as reinforcing biases, reducing human judgment, and increasing environmental impact due to energy-intensive processes. To mitigate these risks, organizations must implement AI responsibly, combining automated support with human oversight, critical evaluation, and ongoing training. Despite the capabilities of citizen developers and AI-powered platforms, collaboration remains essential. The chapter emphasizes the value of cross-functional teams and "creative abrasion," where differing perspectives lead to better, more innovative outcomes. Developers, designers, stakeholders, and users all play distinct but complementary roles in shaping successful software. When these voices are absent, software risks becoming functionally sufficient but lacking in relevance, usability, or impact.

The chapter argues for a balanced model that integrates the speed and accessibility of citizen development with the rigor and user-centered ethos of Design Thinking. Tools and platforms alone are insufficient. They must be accompanied by mentorship, standardized resources, and strategic involvement from professional designers. This approach ensures that citizen development becomes not just a trend, but a sustainable and inclusive mode of digital innovation—one that values empathy, creativity, and human experience as much as efficiency and scale.

Chapter 6: Legal Design Thinking in Software Engineering: A Review of User-Centered Innovations in Legal Technology

The chapter titled "Legal Design Thinking in Software Engineering: A Review of User-Centered Innovations in Legal Technology " presents a detailed exploration of how Legal Design Thinking (LDT)—an adaptation of traditional design thinking—can transform the development of legal technologies by prioritizing empathy, accessibility, and user-centric innovation. As digital transformation reshapes legal practices, LDT emerges as a necessary methodology to bridge the complexity of legal systems with the need for more transparent, intuitive, and equitable legal services.

The chapter begins by grounding LDT in the core principles of empathy, ideation, prototyping, and iterative testing, explaining how these design thinking elements are reimagined for the legal context. Empathy helps uncover the real needs of legal users, ideation fosters collaborative innovation, prototyping enables tangible development of tools, and iterative testing ensures continuous refinement. These principles are then shown in action through real-world applications aimed at improving client engagement, democratizing access to justice, and streamlining legal workflows. By examining software solutions that operationalize LDT—such as Juro, LawGeex, DoNotPay, and LegalZoom—the chapter illustrates how user-centered design simplifies complex legal processes and enhances service delivery. These tools improve legal document comprehension, automate routine tasks, and make justice more accessible for underserved communities. Platforms like Casetext, Modria, and

ROSS Intelligence demonstrate how AI and legal tech can combine with design thinking to boost research efficiency, resolve disputes, and personalize services.

The chapter also explores challenges in integrating LDT with software engineering, including technical hurdles, ethical concerns, and regulatory compliance. It addresses the difficulty of translating legal reasoning into usable software, the risks of AI bias, and the need for clear, accessible interfaces in multilingual environments. Still, opportunities abound—particularly in AI-driven automation, blockchain-based transparency, and collaborative, interdisciplinary innovation between legal professionals, designers, and technologists.

Success stories reinforce the value of LDT: LawGeex transformed contract review with AI; Law for All expanded access to justice in South Africa; Ravn automated privilege analysis; Deloitte Legal enhanced client services through empathy-driven design; and projects like Justice Innovation and Pretutela simplified dispute resolution and legal filing. Creative initiatives such as the Escazú Agreement comic for Brazil's Chiquitano people highlight how visual law and co-design can make legal content culturally and contextually inclusive.

The chapter argues that Legal Design Thinking is not merely a trend but a strategic and ethical framework essential for modernizing legal systems. It calls for future research into AI personalization, standardized evaluation metrics for design-centric legal tools, and institutional frameworks that support interdisciplinary collaboration. Ultimately, the integration of LDT with software engineering is positioned as a transformative approach to making legal services more efficient, accessible, and just in the digital age.

Chapter 7: Fostering Creativity in Agile Education—A Comparative Study of Students and Software Practitioners

The chapter presents a comprehensive exploration of how gamified learning methods can be used to teach agile methodologies while simultaneously enhancing creativity among students and software development practitioners. Central to the study is the use of a specially developed educational resource, DesignScrum, which integrates Scrum principles with Design Thinking techniques in a game-based learning environment. The study investigates how different demographics—ranging from middle-grade students to senior software practitioners—perceive and benefit from this approach, analyzing their understanding of agile concepts, enhancement of creativity, motivation, and user experience.

The study involved six distinct experiments with 173 participants grouped by education level and professional experience. Each group engaged with the DesignScrum resource, completed pre- and post-intervention surveys, and underwent observational and expert evaluation. Results revealed that practitioners generally showed stronger understanding of agile concepts, driven by their real-world experience, while university-level students displayed the greatest creative potential. Interestingly, creativity appeared to decline with professional experience, likely due to increasing focus on operational efficiency and reduced opportunities for experimental thinking in real-world environments.

Gamification was widely appreciated across all groups, though its appeal slightly diminished among more experienced professionals. Participants favored gamified learning for its motivational and engaging nature, especially among younger and less experienced learners. Prior collaboration among team members also had a notable positive impact, improving both creativity and agile comprehension by fostering better communication and trust.

Quantitative data validated the consistency and reliability of participant responses using statistical methods like the Intraclass Correlation Coefficient (ICC). The study also identified potential limitations, including a geographically localized sample, reliance on self-assessment surveys, and the need for broader interdisciplinary integration. Despite these, the findings support the conclusion that DesignScrum is a viable tool for promoting both agile fluency and creative thinking in diverse educational and professional settings. The chapter advocates for future research into integrating technology, such as AI and IoT, to further personalize and enrich gamified agile education.

Chapter 8: Design Thinking in Practice - Innovation in the Conceptualization of a Mobile App

The chapter titled "Design Thinking in Practice - Innovation in the Conceptualization of a Mobile App" presents a detailed and practical application of the Design Thinking methodology in the conceptualization and development of a mobile application tailored for motorcycle enthusiasts in Mexico. It begins by positioning Design Thinking as a vital tool in modern software development, particularly in mobile applications where user experience, innovation, and adaptability are crucial. The chapter explains that traditional development methods often fall short in dynamic, user-driven environments, and Design Thinking—by emphasizing empathy, creativity, and iterative testing—fills this gap effectively.

A central theme is the importance of UCD and empathy-driven research. The study begins with an exploratory phase involving interviews, observations, and persona development to understand the unique challenges faced by motorcyclists attending events, such as lack of centralized information and difficulty coordinating personal schedules. From these insights, clear focus areas and problem definitions are established. The chapter then outlines how brainstorming sessions led to innovative solutions—most notably, the concept of a mobile app to centralize event information and a complementary Facebook page to foster community engagement.

The ideation and prototyping phases are described in detail, including the selection of ideas, mockup creation using tools like Pencil Project, and development using the Flutter framework. The testing phase follows, where prototypes were evaluated by real users, leading to iterative improvements based on feedback. Key enhancements included larger font sizes, state-based filtering for events, and an option for users to sponsor content within the app.

The chapter illustrates the full Design Thinking cycle—from empathize, define, and ideate to prototype and test—culminating in the successful deployment of the "Eventos Biker México" mobile app and its associated Facebook page. The final product addresses user pain points, fosters community, and leverages feedback for continuous improvement. The discussion and conclusion emphasize how this methodology fosters deeper user engagement, reduces risk, and drives innovation. It demonstrates that Design Thinking, when thoughtfully applied, bridges the gap between user needs and technological solutions, offering a scalable, human-centered approach to mobile application development.

CONCLUSION AND CONTRIBUTION TO THE FIELD

The book *Innovative Design Thinking Approaches in Software Engineering* makes a compelling and timely case for transforming how we design, develop, and experience software in the age of digital acceleration. Grounded in empathy, creativity, and continuous iteration, the book establishes Design Thinking as a foundational methodology that aligns technical excellence with human insight. This shift from process-driven engineering to human-centered innovation is no longer optional—it is essential for building meaningful, ethical, and sustainable digital systems.

Each chapter in this collection contributes uniquely to this vision. From historical analysis and philosophical grounding to AI-enhanced design tools and real-world case studies, the book spans academic, industrial, and experiential domains. It explores how Design Thinking integrates with modern software development practices such as Agile and DevOps, how it empowers citizen developers and legal technologists, and how gamified and empathy-driven models reshape learning and collaboration. Through these varied lenses, readers are presented with a multifaceted, interdisciplinary framework for applying Design Thinking across different sectors and contexts.

Key contributions of the book include the formalization of hybrid methodologies like FusionFlow, which blend Design Thinking with AI and Agile for scalable, user-centric development. It also provides robust discussions of ethical challenges—such as bias, accessibility, and governance—and offers actionable strategies for responsible innovation. By addressing both strategic and tactical dimensions of design, the book empowers engineers, educators, researchers, and leaders to co-create software that is not only efficient and intelligent but inclusive and emotionally resonant.

As the technological landscape continues to evolve—with increasing emphasis on AI, IoT, remote collaboration, and decentralized innovation—this book offers a forward-looking guide to navigating complexity with clarity. It challenges conventional practices, foregrounds the importance of empathy, and elevates design literacy as a core competency in software engineering.

Finally, I have the pleasure to say that this book is more than a reference—it is a call to action. We invite readers to embrace Design Thinking not as a trend, but as a critical mindset and method for shaping the next generation of digital experiences. By doing so, software development becomes not just a technical endeavor, but a profound opportunity to create systems that are meaningful, responsible, and built for the diverse needs of real people.

Acknowledgement

This book represents the culmination of a collective endeavor marked by intellectual collaboration, academic generosity, and unwavering personal commitment. Its realization would not have been possible without the invaluable contributions and steadfast support of numerous individuals and institutions, each of whom deserves my deepest and most sincere appreciation.

In particular, I wish to express my profound gratitude to the Tecnología Educativa I+D+i Research group (UAS-CA-303) and the Facultad de Informática Mazatlán at the Universidad Autónoma de Sinaloa. Their dedication to academic excellence and research innovation provided the collaborative and supportive environment essential for the development of this work.

This publication also stands as a testament to the insightful contributions of a distinguished group of scholars and professionals whose chapters have significantly enriched the discourse surrounding Design Thinking in software engineering. To all contributing authors: your commitment, academic rigor, and forward-thinking perspectives have greatly enhanced the depth and relevance of this volume. Your work serves not only to elevate the quality of this book but also to advance the field by promoting a more empathetic, inclusive, and visionary approach to software development.

It is our collective aspiration that the ideas presented herein will inspire ongoing dialogue, inform evolving practices, and spark meaningful innovation in the dynamic intersections of technology, design, and human-centered thinking.

José Alfonso Aguilar-Calderón expresses his heartfelt gratitude to his beloved wife and son for their understanding during the time dedicated to his book.

Chapter 1
Revolutionizing Software Engineering:
Innovative Design Thinking Approaches

Subhadip Kowar
https://orcid.org/0009-0005-7758-4635
Brainware University, India

Sneha Mukherjee
Brainware University, India

Shramana Ghosh
Bengal Institute of Technology, India

ABSTRACT

This chapter examines how Design Thinking is revolutionizing software engineering by shifting the focus from purely technical execution to human-centered innovation. It presents Design Thinking as a methodology grounded in empathy, creativity, iterative prototyping, and interdisciplinary collaboration. The chapter traces its evolution from design and architecture to its current role in software development, highlighting its integration with Agile, UX, and HCI practices. Through practical principles and real-world case studies in sectors like e-commerce, healthcare, and EdTech, it demonstrates that the creation of software that is not only functional but also intuitive, inclusive, and impactful. Ethical considerations such as accessibility, privacy, and sustainability are also addressed, emphasizing the responsibility of software engineers to design with purpose. Challenges related to implementation, such as resistance to change, resource constraints, and scaling, are critically analyzed

DOI: 10.4018/979-8-3693-9531-8.ch001

INTRODUCTION TO DESIGN THINKING IN SOFTWARE ENGINEERING

It brings new approaches to software engineering about design thinking, which flips things upside down from pure technical specifications of people. Essentially, it relies on an understanding of the users and defining the needs, then brainstorming ideas for how one would solve those problems, followed by rapid prototyping of an idea to test what actually works. In contrast with a strictly process-driven approach, it inspires curiosity, collaboration, and flexibility—virtues for a fast-paced user-driven world.

Originally conceived of as applied to architecture or product design, Design Thinking is increasingly applied to the software engineer's problem solving of tough problems. This process begins with empathy-listen and observe so that pain points in the user can be attended to and needs uncovered which users may not even know exist. From there, they use ideation with a cycle of creating prototypes, then testing, balancing imagination and pragmatism.

This is the approach agile development follows. Agile development continually improves and responds. Early and frequent feedback from users minimizes the risks of a team while making software developed intuitive and meaningful. Collaboration and shared ownership bring all developers, designers, and stakeholders together. Software engineers will create experiences that matter, not products with design thinking. Here is how it changes the game with real-life examples on how to implement it.

The goal of the chapter is to redefine the practice of software engineering by presenting Design Thinking as a transformative methodology that prioritizes empathy, creativity, and user-centered innovation. It aims to shift the developer's mindset from technical execution to human-centered problem solving, emphasizing collaboration, ethical responsibility, and continuous iteration. The chapter demonstrates how software should not merely function but must also meaningfully respond to real human needs and contexts.

The chapter structure is as follows: Section 2 explores the historical context and scholarly foundations of Design Thinking, tracing its evolution from product design to software. Cites Tim Brown, Beckman, Sy, and others as foundational voices. Connects Design Thinking with Agile and UX practices. Section 3 compares Design Thinking with: Agile, Lean and Waterfall and highlights hybrid adoption (e.g., SAP, IBM) and helps teams choose methodologies best suited to project culture and scale. Section 4 addresses ethical software design by focusing on: accessibility and inclusion, data privacy and transparency, bias detection and mitigation, responsible innovation and long-term thinking and stakeholder dynamics and fair trade-offs. Section 5 advocates for rigorous understanding of problems such as empathize deeply, the use techniques like journey mapping and the "Five Whys", rely on both qualitative and quantitative data, collaborate across roles and stay agile but avoid over-simplification. Conclusions are detailed at the end.

BACKGROUND AND LITERATURE REVIEW

Design thinking is increasingly recognized as a transformative force in software engineering, centering creativity, empathy, and end-user value in the development process. Booch (2016) argues that the future of software engineering lies in embracing broader perspectives that integrate human needs with technological capabilities. Norman (2013) emphasizes the significance of intuitive and user-centered design, laying a foundational argument for embedding empathy in software processes.

Human-centered design (HCD) plays a critical role in this shift. Spencer, Toshniwal, and Weiss (2022) present methods and case studies that illustrate how HCD improves software relevance and usability. Heuristic evaluation techniques, such as those proposed by Nielsen and Molich (1990), further support the alignment of software features with human cognition and expectations.

Brown (2009) and Meinel and Leifer (2022) explore design thinking as a mindset that fosters innovation by merging functionality with deep understanding of user context. Alavi and Carlson (2022) highlight its potential to reshape software development methodologies, advocating for its integration with agile frameworks to enhance responsiveness and creativity.

Involving end-users throughout the development process is critical. Heck, Ali, and Zaidman (2023) propose a structured framework to embed user feedback, reinforcing the value of collaboration and iterative improvement. Gutwin and Greenberg (2002) provide theoretical grounding for such collaboration, underscoring its importance in co-creating meaningful software.

Ethical considerations, as discussed by Beyer (2021), remind developers that technology must not only work well but also do good. Ralph and Wand (2016) and Zimmerman, Stolterman, and Forlizzi (2010) contribute formal perspectives on design and research methodologies that support innovation grounded in user needs.

Together, these works affirm that design thinking—when intertwined with agile, ethics, and user involvement—has the potential to revolutionize software engineering by making it more human-centered, adaptive, and impactful.

INTRODUCTION TO DESIGN THINKING IN SOFTWARE ENGINEERING

It brings new approaches to software engineering about design thinking, which flips things upside down from pure technical specifications of people. Essentially, it relies on an understanding of the users and defining the needs, then brainstorming ideas for how one would solve those problems, followed by really rapid prototyping of an idea to test what actually works. In contrast with a strictly process-driven approach, it inspires curiosity, collaboration, and flexibility—virtues for a fast-paced user-driven world.

Originally conceived of as applied to architecture or product design, Design Thinking is increasingly applied to the software engineer's problem solving of tough problems. This process begins with empathy-listen and observe so that pain points in the user can be attended to and needs uncovered which users may not even know exist. From there, they use ideation with a cycle of creating prototypes, then testing, balancing imagination and pragmatism.

This is the approach agile development follows. Agile development continually improves and responds. Early and frequent feedback from users minimizes the risks of a team while making software developed intuitive and meaningful. Collaboration and shared ownership bring all developers, designers, and stakeholders together.

Software engineers will create experiences that matter, not products with design thinking. Here is how it changes the game with real-life examples on how to implement it (Booch, 2016).

Empathy-Driven Innovation

It, pretty much, starts with what users struggle through and with; their behavior; and what they aspire toward. The user-centric form of thinking enables developers to have a go at issues that, in real life, fall far beyond the scope of functional requirements, taking into consideration the areas of usability, accessibility, and emotional involvement here again. Using tools like the persona of the user, a journey map, and workshops on empathy that bring in actionable insights for solution design helps guide the developers once more.

Breaking silos in development

Significance of design thinking towards software engineering is that this brings together cross-functional teams. It is a linkage that brings developers, designers, product managers, as well as the final consumers together. This wide perspective balances the team while the technological and creative fields harmonically blend.

Ideation sessions together with rapid prototyping become tools to break silos and deliver continuous feedback.

Iterative Prototyping Testing

Design Thinking encourages iterative cycles of prototyping and testing of ideas by engineers to help evaluate their ideas early and frequently enough. It reduces the risk of expensive rework associated with usability flaws and technological constraint exposure early. Combining this iterative approach with agile methodologies completes an excellent synergy of exploration within concepts and structured software delivery.

Solving complex problems with systems thinking

Modern software solutions are built in complex ecosystems where the engineers must take into consideration a wider view of system-level interactions. Correspondingly, the structured framework of Design Thinking, as an extension of systems thinking, lets the teams model and assess inter-component connections in terms of scalability, reliability, and performance.

Driving Creativity with Constraints

Software engineering constrains the design process based on budget, timelines, and technical capabilities. Design Thinking flips the constraints as opportunities for innovation. For instance, when challenging the problems into "how might we" questions, the engineers will have creative minds activated with the limitations set for practical applications.

The Evolution of Design Thinking in the Software Industry

Design thinking is that much of an approach that changes the way in which the software is being developed. This stream ranges from architecture and industrial designing to the lowest level of the world of software development in order to innovate and lead it in a path around the user. This is a reflection of changing natures in technologies and changing user expectations through the history of design thinking by which developers and designers collectively bob in reflection reflects how they have been bobbing (Norman, 2013).

1. The Early Years Function over Form (1970s-1980s):

It was a time of young software development that had things needing to be right rather than look right; the end-users cared little how they were eventually going to use them. The basic productivity was work by engineers toward systems that worked and were reliable with little concern for form. This was highly rigid by the so-called waterfall model, whereby every step was defined, and there was little scope for creativity. This made the interfaces appear unattractive and more technical. They seemed to be far more suitable for engineers rather than the end-users. Although this phase helped establish structured development, the human factor was even painfully missing in this phase.

2. Towards the User (1990):

Everything changed in the 1990s. With personal computers now deployed everywhere, software had to be accessible to non-technical users. This was user-centered design, where usability and making interfaces more intuitive began getting its due importance. For the first time, the spotlight went on to user needs and experience. The term “design thinking” hadn't really been used yet, but its basic ideas-even beginning to understand users and iteration on designs-started getting into the conversation.

3. Agile Team Collaboration (2000):

The Agile movement and new working model appeared very comfortably in the early years of design thinking in the 2000s. Agile encourages teams to work on short flexible cycles and improvise work based on feedback. Designers, developers, and product managers began to collaborate closer with each other, and it can be said that design thinking becomes the glue that stuck various perspectives together. Prototypes, mockups, and user testing became routine tools, which means they are easier to include the user.

4. The UX Boom (2010):

Design thinking is more of a buzzword than a term in the world of 2010s tech. Methods propagated by current companies, such as IDEO and Stanford's d.school, whereas terms like “empathize” and “prototype” are huge debates in software teams. Smartphones and mobile apps started threatening to produce class problems but will help them “invent” software that is not only functional but enjoyable as well. Accessibility and inclusion now center stage. Software would now reach all through all channels as well as not only to the privileged few chosen.

5. Today AI boom and beyond:

Thus finally, in this world of artificial intelligence, internet of things, and virtual reality design thinking has emerged one more time.These AI tools make them understand consumer behavior in ways that could never be understood before and give them insights into creating personalized and intuitive experiences. And with this comes its fair share of challenges in data privacy and ethics in design. Impact now is as much about the people that the technology has on them as it is about creating great products.

6. A Collaborative Future ENC:

Modern thinking through design is very team and collaborative creativity. Such ease of collaboration around the world in real-time brings tools such as Figma and Adobe XD. Teams can create systematic-yet-innovative experiences due to standardized design systems such as Google's Material Design. Significant is the shift of developers, designers, and users blurring lines within that creates this very collaborative ecosystem.

Key Principles and Concepts of Design Thinking in Software Engineering

Design thinking has started to alter the nature of software engineering, and it brings the solution whereby human beings can figure out and solve real human problems. It influences people to center their developers towards the true needs of users, promotes creativity and collaborative practice in problem-solving without dogmatic or linear methodologies which have a flexibility viewpoint upon failure, taking failure and learning it as an experience while enhancing and brings diverse perspectives and explores unique insights into developing the most intuitive and impactful solution. By combining empathy, experiment, and iteration, it can ensure that software is functionally meaningful to users as well. This is actually changing the landscape for the way teams innovate so that more software development becomes more responsive and user-centric. So, let's examine what are the essentials of design thinking and how its impact expands in software engineering practices below (Spencer, Toshniwal et al., 2022).

1. Start with Empathy: Walk in the User's Shoes:

That's where empathy starts, ostensibly on the shores of Scotland. When creating applications we have to take into account the users—what they face daily, what they lack, and what they want to achieve. This entails looking at the situation objectively by interviewing and understanding how a user goes through his activities. Almost always, whenever we truly stand in the shoes of the user, we are able to develop good software that tackles meaningful problems not just symptoms of problems.

2. Define the Problem Clearly:

Major problem areas should first be outlined before proceeding to solutions. In software engineering this is taken to mean searching for the root causes of problems. That fused problem statement can guide the entire team throughout the process and allow us to focus on the problem and not the symptoms.

3. Collaborate to Generate Ideas:

After we have clarified what the problem is, we have to step back and go for the grand vision. The Lean Idea Management process is about defining ideas and looking for opportunities to give them a voice. Such procedures as brainstorming or drawing general notions reveal ideas to teams. Teamwork makes the dream work—having designers, developers and stakeholders is immensely valuable as when people of different specializations brainstorm they come up with something new.

4. Build Prototypes to Explore:

Prototyping illuminates where ideas go. No matter if it is only a rough drawing on paper or a physical model, a prototype allows students to develop ideas rapidly and discover which one feels right without creating large pieces of work. This is particularly a useful step in cultivating software engineering where teams are allowed to test available options, and this does not involve the use of many resources. It's a very beneficial approach to begin to get an understanding of how a potential audience will respond to an idea before investing time and money into it fully (Brown, 2009).

5. Test and Refine with Real Feedback:

The real exciting part comes with testing. The objective is to take the prototypes and present them to real users to find out what is effective, equally as important what is a failure and why. The concept of 'defect' is a misnomer in testing – it's not about finding faults but in finding things that could make the solution that much better. This kind of testing assures that the product meets the user requirements in the final product development.

6. Keep It Human-Centered:

Contrary to community marketing or lean start-up, Design Thinking is first of all about people. Software development should support the notion where every line of code, every line drawn at the design phase, and many other features should be produced with the belief that the software will have a positive impact on the user. It's about changing the paradigm of thinking from "What can we build?" to "What do people need?"

7. Break Down Silos & Work as One Team:

Design Thinking is a team activity through and through. It insists that interdisciplinary teams—designers, developers, business analysts to work from conception. We eliminate barriers and make sure everyone has the same understanding that any decision made must be technically and user-friendly possible.

8. Embrace the Unknown:

Acceptance of the unknown in software engineering is an attitude that breeds creativity and innovation. Uncertainty scares, but it is from those very scary moments that often come some of the best revolutionary ideas. The creation of solutions that redefine the experience of the user opens up when the process of curious inquiry looks into ambiguous challenges or emerging technologies.

Teams overcome uncertainty by testing and prototyping their ideas, learning from them, which means they are not so far-fetched concerning users and the market situation. This means challenges should be treated as opportunities to learn rather than as things to flee from.

This again collaborates. People from different backgrounds who collaborate come up with new ideas that challenge ambiguity in new approaches to address it. Not only do problems have to be solved but even imagining possibilities and making software which may well change the world itself is included.

USER-CENTERED DESIGN AND HUMAN-COMPUTER INTERACTION

A Brief Outline Of User-Centered Design (UCD):

The acronym UCD stands for User-Centered Design, which in its purest form is concerned with people within the entire process of developing software. It's the approach that guarantees that the software I develop does not only solve the existing problem but is also meaningful and easy to use. Conducting actual users every process, such as usability testing and feedback, UCD delivers not only results that are efficient and functional but also enjoyable.

How UCD and HCI Work Together:

HCI is the foundation of UCD. It allows an understanding of how people engage with technology to lead us to create interfaces that appear 'natural'. It proves that such concepts as reducing the amount of mental effort or giving clear feedback from HCI help to improve the software a lot. UCD and HCI combined together ensures a strong bond of Science and Empathy, thereby building tools that are unique, serving the needs of the end users.

Some elements of UCD important to software design are discussed in the following section:

Listening to Users: This means that the best designs have to begin with the understanding of the people who will use different designs. Interviews, questionnaires, observation of humans' activity within their working process can reveal true and real needs from the software.

Building and Improving:

The construction of early mockups and feedback on them allow minimizing losses in the further work process. That is the process of constructing a new product, the process of evaluating the results and then optimizing the product.

Making It Accessible: Amazing designs are inclusive designs. Taking into account those who have disabilities or lower technical literacy means everyone may use the software to their advantage (Alavi & Carlson, 2022).

Thinking About Context: When people use software applications, they work within certain contexts which are not irrelevant to usage. This way, creating tools that would fit their environment, even if they work in quite an office or are more active in some other manner.

Introducing Creativity in UCD through Design Thinking:

In summary, while sharing a common goal of putting people first, the idea of Design Thinking elevates the concept of User-Centered Design by adding to that spark provided in terms of exploration, experimentation, and re-imagining the solution to it.

Essentially, Design Thinking allows for creative exploration of ideas. It challenges members to think outside the box without fear of failure and allows them to come up with rather unconventional ideas. Techniques involved are mind mapping and storytelling, bringing ideas to life, allowing teams to view the problems from another angle, as well as viewing their solutions.

It's really a very powerful tool especially in terms of storytelling. User personas and mapping the journey of such personas would ensure teams step into users' shoes and design experiences not only functionally but emotionally as well.

Rapid prototyping is another form of creativity. Making simple prototypes early and testing them allows rapid gathering of feedback and evolution of an idea. One learns in the process. With design thinking, a collaborative practice also thrives. Brought together are disparate perspectives--designers, engineers, analysts, and users that make it an exciting environment, where ideas collide and innovation flourishes.

Through empathy, the UCD teams can pair it with Design Thinking in order to bring practical and inspiring solutions in software creation.

Real-Life Impacts of UCD:

Of course, it is not always easy to stay in the mainstream of thinking about users. Many a time, the teams are faced with contradicting objectives, for example, working within a set budget constraint or use of limited time. Another challenge is the identification of the large-group characteristics based on the small sample results. And let's not forget about the fact that designers, developers, and researchers are always a bit hard to manage at the same time.

The Future of UCD and HCI:

Technology advances rapidly, and so does the approach to designing for people. Advanced methods in artificial intelligence, augmented reality, and smart devices are promising incredible opportunities for customization and engagement. Conceive applications that learn your working style or instruments that guess what tool you might require next. However, we also have to be more conscious about other factors such as privacy and fairness while developing such systems. Taking it to the third-Gen AI advancement further, the brain-computer interfaces could revolutionize human's interaction with the machines making it even easier and more open.

Depth of Analysis

In software engineering, depth of analysis is what differentiates good solutions from middling ones. Perhaps nothing is better than really taking one's time to finally understand the problem. Design thinking takes its roots deep into an appropriate depth of analysis so that the teams start with observations in ways not just created for observations but meaningful insights leading to innovative and user-focused solutions.

Starting with Empathy

Design thinking starts with empathy. That is, it begins with the most basic things: talking to the users, seeing how they use the system, and listening closely to frustrations and needs. In this way, solutions are not so much assumed but will emerge from a deeper understanding of who the software will be serving.

To the Heart of the Problem

This encourages one to trace problems to its core rather than accelerating and rectifying the signs. Techniques include repeated "why" questions and cause and effect mapping, giving the team perspective in the broad scheme of things. Solutions implemented would be way more effective if truly the correct problems were being handled.

Let Data Tell the Story

Numbers count too. Analytics, user behavior data, and system performance metrics are fantastic evidence to back up observations. For example, heatmaps can suggest where users get stuck, and A/B testing can help confirm which design decisions work best. Combining that quantitative data with real user stories creates a much more complete picture.

Learning Through Prototypes

Prototypes are where analysis meets action. Pre-design prototypes can be quickly used to test ideas and rapidly get fast feedback back into teams. Often usability testing reveals things that preliminary analysis could not even suggest, and so refinement and iteration can happen before ever being fully committed to a design (Nielsen & Molich, 1990).

Collaboration Brings Depth

There is no one right answer. Over the analysis, a group of designers, developers, and business experts combine so that different viewpoints about the problem are layered over, and the final solution takes care of technical issues, user needs, and business goals.

Stay Focused and Flexible

While deep analysis is required, it needs to be taken forward. Agile approaches avoid overthinking and encourage solution-focused thinking that is testable and, hence, can be iterated.

Finally, it is not about overcomplicating things but bringing things from the other end and asking the right questions to design products or services that would make a difference for people.

Case Studies and Success Stories of Design Thinking in Software Engineering

This means that the game in software engineering changes through design thinking-brings a new approach through which teams face problems and deliver solutions that really connect with users. Let us look through examples of applications and success stories in this chapter that put this approach to life in action. By putting the person at the center of the process and listening to his or her needs while working collaboratively across teams until a best solution is produced, developers can move from just churning out functional products toward ones that really matter (Meinel & Leifer, 2022).

These stories illustrate how big and small companies embrace design thinking to innovate, solve tough challenges, and deliver remarkable results. Whether it is a startup shaking up an entire industry or a long-established business reimagining its digital strategy, each case illustrates how this mindset turns ideas into impactful solutions.

As we work through these examples, you will find that design thinking bridges that gap between theory and practice and is a robust tool with which to craft software to solve today's problems and foretell tomorrow's needs. These stories are not success stories; they are journey stories about learning, adaptation, and difference for business and for the people whom they serve.

1. Improving User Experience in Electronic Commerce Systems

Due to the research design, one of the leading e-commerce companies applied the design thinking approach to transform its e-commerce shopping experience. By conducting the empathy map and user journey, the team noticed mixed learning from Product Discovery and product Check Out. Feedback and prototyping cycles resulted in changing the interface and cutting the cart abandonment to a 25 percentage point. This success proves that only after involving the customer, focused on specific solutions, such iterative feedback and quick prototyping are effective.

2. This paper focuses on the topic – "Streamlining Healthcare Management Systems"

A software engineering team of a company which was hired to build a healthcare management platform used Design Thinking in order to solve the problem of inefficient work of hospitals. The multidisciplinary team enacted an anthropological approach to problem finding, interviewing doctors, nurses, and administrative staff who identify the following key problems in appointment scheduling and patient data management. The result was the high-value platform that has led to the increase of 40% in the scheduling effectiveness based on the patients' surveys.

3. The Impetus for Innovations in Wind and Solar Energy Technologies

A mobile application product for micro investment was designed and developed by a FinTech startup using Design Thinking. Based on investment behaviour of millennials, ideation workshops and co-create sessions were used as part of the ideation stage. The end product was a hybrid, combining accurate financial recommendations interfaced with a clean and easy-to-navigate design: they expanded the user base of the application twice in six months. This success demonstrates how learning from the use of participatory design techniques can help in identifying these sub-markets for targeting.

4. Optimising DevOps Practices Using Cross-Functional Teams

A global software enterprise adopted Design Thinking to enhance its DevOps value stream. Working with developers, testers, and operations teams in specific workshops allowed the organization to define crucial and emerging bottlenecks in the CI/CD process. An efficient system for deploying resources shaved deployment time in half and began to establish multidisciplinary ideas on the best practices for a business.

5. Some Characteristics of Educational Software Design for Accessibility

A case on learners with disabilities in an EdTech company used Design Thinking to create the learning platform. Involving the educators, accessibility experts and students, the team was able to produce the work satisfying the WCAG requirements yet providing the chances for the adaptation process. Market access went beyond just broadening a client base, and the platform even received awards for product accessibility(Zimmerman, Stolterman, & Forlizzi, 2010).

CHALLENGES AND LIMITATIONS OF IMPLEMENTING DESIGN THINKING IN SOFTWARE PROJECTS

Software design thinking is an exciting ride, but a real challenge. Its user-centered approach is great, but its integration is not always smooth with the fast-paced world of software development. The exploratory and iterative nature of design thinking often clashes with structured realities, deadline-driven realities of many projects. It's really tough to adjust processes and mindsets in adopting this new way of working.

This is no easy task in organizations that have a traditional development background. As far as time, budget, or the availability of qualified team members are involved, this only means the lack of resource makes it more challenging to devote effort necessary for true empathy with users, developing prototypes, and then perfecting ideas based on feedbacks.

To say nothing of trying to balance off the countervailing expectations emitted by diverse stakeholders of the system itself other than also meeting technological as well as being achieved business goals within that creative solution. Communications themselves, plus collaborations are those bedrock attributes of design thinking and could, conversely even become another challenge, yet one of how to make them happen across a distributed team. First of all, there is natural resistance to change: skepticism of the process, or just a simple refusal to leave the comfort zone of existing workflows. These have to be overcome before design thinking can be ready to start revolutionizing, in earnest, the current software engineering practice.

1. Resentment to Change

Cultural Barriers: Most organizations function in a particular way or manner. Even Agile, by following strict hierarchy or waterfall methodology, sometimes feels like trying to turn a ship while attempting to get everyone on board and working in a more collaborative and iterative manner.

It calls for a mindset of empathy, trying, and failure. This is pretty a number of mental shifts when the teams are those whose linear processes and sureshot results are the norm.

2. Time and Resource Constraint

Time Constrained: In general, software products work under highly aggressive schedules. With such huge pressure for better customer knowledge and innovative solutions, this is considered a kind of luxury that teams cannot afford to part with.

Resource Intensive: Workshops, interviews, and prototypes all take dedicated time, money, and effort. That is too much of an imposition to stretched organizations.

3. Scaling Design Thinking

Where design thinking works very well with small, focused teams is much harder to apply to the larger, cross-function project work. With a bigger team, the collaboration, agility, and alignment become a challenge.

4. Coordination with other approaches

Methodology Misfits Design thinking does not play well with the current workflow: Agile and DevOps, for example. An Agile sprint cycle conflicts with an exploratory phase within design thinking, which at times is frustrating or set up to be disappointed.

Tooling Issues: In the development pipeline, it might be more work and could be difficult for some teams to integrate design thinking artifacts like empathy maps or user personas.

5. Stakeholder Buy-In

Proof of Concept: The near-term output of design thinking is not necessarily delivered with low-hanging fruit that one can quickly measure, often providing the stakeholder with reason to doubt investment in time and resources. He says things like, "What's the ROI?"

Priorities: Teams with clear priorities, either business or technical feasibility, do not feel like digging into understanding the needs of the users very deeply. Without that buy-in, it is tough to catch design thinking.

6. Prototyping and Iteration Challenges

Technical Limitations: Prototypes that result from design thinking often require iteration once they have been translated into functional software. Sometimes, the output may differ significantly from what was envisaged.

Iteration Fatigue: One risks entering an iteration cycle that leads to not really solving the problem but in delay and frustration.

7. Skills Gaps

Design thinking is not a process. It requires experience: user research, leading workshops, rapid prototyping. Most teams do not possess this kind of expertise; thus the entire process becomes too complex and ineffectual.

8. Ethical and Practical Issues

Data Privacy: All the knowledge about users bears extremely sensitive information; operating very strict regulations like GDPR and CCPA makes the whole business a little too confining and abides with breach issues.

Overemphasis on the users: Pursuit of user-centered design puts overriding emphasis on individual needs and tends to overshadow other major factors, including scalability, long-term sustainability, or broader societal impact.

Comparative Analysis

This is one very critical tool for assessment into how different approaches and methods do influence outcomes within software engineering. Along with design thinking, they achieve the balance of both the pros and cons of using other approaches as ways to solving problems, improvement in user experience, and coming up with inspirations. These design thinking have traditionally been compared to approaches in software development that include methodologies like Agile, Lean, and the traditional waterfall model. All of the design thinkings in its own value have been focusing on trying to understand someone's needs by being empathetic. Comparing that with Agile where there is this great leaning and short iterations and in one sort of an approach towards "cutting out the waste," if one would want to put that way, this design thinking still depends much upon finding the difficulty of people with challenge exploration where solutions will come through prototyping and testing. Having said that, Agile and Lean are stronger in the delivery and the efficiency approach while comparing the approach in place; however, it stays on track even till the point of deliverables getting in sync with the real user's expectations by incorporating design thinking. Even though paying closer attention to the specific tools and techniques applied under the umbrella of design thinking, such as journey mapping, brainstorming, prototyping, their respective participation can also be encountered. All the aforesaid tools therefore stir teamwork and inspire creativity, making teams imagine possibilities than fine-tune existing systems with something like gathering software requirements. These differences help a team to know which tool will be applied best for a given project timeline.

More than that, case studies over real-life make a further step in explaining the benefits of comparative analysis. All design-thinking-friendly organizations like IBM and SAP will have greater user satisfaction, lesser cycle time while developing, and successful product adoption. This advantage of the traditional method can be clearly explained by a comparative study over an organization using that method (Heck, Ali, & Zaidman, 2023).

Generally, comparative analysis also helps ascertain the role methodologies fit within the organizations' cultures. Start-ups and smaller scale enterprises will most often do well with flexible design thinking having high innovations. Conversely, the large scale with a higher structured methodology will best thrive using the Agile or the waterfall methodology. In understanding such differences, firms will determine their specific best-suited approach.

In simple words, comparative analysis can make the group of software engineering take responsible thought decisions. Taking the strength point of design thinking, limiting its usage with various methodologies, creating a combination to include innovation, effectiveness, and meeting user satisfaction: this is easy and capable of making profoundly transformative results happen.

Ethical Considerations in Design Thinking for Software Engineers

One of the great methodologies for developing user-centered software is design thinking. With it, all the ethical responsibilities are incorporated and cannot be overlooked by developers. Simultaneously, while designing to understand and fulfill all the needs of the users, it becomes possible to increase accessibility, inclusion, and responsibility of technology with ethics at every step. Some of the very important areas in which ethical thinking plays a very crucial role are as follows:

Design for All

Much of design thinking has to do with walking in users' shoes. Whose do we wear? If narrow, we leave many out of the equation. Meaning when we include all - people from all walks of lives: culture, ability and experiences - it means, therefore, it works for all of us and for not a few.

Protect User Privacy

Useful software creations often need gathering and processing information about its users. Dealing with such information in a responsible manner then very much becomes part of the equation. Here too, transparency is key to such systems: users need to be clearly aware of how their data are being used, and they have to be in control at any moment in time. Trust and security must be a first call for ethical design.

Bias removal

Sometimes, biases creep into our designs unknowingly, and this is usually through the data we use or even assumptions we make. In case one is not careful, such biases may lead to unfair outcomes for certain groups of users. Ethical design thinking is taking time to test for and remove such hidden issues among other things.

Creativity with Caution:

It is design thinking: think big but pause to see if this idea might have bad ripple effects. Would such a feature inadvertently hurt someone? Might this be used in not-so-great ways? Asking those questions leads us toward solutions that are innovative and safe, thought-provoking, and at the same time.

Thinking long-term

In the rush to fulfill immediate needs or deadlines of users, it is easy to lose sight of the bigger picture. However, ethical design thinking challenges the mind to think about the future. Is our software environment-friendly? Does it provide support to social progress? These are the kinds of questions that help us to design with purpose.

Making Technology Accessible

Accessibility is a must-have, not to have. This makes software inclusively designed for the target users with disabilities. One should not work on compliance but ensure he or she creates tools used by everybody regardless of capabilities.

Navigating Stakeholder Pressure

Enough, business objectives and ethics forming good software often contradict each other. All stakeholders can come for any business in design thinking workshops and can openly address every obstacle that stands against them, but finding what will benefit both the business and the users becomes simpler once all the voices have been heard.

Depth of Analysis

It is in software engineering that the depth of analysis really brings design thinking to life. No more scratching on the surface, but going straight into the heart of understanding what the users really need and want, what technical challenges are going to be there, and what business objectives are involved in this. In that way, what is created shall be functional, and it will have an impact.

In the empathize phase, this is time spent getting really deep understanding through interviewing, surveys, and observation-really listening for what's being said but, more importantly, what's left unsaid. Then there's the define phase where it connects the dots so that the problems are clear-cut to focus on solutioning. This hard work makes up a very good base for the ideas to start flowing on their own, innovative and practical at that(Gutwin & Greenberg, 2002).

Prototyping and feedback lead to many opportunities for testing and yield results confirming that solutions are in the right place. Journey mapping or asking "why" a few times ensures that designs can really hone in so they truly meet the needs of the users.

When such thoughtful analysis is implanted in the process, software teams produce products that solve problems but also delight users and effect meaningful change.

The Future of Design Thinking in Software Engineering

Design thinking is going to be that much more key in the future of software development. More importantly, with the progress of technology and the desire to get smarter, simpler, or even more meaningful interactions, it is at its core as it is based on being empathetic and a creative problem-solving approach when dealing with building software meant to really resonate with people. Let's look at how, in this environment, design thinking might evolve in the future.

1. AI and automation as co-creators

Imagine this future where AI tools are supposed to come up with ideas together with human beings in the future instead of only assistance. Generative AI, for instance, can provide ideas on designs or even mock-ups, based on users' data and is still improving with time. They will then allow engineers and designers to further develop and test ideas rather than having to start all over again from square one. Thus, the process of creativity accelerates and becomes more dynamic. However, for example, automated usability testing will provide immediate feedback for teams to make the required adjustments on the fly.

2. Work Smarter with Agile

Agile development is agile in nature, hence fast and flexible too. Design thinking fits the bill perfectly, as together they open up continuous loops of user feedback. Meaning that in an environment as fast-paced as one with lots of development activity, teams will stay attuned to what users need. Their blend, often referred to as "DesignOps," likely will become the new standard in this industry.

3. Tearing Down Silos

The near future would see software engineering more of a team discipline than just design, coding, product management, or data science. Design thinking involves collaboration in that each individual sees from the eyes of the end-user. Tools shared, like personas or experience maps, can bring a common language to help everyone stay on the same page.

4. Designing for Ethics

As technology becomes stronger, it poses very big questions on how to use it more responsibly. Design thinking may take an element of ethical foresight-imagining the far-off consequences of a product on the world or the environment. Teams start testing for ethical considerations as well as they do for usability.

5. Let data tell the story:

Further information streams in about the future to identify exactly what will assist users and what needs to be created by the tools, used for design in finding pattern and points of pain, or areas that aren't even intuitive. So the art and science are a better invention when designers' work and decisions rest upon the assumption of the truth based on real data, not just assumptions.

6. Build for Everyone

The future of software will not compromise on inclusions and accessibility. Such brainstorming on ideas about how features can be good for diverse users may well involve design thinking workshops with either the handicapped or with those from the less privileged sections of society. This idea can then be experimented using emerging tools like augmented reality.

7. Become Adaptive to Emerging Tech

New technologies such as IoT, blockchain, and edge computing force us to rethink ways we design software. Imagine how IoT systems are all about thinking of the whole network of devices, where blockchain is all about trust and transparency. New such dimensions are forcing design thinking to wonderful adjustments (Beyer, 2021).

8. Testing with Digital Twins

What if you could test a design in a virtual replica of the real world before it is built? That's what digital twins promise: digital versions of systems or devices, allowing us to simulate how users will interact with them. This could make the design process as precise and reliable as anyone has ever dreamed.

9. Sustainable Software by Design

By implication, it will be concerned with sustainability in software engineering. Therefore, the software to be developed will be efficient, durable, and adaptive. Perhaps this may be the time when easier-to-upgrade modular systems will be constructed, or the solutions can consume less energy.

CONCLUSION AND KEY TAKEAWAYS

Design thinking shaped the approach to software engineering. Not a process of writing codes anymore, but now, it's the process that understands people. Through empathy, collaboration, and creative problem-solving, software engineers now create solutions that resonate with users and actually solve their problems.

This is a methodology, but one that counters the approach of more traditional developments. It inspires teams to look beyond what requirements are for this technical piece and how we make software really work, beyond making a real difference. Software engineers can do this: flexible, scalable, and equipped to face tomorrow's challenges by embracing iterative design and constant feedback.

Design thinking also brings ethics to the fore, reminding us of the fact that technology is about people and not vice versa. Whether it is about accessibility, protecting user's right to privacy, or bringing up the issue of inclusivity, it keeps the human element front and center in the work done by the developers.

1. **It's All About the User:** In a nutshell, at its core, design thinking is about understanding and solving problems for people. Focus on the user needs-this is how we build software intuitive, useful, and impactful.
2. **Teamwork Makes the Dream Work:** Teamwork is fuel to creativity and innovation. Break down silos: make it the way to better solutions and stronger teams.
3. **Learn, Test, Repeat:** Design thinking is a loop of ideas. Test them, get some feedback, and refine. In that way, the final product changes to grow with the needs of the user.

4. **Ethics Matter:** Software engineers need to think about much more than functionality in this world. How does our work impact privacy, for example, or inclusivity, or fairness? Questions like these must guide our designs.
5. **Future Fit:** It addresses not only what exists in the present but also makes change adaptable, sustainable, and ripe enough to enter the world.
6. **Real Stories, Real Impact:** These case studies will show that these ideas of design thinking are bringing innovation and answering the complex questions by which one can be successful in almost any industry in paving the way for others.

Ultimately, design thinking is not about doing better software but doing software that makes life better. It's more about how one can blend creativity with technology and humanity in such a way that what they create really matters.

REFERENCES

Alavi, M. M., & Carlson, P. (2022). Design thinking: An innovative approach to software development methodologies. In *Proceedings of the 2022 IEEE International Conference on Software Engineering (ICSE)* (pp. 356–363). IEEE. https://doi.org/ DOI: 10.1145/3377811.3381396

Beyer, S. (2021). Ethical considerations in human-centered design for software development. *Journal of Ethics in Information Technology*, *23*(2), 129–138. DOI: 10.1007/s10676-021-09581-y

Booch, G. (2016). The future of software engineering. *IEEE Software*, *33*(1), 20–24. DOI: 10.1109/MS.2014.16

Brown, T. (2009). *Change by design: How design thinking creates new alternatives for business and society*. Harper Business.

Gutwin, C., & Greenberg, S. (2002). The mechanics of collaboration: Developing a theoretical framework for collaborative software. [CSCW]. *Computer Supported Cooperative Work*, *11*(1–2), 83–102. DOI: 10.1023/A:1015249122500

Heck, P., Ali, R., & Zaidman, M. (2023). A framework for involving end users in software engineering processes. *Empirical Software Engineering*, *28*(3), 783–811. DOI: 10.1007/s10664-022-10136-2

Meinel, C., & Leifer, L. (2022). Design thinking research: Building innovation eco-systems. In *Understanding innovation: The role of design thinking in software engineering* (pp. 45–67). Springer.

Nielsen, J., & Molich, R. (1990). Heuristic evaluation of user interfaces. In *Proceedings of the SIGCHI Conference on Human Factors in Computing Systems* (pp. 249–256). ACM. DOI: 10.1145/97243.97281

Norman, D. (2013). *The design of everyday things: Revised and expanded edition*. MIT Press.

Ralph, P., & Wand, Y. (2016). A proposal for a formal definition of the design concept. *Design Science*, *2*(4), 1–22. DOI: 10.1017/dsj.2016.2

Spencer, J. R., Toshniwal, S., & Weiss, A. M. (2022). Human-centered design in software engineering: Methods and case studies. *IEEE Transactions on Software Engineering*, *48*(4), 1080–1094. DOI: 10.1109/TSE.2021.3112345

Zimmerman, J., Stolterman, E., & Forlizzi, J. (2010). An analysis and critique of Research through Design: Towards a formalization of a research approach. In *Proceedings of the 8th ACM Conference on Designing Interactive Systems (DIS)* (pp. 310–319). ACM. DOI: 10.1145/1858171.1858228

Chapter 2
Leveraging Artificial Intelligence Techniques in Design Thinking Tools for Software Engineering

C. V. Suresh Babu
https://orcid.org/0000-0002-8474-2882
Hindustan Institute of Technology and Science, India

Mala Raja Sekhar
https://orcid.org/0009-0007-6841-8330
Hindustan Institute of Technology and Science, India

A. Sachin
Hindustan Institute of Technology and Science, India

Bala Brindha
Hindustan Institute of Technology and Science, India

ABSTRACT

This chapter explores the integration of AI techniques into design thinking tools for software engineering, aiming to enhance problem-solving, innovation, and user-centered development processes. The study focuses on software engineers, designers, and technology-driven organizations seeking to optimize software development work-flows through AI-powered design thinking. The methodological approach includes a comprehensive review of existing AI applications in design thinking, an analysis of AI-enhanced prototyping and ideation tools, and case studies demonstrating their effectiveness in real-world software engineering scenarios. The findings reveal that

DOI: 10.4018/979-8-3693-9531-8.ch002

AI-driven design thinking tools streamline ideation, improve decision-making, and enhance user experience modeling, ultimately accelerating software development cycles. The chapter concludes that AI integration fosters a more adaptive, efficient, and innovative approach to software design, with significant implications for improving software engineering practices. .

1. INTRODUCTION

Software engineering has entered a transformative era where user-centric innovation and rapid adaptability are no longer luxuries but necessities. The evolving expectations of users, coupled with the increasing complexity of digital products, demand a rethink of conventional software development methodologies. This chapter begins by introducing the foundational ideas of design thinking and its growing influence in software engineering, especially in the context of rising AI integration. It also outlines the chapter's purpose and scope, preparing the reader for an exploration of how artificial intelligence is reshaping design thinking practices to meet modern software engineering challenges.

Design thinking is an empathetic approach that generates innovation and iterative testing to solve complex problems. This approach is applied in software engineering to create functional and aesthetically appealing solutions for users. Methodology Some of the stages involve empathizing with users, defining problems, and development of ideas, prototyping, and testing. Strength is in its iterative nature: design thinking reinforces itself in feedback loops, enhancing what should be high-quality products in software. Any landscape as rapidly shifting as that of software engineering-from a field whose users' expectations shift and evolve at once subtly and profoundly-design thinking offers a flexible structured framework. Traditional software development processes such as the Waterfall or Agile methodologies strongly orient towards technical performance and adhering to the deadline but miss the target when it comes to changing user requirements. Design thinking bridges this gap by placing the user at its center. Ingraining the concepts of design thinking into the processes of engineering software ensures that the products are both technologically robust and appealing to users (Buchanan, 1992).

The rise of Artificial Intelligence (AI) in software development signals a paradigm shift in how developers approach solving problems, efficiency, and innovation. AI-facilitated tools significantly impact the way developers write, test, debug, and optimize code. The integration of machine learning, NLP, and deep learning in recent times has transformed software engineering to be more dynamic. Through the automation of certain repetitive tasks, the developers can get assisted by insights into the products and even suggestions on how to enhance the code-that is leading to faster development cycles and higher quality. Some other AI-based tools, such as code completion engines by GitHub's Copilot and Tabnine, are presented as practical examples of how AI could better the productivity of software. The intuition behind what a developer is trying to write next at a time of auto-completing large code segments reduces the overall cognitive load that developers can put into more complex logic and user-centric features. AI helps determine bugs and optimize algorithms in addition to ensuring that all codes are consistent within large projects. This hints at a future where AI occupies its rightful place as a “must-have” co-pilot in software development- procreasing speed, maximally using one's smarter abilities, and efficiency (Flores & Meseguer, 2018).

This chapter will discuss integrating AI into design thinking tools in software engineering. It will then specifically explore how AI tooling could augment various stages within design thinking-ideation, prototyping, and even testing. Design thinking has been proven useful in creating novel software products already because it encourages empathy and rapid prototyping of ideas. However, the largely manual process here might severely limit scalability in very large or quite complex projects. AI certainly can help augment these processes by automating routine tasks and providing data-driven insights that enhance better, more efficient decision-making. In this chapter, we will deep dive into the growing crux of AI and design thinking with tools like Stepsize, Cody, Tabnine, among others. It covers an analysis of the benefits and challenges in using AI-driven tools with the context of software engineering. This would help solve how the tools improve teams' collaboration efficiency, the quality of code written, and the overall time to develop products. The risks of over-automation, technology dependency, and the general need to balance AI with human creativity form some of the potential limitations of AI integration in this chapter. As part of this perspective, this chapter will combine the advantages and challenges to bring forth a more comprehensive overview of how AI might take design thinking forward in software engineering. In this respect, the investigation is set within a more extensive software engineering framework comprising Agile, DevOps, and Waterfall in order to demonstrate how AI-enhanced design thinking can transcend the varied development environments (Razzouk & Shute, 2012).

The remainder of the chapter is structured as follows: Section 2 presents the background and evolution of design thinking in software engineering. Section 3 explores how AI tools integrate with design thinking processes. Section 4 provides case studies and tool analyses. Section 5 offers a comparative analysis of AI-powered design thinking tools. Section 6 discusses the benefits and challenges of AI integration. Section 7 delivers practical suggestions and recommendations. Section 8 outlines future directions for research and practice. Finally, Section 9 concludes the chapter by summarizing key insights and highlighting the road ahead.

2. BACKGROUND

To appreciate the current synergy between AI and design thinking, it is essential to trace the historical evolution of design thinking within the software development landscape. This section presents a detailed background that contextualizes how design thinking transitioned from a product design methodology to a core component of software engineering. It further investigates the limitations of traditional design thinking, laying the groundwork for why integration with AI is not only beneficial but necessary. Understanding these constraints helps highlight the opportunities and improvements that AI-enhanced design thinking can offer.

2.1 Evolution of Design Thinking in Software Engineering

The theory of design thinking has indeed undergone several landmark developments since it was initially developed and implemented into software engineering. Design thinking was much more connected with product design and human-centered innovation out with the software industry. When the development of software became more user-centric, methodologies of design thinking naturally started getting integrated into the software engineering practices. For long, software engineering was much more dominated by methodologies such as Waterfall that focus more on a structured and linear approach to development. Although they were great tools for managing large projects with tight requirements, they did not offer the flexibility needed to tackle changing user requirements. This inflexibility resulted in embracing Agile and other iterative approaches, which emphasize team collaboration, adaptability, and user feedback throughout the development cycle. It ushered in aspects of solving real-world issues by giving more focus on user experience, which is largely a departure from the traditional approach of software development, which is heavily oriented on functionality and performance. Design thinking revolutionized the way a software product would be conceptualized, developed, and iterated. The advent of AI further accelerates this evolution, enabling developers to analyze the behavior of users in real-time and create more personalized and adaptive experiences for the software.

In modern software engineering, design thinking is no longer optional but becomes a fundamental framework when developing software that responds to users' current needs (Carroll, 2012).

2.2 Limitations of Traditional Design Thinking

Though it has been extolled as an ability to market creativity and user-centric innovation, traditional design thinking is marred by a number of drawbacks in the context of modern software engineering. At its core, the greatest limitation that hampers the traditional design thinking is its lack of scalability. Design thinking works very well in closely-knit smaller teams where collaboration and iteration are better appreciated and responded to. However, coordination of a number of iterations across various teams, gathering feedbacks, and implementing changes is tougher when the size of a project gets bigger. In large software engineering environments with design thinking, iterative cycles may slow the development; indeed, this is likely to happen when the working teams are spread over time zones or when working on tight deadlines. The other limitation is its susceptibility to subjective factors. Design thinking is very empathetic and very dependent on the interpretation of user feedback. While this is an important aspect of creativity, this does embed biases or misinterpretations where feedback has not been clearly constructed or analyzed. Success in design thinking when applied to software engineering depends greatly on teams' ability to correctly interpret a balance between needs of the user and the given technical constraints. Most importantly, conventional design thinking cannot take in the assimilation abilities toward data-driven decision making (Suresh Babu et. al., 2025). The amount of available user data in the modern software environment is enormous and can only be meaningfully interpreted through using advanced analytic tools. Traditional design thinking, relying primarily on qualitative methods, fails to leverage these enormous sources of data efficiently. This leads to an inability to seize opportunities to modify products on the spot according to actual user behaviors and preferences. Lastly, traditional design thinking can be time and resource-intensive as it involves workshops, brainstorming, prototyping, and testing with end-users, all of which delay timelines more readily in fast-paced industries like those pertaining to software development (Flores & Meseguer, 2018).

2.3 Introduction to AI-Driven Design Thinking Tools

The emergence of AI-driven tools for design thinking forms a revolution in the general ideas of how one can put together software. These tools include Stepsize, Cody, Tabnine, and so forth. They incorporate the typical design thinking with machine learning algorithms and AI-driven insights to optimize different parts of the software development process. Perhaps the biggest advantage that these AI-powered tools offer is that they allow the developers to automate some of the repetitive work like code completion, debugging, and refactoring, and thus spend more time on higher-level design and problem solving. Other tools, like Tabnine or Cody, apply

AI to predict and make code completions based on the context of where the code is being written. This accelerates code-writing and also introduces fewer errors while coding. Another tool, Stepsize, improves problem identification because it integrates directly into a developer's workflow so that the team can document technical debt as they write the code. It catches problems in real-time, pointing out areas that may go wrong, thus ensuring that flaws are picked up early during the development cycle, saving costly fixes later on. Other tools, such as Codeium and Mintify, focus on AI-assisted debugging with code refactoring that suggests improvements to enhance code quality and execution. These tools analyze the code structure, compare it to vast databases of coding patterns, and come up with improvements that developers might not easily spot. AI-driven tools are revolutionizing both individual productivity and team collaboration in fresh ways. For instance, using Mutable will facilitate better communication and collaboration in Agile development environments, as knowing what is going on in the team dynamics and what is progressing helps improve efficiency. In short, AI-driven design thinking tools will change the style of software engineering by enriching the creative and problem-solving powers of developers (Shepherd, 2020).

3. LITERATURE REVIEW

As design thinking continues to shape modern software engineering practices, its integration with artificial intelligence emerges as a compelling advancement. AI has the potential to amplify every stage of the design thinking process—from empathizing with users to prototyping and testing solutions. This section delves into the specific ways AI tools are being incorporated into design thinking frameworks, thereby enhancing their scalability, precision, and responsiveness. Through real-world examples and current applications, the discussion will show how AI doesn't replace human creativity but rather augments it to build more adaptive, user-focused software.

3.1 Design Thinking Strategies in Software Development

Design thinking has become a revolutionary strategy in software development centered on user-centered innovation through iterative problem-solving. In contrast to conventional methods, including the Waterfall model, characterized by a linear, step-by-step process, design thinking values flexibility, empathy, and creativity. The drawbacks of Waterfall result from its rigidity in addressing changing user needs, which results in inefficiency within dynamic software development environments. In reply, Agile and Lean principles brought forward iterative feedback loops that foster flexibility and ongoing improvement. While Agile principles focus on quick prototyping and incremental delivery, however, they do not always include the profound user empathy and ideation methods that characterize design thinking (Brown, 2009). Design thinking extends Agile principles further by promoting collaboration between cross-functional groups and emphasizing heavily user experience. Evidence indicates that software engineering teams using design thinking principles create more innovative solutions and attain greater user satisfaction (Cross, 2011). Emphasizing user empathy, design thinking helps developers foresee pain points and iterate solutions accordingly. One of the strengths of design thinking is that it is collaborative in nature, involving multidisciplinary teams iterating on problem definition, ideation, prototyping, and testing. But as Razzouk and Shute (2012) point out, although design thinking has been successful in small groups and startup settings, making it work at large, distributed teams is a challenge. AI allows software development teams to become more efficient and preserve the iterative approach of design thinking without sacrificing creativity and user-centricity.

3.2 Past Research on AI Tools in Software Development

The application of AI in software programming has been widely researched, and studies have projected that it will automate routine operations, enhance decision-making, and enhance productivity in general (Suresh Babu et al., 2025). The tools powered by AI aid several facets of software development, from code generation, bug identification, refactoring, and testing. Kim et al. (2018) had looked into whether machine learning-based algorithms could facilitate the automation of code snippet construction to save manual labor and prevent coding errors. Artificial intelligence-driven tools like Tabnine and Cody use deep learning to offer real-time code completion recommendations, cutting down drastically on the mental effort required of developers. Ray et al. (2020) investigated the use of AI in technical debt management, illustrating how tools such as Stepsize offer real-time feedback that enables developers to resolve potential issues ahead of time before they become problematic. Likewise, Tufano et al. (2019) examined AI-based debugging tools, including Codeium and Mintify, that leverage machine learning models trained on large datasets to identify inefficient code patterns and suggest optimizations. Platforms such as Mutable leverage AI to monitor teamwork dynamics, document the progress of a project, and offer live feedback, such that teams always remain on course. Nevertheless, Filkov and Devanbu (2020) warn against adopting AI in software development as there are pitfalls in overtrust of automation, alongside ethical considerations on biased choices.

3.3 Gaps in Current Literature

Although there is extensive research on both AI in software development and design thinking as separate areas, studies that explore their intersection remain scarce. Most existing literature focuses on AI's ability to automate technical tasks, such as code generation and debugging, rather than its potential to contribute to creative problem-solving, ideation, and prototyping in design thinking. One critical gap in current literature is the lack of research on AI's role in the ideation phase of design thinking. Another important gap is the scalability of AI-augmented design thinking in large-scale organizations. While research shows that AI enhances productivity in small or medium-sized teams, there is limited research on how AI-facilitated design thinking can be effectively applied in enterprise-level projects with multiple stakeholders, distributed teams, and intricate workflows. The issue is how to make sure that AI integration does not introduce extra coordination overhead or upset established team dynamics. Furthermore, there is not enough research on the ethical consequences of AI in making design decisions. Because AI models are trained using past data, they are vulnerable to biases that can unwittingly affect software design decisions

3.4 Relevance of AI-Driven Tools in the Design Process

AI-driven tools are increasingly relevant in the design thinking process, especially as software engineering projects become more complex. These tools have the potential to aid various stages of design thinking, ranging from ideation through prototyping and testing, by automating repetitive tasks, processing large datasets, and speeding up iteration cycles. During the ideation process, AI-based tools scan user data, recognize patterns in behavior, and produce insights that are used to drive problem-solving. For instance, AI can scan vast amounts of user feedback, survey data, and market data to recognize unmet needs and thus assist teams in developing solutions that are better attuned to actual demands. Instead of displacing human creativity, AI is an augmentation tool that facilitates the brainstorming process by offering data-driven inspiration. By reducing the time spent on coding manually, AI allows teams to quickly iterate and improve their prototypes. During the test phase, quality assurance and debugging tools powered by AI assist the developers in determining and fixing the problems more quickly.

4. METHODOLOGY

In this chapter, research methodologies will be a mix of qualitative and quantitative approaches through exploring the utilization of AI-driven tools for design thinking in software engineering. The case study method will dominate the data-gathering process in order to understand properly the reality where AI tools are applied in software engineering projects. Case studies have been chosen based on a cross-section of industries that could help demonstrate the wide applicability of design thinking with AI enhancement. Beside case studies, a comparative analysis will be carried out that would compare traditional design thinking methods against AI-enhanced ones.

4.1 Case Studies: Design Thinking Powered by AI in Software Development

Case Study 1: AI-Powered Agile Software Development

Tabnine, an artificial intelligence code-completion system, was deployed in an Agile software development organization globally to improve productivity. Slow iterations, repeated coding efforts, and debugging inefficiency were issues facing the company. Through incorporating Tabnine in the development cycle, the organization shaved off 40% of the coding time and increased software delivery speed. Evidence was presented that the rate of defects decreased by 35%, with AI-enabled debugging catching potential mistakes prior to deploying code. Flow efficiency improved for developers by 25%, since AI enabled them to concentrate on higher-level issues rather than trivial coding.

Case Study 2: AI-based Bug Detection and Code Refactoring

A fintech company that focuses on AI-based financial solutions implemented Bugasura and Mintify for bug tracking and code refactoring, both of which are automated. Prior to integration, the company invested considerable resources in manual debugging and post-deployment bug fixing. With AI, they were able to detect and fix 95% of the code inefficiencies prior to production, lowering post-launch bugs by 50%. Code analysis using AI enhanced system reliability and decreased technical debt, allowing for quicker updates and smooth user experience enhancements.

Case Study 3: Technical Debt Management and AI:

A mid-sized SaaS firm creating enterprise collaboration software incorporated Stepsize, an AI-based technical debt management tool. Their earlier process was plagued by untracked code inefficiencies, resulting in long-term maintenance issues. With AI-powered documentation and real-time monitoring, the company cut refactoring costs by 30% and reduced system crashes. The development team also enjoyed automated feedback on stale code sections, making it maintainable for the long term.

4.2 Comparative Analysis: Traditional vs. AI-Enhanced Design Thinking

Traditional Design Thinking and AI-Augmented Design Thinking are two concepts that together open different advantages to be included in the thinking process when using AI. Traditionally, design thinking involves only human creativity, collaboration, and empathization requirements for the development of user-centric solutions. Such processes are time-consuming, and the outcome depends on the reception of it at the end, through users' feedback. Traditional design thinking suffers greatly in terms of scalability, especially in large and sophisticated software engineering projects. The iterative cycles of prototyping and testing can slow down the development process because each cycle will take more time.

Automated testing, in particular, allows teams to quickly validate their ideas and move forward with more confidence. Moreover, AI can enhance collaboration in distributed teams by providing real-time insights into project progress and team dynamics. However, the comparative analysis also highlights some challenges with AI-enhanced design thinking. While AI tools are excellent at tasks automation and answering data-driven information, they often fail to capture the levels of empathy and instinct human beings bring to the table. Overreliance on AI may thus lead to loss in human-centric focus most inherent to design thinking; thus, only the best results would be achieved if AI were used to augment rather than replace human creativity (Flores & Meseguer, 2018).

4.3 Application Development Methodologies (Agile, DevOps, Waterfall)

Though design thinking captures well the agility of modern software development approaches like Agile and DevOps, it poses somewhat stronger challenges to the more traditional models like Waterfall. Agile methodologies emphasize flexibility, iteration, and constant feedback from users-all of which match perfectly with the basic principles of design thinking. Within the Agile environment, AI tools accelerate the pace of iterations by automatically coding, debugging, and even generating rapid prototypes. For instance, in an Agile sprint, it could force a developer to write functionally correct code in time, although Stepsize tracks and prioritizes technical debt without slowing down the iteration process (Daugherty & Wilson, 2018).

4.4 Justification for Chosen Methodology

There is justification for the usage of such a research methodology as a combination of cases with comparative analysis and surveys to study the practical and theoretical aspects of integrating AI in design thinking in software engineering. Case studies carry real examples about how the AI-driven tools improved the process of design thinking and offer insight on various points of interest, including points of strength and challenges faced by teams in different industries. These case studies are necessary to truly understand the impact of AI on design thinking and how it radically alters the traditional workflows in the design of software. In contrast, comparative analysis offers one a chance to explore the contrast between traditional and AI-assisted approaches in design thinking.

These surveys will capture the experiences and opinions of developers, designers, and project managers who use AI in their day-to-day workflows. Such data is essential in identifying the common challenges, including any resistance to AI adoption or difficulties in balancing AI automation with human creativity. The combination of these methodologies ensures a comprehensive and multi-faceted exploration of the topic, providing both empirical data from real-world applications and theoretical insights from comparative analysis (Shepherd, 2020).

5. ANALYSIS OF AI-POWERED TOOLS FOR DESIGN THINKING

With the surge in AI adoption across software development, a variety of tools have emerged that support and enhance design thinking practices. However, to make informed decisions about tool selection and integration, it is important to analyze these solutions in depth. This section provides a comparative analysis of leading AI-powered tools used in design thinking, evaluating them on functionality, adaptability, user experience, and alignment with different phases of the design process. By understanding the strengths and limitations of each tool, software teams can better tailor their workflows to achieve optimal innovation and user satisfaction.

5.1 Step Size: Improving Design Documentation and Problem Identification

Stepping into technical debt management, Stepsize is a recent tool from the AI end designed as a resource for developers to track technical debt by improving design documentation and problem identification. Technical debt refers to the implied cost of additional rework caused by choosing an easy solution now instead of a better approach that takes more time. Thus, keeping control over a piece of software over its lifetime is the task of managing technical debt. This is caught early on by technical debt, which is what Stepsize allows its teams to address before it turns reactive. Stepping it up also facilitates collaboration among team members by centralizing technical debt documentation making it easy for everyone to keep in step with what is happening on the project from a technical standpoint. By automating identification and documentation of technical debt, Stepsize enables teams to concentrate more on creative problem-solving and user-centered design. This should lead to higher overall quality of the software product (Devanbu, 2020).

5.2 Cody and Tabnine: Automating Code Generation in the Design Process

Cody and Tabnine are AI coding tools that help developers speed up the design thinking process as they outline code, possibly or generated from the machine. They utilize machine learning algorithms to predict the completion of code pieces within the context of the code being written. It makes the development process much more cohesive and efficient because of how the new code meshes with the existing code. This helps to speed up the production of code similarly for rapid prototyping and for the iterative testing phases of design thinking. Cody and Tabnine show the power of AI when applied to the streamlining of the design thinking process. They enable developers to iterate far more quickly by automating routine coding tasks and reducing the time invested in debugging and refactoring which ultimately lead to better quality and efficiency in software development (Moon, 2018).

5.3 Mutable: Enhancing Collaboration in Agile Development

Mutable is a collaboration and communication tool that works with the help of AI to support the design thinking process in Agile development. Agile development is such that there is collaboration required efficiently, in the case of large or distributed teams. Agile, at every stage, insists on very short cycles of development, high feedback during continuous integration, and makes it possible for the team members to be on the same page through communication at every stage.

The problem that Mutable addresses is to provide real-time insights into team dynamics, project progress, and potential bottlenecks so that teams can stay on track and collaborate more efficiently. Mutable uses AI to monitor team activities, track progress on tasks, and make sense of the communication patterns in a way to give project managers a clear overview of the status of the team at any time. To say, for instance, when a person doing a particular task is stuck, or a bottleneck is identified in the flow of work, Mutable can notify the project manager to intervene promptly and set things right. This real-time visibility into team performance ensures that problems are addressed before they escalate, maintaining the momentum of the Agile cycle (Meseguer, 2018).

5.4 Codeium and Mintify: AI for Debugging and Code Refactoring

Codeium and Mintify are AI-driven tools for debugging and code refactoring, both of which are concerned with the prototyping and testing phases of the design thinking process. They help in the identification of issues within the code, suggest improvements, and optimize performance, stability, and scalability.

This means that if a developer writes a piece of code that has a tendency to be performance bottleneck-prone, for instance, then Codeium flags it and could recommend a more optimal solution. That is very valuable especially in design thinking, where maintain focused approaches toward user needs and functionality require that the technical problems are addressed as soon as possible. Codeium and Mintify advance the efficiency of the design thinking process by automating key aspects of debugging and refactoring thus allowing for faster iterations towards higher-quality software outcomes (Bavota, 2019).

5.5 Grit and WhatTheDiff: AI-Powered Change Management and Code Comparison

Grit and WhatTheDiff are change management and code comparison tools, two aspects of the software development lifecycle which are particularly important in the stages of design thinking development and iteration. In design thinking, rapid prototyping and testing depend on effective change management within the codebase, or there is a possibility that the momentum and feedback from users will not drive the product toward its evolution. Grit aims to help development teams effectively manage changes across complex projects. What The Difference does is allow developers to instantly see exactly what has been changed between one version of code and another and thereby provides an easier form of understanding of the changes and avoids the unintended side effects. As an example, if a developer changes the code in one block to optimize some functionality, WhatTheDiff would provide insight on any related blocks of code that may be impacted, thus ensuring the new functionality would thoroughly be tested and validated (Moon, 2018).

5.6 Bugasura: Enhancing Bug Tracking and Issue Resolution

Bugasura is an AI-powered bug tracking tool that allows the process of adding to be speeded up in the problem-solving process when it comes to software development. The efficient tracking of bugs in the process of design thinking includes actual feedback loops used when perfecting the product based on real-world testing in the testing and iteration phases. Bugasura simply streamlines the process by intelligent bug tracking and issue resolution capability to ensure that bugs are identified, documented, and solved as fast as possible Thus, this minimizes the length of time developers spend on handling bugs or troubleshooting. Consequently, it accelerates the iteration process so that prototypes can be tested and refined rapidly (Bavota, 2019).

6. DISCUSSION AND FINDINGS

While the integration of AI into design thinking processes unlocks a host of advantages—such as faster prototyping, improved user insights, and enhanced collaboration—it also introduces a range of new challenges. This section critically examines both sides of the coin, offering a balanced view of how AI-enriched design thinking can benefit software engineering, while also identifying the pitfalls such as over-automation, ethical dilemmas, and dependence on technology. The discussion aims to equip developers, designers, and project managers with a realistic understanding of the opportunities and limitations in this evolving landscape.

6.1 How AI Enhances Ideation, Prototyping, and Testing in Design Thinking

AI has fundamentally changed the design thinking process through strengthening the ideation, prototyping, and testing phases. These stages are essentially the building blocks of building great innovative, user-centric software solutions, and AI-driven tools make them more efficient and effective. In this respect, the ideation phase is crucial in analyzing ample amounts of data to generate insights in developing new ideas. Tools like Stepsize also track technical debt during the ideation phase where such ideas being created are not only user-centric but technically feasible as well.

Tools such as Tabnine and Cody, during the prototyping phase, can actually generate code much faster and more efficiently so teams can deliver a working prototype possibly in a much reduced time frame. These tools can even foretell code patterns that may be suggested to reduce the cognitive burden of developers while speeding up the development cycle. Furthermore, AI-facilitated prototyping tools can simulate user interactions with the software even further to give crucial feedback before the actual build-out of the product. This helps them identify early problems and called for needed adjustments that may make the prototypes more refined and effective (Wilson, 2018).

6.2 Real-World Case Studies: Successful Integration of AI Tools

There are several real-world case studies that have successfully integrated AI tools into the design thinking process and are therefore demonstrating practical benefits in using AI to improve software development. A very good example would be from a very large e-commerce company, which has already infused AI-powered code-completion tools such as Tabnine within the development workflow. The company was experiencing problems with its iterative development process-a huge point of concern, particularly when it came to prototyping and testing. Thus, the firm identified and focused on technical debt as it was incurred. In this manner, technical debt did not balloon into bigger problems at the later stages of the project: through proactive management of technical debt, the firm is free to focus its attention on innovation and user-centric design while ensuring that software remains technically sound. The third case study is about an AI-powered financial technology startup, where it used Bugasura and Mintify for bug tracking and code refactoring. It was designing a new mobile banking application and was given a very short deadline to produce a working prototype. By leveraging Bugasura for automated bug tracking and Mintify for refactoring, the startup was able to iterate pretty fast and solve the issues quickly. The result was a fairly stable and user-friendly app delivered on time with almost negligible issues in the post-launch scenario (Devanbu, 2020).

6.3 Challenges of AI Integration: Overcoming Resistance and Human Oversight

While AI-driven tools can potentially significantly enhance the process of design thinking, its integration into workflows can turn out to be quite challenging. One major challenge has been the resistance towards it. Most development teams have traditional workflows to which they are accustomed. Being used to the usual workflows, they could be reluctant to change because they fear that automation might supplant human creativity or reduce their own role. These AI-driven tools are used only by the right amount of human oversight and correctly. Now, of course, AI can automate many of those tasks, but it is still far from flawless. For instance, an AI automated code generation tool may propose an answer that is technically correct but does not align with the goals of the project or the needs of the user. Thus, there must always be a delicate balance between the use of automation and human judgment. There must be active participation from developers and designers in making decisions through the assistance of tools developed using AI, rather than replacing it with their ability (Kunz, 2020).

6.4 Key Findings on the Impact of AI in Design Thinking

Introducing AI tools to the design thinking process has influenced the software development process in so many ways that have resulted in key findings. First, AI enhances significantly the speed and efficiency of the design process. Applications like Tabnine and Cody reduce the hours which developers take in doing routine coding, leaving them ample time for ideation and problem-solving. This acceleration is highly valued in Agile and DevOps environments because it matches the fast-paced need to iterate rapidly enough to keep in step with users' needs and still remain competitive in the markets. AI tools also speed up the testing and debugging stages, where identified issues are resolved quickly, thereby speeding up the development. There's also the challenge AI will bring to design thinking, including resistance and lack of oversight. As AI will surely enhance efficiency, one of the fragile balances between automation and human creativity has to be maintained. Thus, teams using AI tools have to be highly managed so that the process of design thinking stands firm with its human-centric element. Conclusion: AI transforms the process of design thinking through enhancing efficiency, quality, and collaboration in proper oversight so it is not overly dependent on automatio (Bavota, 2019).

6.5. Suggestions and Recommendations

As AI becomes more intertwined with design thinking, it is imperative for practitioners to adopt strategic approaches that ensure successful implementation and long-term impact. This section offers targeted suggestions and recommendations for developers, designers, educators, and decision-makers aiming to integrate AI into design thinking workflows. Drawing from the insights, analyses, and case studies discussed in earlier sections, the recommendations focus on best practices, ethical considerations, and organizational readiness to embrace this convergence effectively and sustainably. Some best practices have to be adopted to ensure proper integration of AI with the design thinking process. First and foremost, AI should not be looked at as a substitute but an augmentation tool. In fact, AI has been more effective in augmenting human capability in the creative decision-making space rather than attempts to automate.

The education and training of the teams are also important. AI-driven tools can be pretty complex, and without proper training, the team members would not work effectively with them. Regular training sessions and perfect documentations about the best usage practices for AI tools can help bring out the best from these technologies. A culture of experimentation in which experimentation is encouraged will help the teams to work over the resistance to change. The third issue is indeed about the balance between automated and human forms of oversight. As automation can be used for such processes as code generation and testing, there is, however, an inescapable human element to factor in, namely oversight, to ensure solutions are in line with user needs and delivery of the project. This iterative approach lets teams test and refine AI usage while ensuring that AI adds value instead of disrupting workflows (Wilson, 2018).

AI tools selection is one of the defining steps in ascertaining that AI benefits the design thinking process. The major element in selecting AI tools will be their relevance to the needs at which they are supposed to work. For instance, if a team is focused on improving code quality and speeding up the generation of code, tools like Tabnine or Cody, which offer AI-powered code suggestions and completions, would be incredibly useful. These can save developers hours in routine coding tasks and free up the developers' time for other forms of creative and problem-solving work. Similarly, if the application surrounds technical debt management and good code, then Stepsize should be the tool of interest, since it naturally tracks and will automatically prioritize what parts of the codebase need work. It's also important to consider how AI tools handle large datasets, particularly in terms of performance and response times.

Cost and licensing is another important question. Most of the AI tools come with free options, but require payment for functionalities in premium editions to unlock certain features of a project. The teams should also estimate the investment costs in comparison to the productivity gains and the better quality of the code (Meseguer, 2018).

One of the biggest obstacles in implementing AI to the design thinking process is finding a way to balance automation with human creativity. While AI-driven tools can automate a lot of repetitive code generation and debugging tasks as well as testing, they definitely shouldn't overshadow the creative and empathetic aspect so critical for providing user-centered solutions. In order to strike that balance, a very important step would be identifying the limits of AI so it's known where human input can't be replaced. For the first, automating human creativity. The use of AI tools in this example like Tabnine or Mintify could well aid the developer by giving propositions and automating most of the mundane work while proper decisions about designing, structuring, and an interface friendly to user would be provided or should be held by humans. After all, developers and designers understand better the users' needs for a project, its goals, and even ethical considerations that an AI can't. One way to strike a balance between automation and creativity is by making collaboration happen among team members. Teams should, from time to time, check whether AI is enhancing or inhibiting the creativity and productivity among the team members. An iterative approach by teams can ensure refinement in the use of AI for striking the right balance between human input and automation (Kunz, 2020).

The use of AI in the design thinking process may pose quite a few barriers, such as resistance from team members, technical challenges as well as over-reliance on automation. However, several strategies exist that teams can adopt to overcome such barriers and integrate AI tools into their workflows successfully. First comes the introduction of openness and experimentation. The fear of change or simply a misunderstanding of how AI can be related to jobs often acts as a big defense. Teams, therefore, need to create an environment encouraging teams to experiment with AI tools. This can be done by providing workshops and training along with hands-on experience with AI tools, demystifying AI and showing the actual enhancement of their work through it. Once the team gets comfortable with those tools, AI can then be introduced to other stages of the design process, such as testing or prototyping. Gradual introduction of this sort is easier for teams because they fine-tune how they use AI over time. Finally, one has to address over-reliance concerns. The teams should draw clear lines on when and how AI tools should be used and make sure they do not undermine human principles of design thinking. Proper collaboration will ensure that a technology solution does not prioritize itself above the human-centric principles of design thinking and that it is used responsibly and effectively (Meseguer, 2018).

7. FUTURE SCOPE FOR RESEARCH

The convergence of AI and design thinking is still in its formative phase, with much potential left to be explored. This section looks ahead to the future of software engineering, highlighting emerging trends, anticipated innovations, and strategic recommendations for researchers and practitioners. Whether it's the rise of adaptive UX, AI-assisted brainstorming, or ethical AI design, this part of the chapter offers insights into where the industry is heading and how teams can prepare to harness the next wave of change in user-centered, intelligent software development.

7.1 Emerging Trends in AI-Driven Design Thinking

As AI technology continues to evolve, several key trends are shaping the future of AI-driven design thinking in software engineering. These trends highlight how AI will further integrate into the ideation, prototyping, and testing phases of design thinking, making processes more efficient, scalable, and user-focused.

1. AI-Driven Generative Design

Among the most promising developments is the application of AI-generated design solutions. Generative AI applications scan for constraints, user data, and functional needs and automatically develop several design options (Suresh Babu & Adhithya, 2023). Such a strategy accelerates the ideation process, whereby teams can choose the best-performing design using insights generated from data over intuition. Autodesk is already applying AI generative design to optimize UI/UX processes in software engineering.

2. AI and Virtual Reality (VR) for Prototyping

AI combined with VR and AR technologies will change software prototyping forever. AI-powered VR simulations enable teams to validate user interactions in a virtual environment prior to actual development. It gives instant feedback on usability, eliminating expensive iterations. AI-powered VR is especially beneficial in gaming, healthcare, and immersive UI development.

3. Predictive UX & AI-Based Emotion Recognition

AI can now be used to monitor user behavior, eye movement, and facial recognition to identify emotions while interacting with products. Predictive UX software can predict user frustration, levels of engagement, and preferences and make real-time design changes. This is increasingly being adopted in e-commerce, SaaS sites, and mobile apps, where personalized experiences are key to user retention.

4. Self-Learning AI Systems

Next-generation AI-based design thinking will include self-improving AI models that evolve independently. These models will improve UI/UX designs with automated updates based on ongoing user interaction, optimizing software incrementally without the need for manual updates. This innovation holds promise for applications in automated A/B testing, dynamic interface adaptation, and adaptive software workflows.

5. AI-Enhanced Collaboration for Distributed Teams

As remote work becomes the norm, AI-powered project management tools will become more streamlined for communication, task assignment, and workflow analysis. AI-powered software such as Mutable is already assistive in helping remote teams achieve greater alignment by giving them live insights into team dynamics, project bottle-necks, and tracking progress. AI will continue to be more involved in breaking down global development teams' silos and enabling easier collaboration.

7.2 Critical Analysis: Balancing AI and Human Creativity in Design Thinking

While AI tools offer many benefits in design thinking, they also have challenges that need to be well thought out. A balanced strategy ensures that AI complements and does not substitute human creativity. Next, advantages of AI in Design Thinking and problems and weaknesses are listed.

Advantages of AI in Design Thinking

- Increased Efficiency and Speed: AI speeds up design cycles by automating routine tasks like prototyping, debugging, and user data analysis, allowing designers to concentrate on high-level problem-solving.
- Data-Driven Insights: AI is able to analyze large volumes of user data to identify trends, optimize designs, and enhance decision-making based on behavioral patterns.
- Increased Accuracy and Consistency: AI eliminates human errors in software development, providing more consistent and reliable design iterations.
- Scalability and Automation: AI allows big-scale design flows, aiding in the control of intricate tasks through distributed systems.

Problems and Weaknesses

- Weakened Human Instincts: Though extremely capable, AI lacks intuition, creativity, and contextual comprehension in comparison to that of human designers.
- Bias and Ethical Concerns: AI algorithms carry through on present bias in data through training with subsequent unintentional discriminative impact within design solutions.

- Risk of Over-Reliance: Over-reliance on AI tools can limit designers' critical thinking and independent thinking skills, which could lead to the dampening of innovation.
- Lack of Transparency: Most AI systems are “black boxes” whose workings are hard to comprehend or defend when using AI-based design decisions.
- Striking the Right Balance: AI as a Creative Partner In order to maximize the potential of AI without sacrificing human creativity, organizations must embrace an AI-human collaborative model in design thinking. These strategies include:
- AI-Augmented Ideation: Leverage AI as an inspiration tool and not a decision-maker, so human designers can improve and authenticate AI-created concepts.
- Ethical AI Deployment: Regularly auditing AI models for fairness, transparency, and consistency with human values.
- Hybrid Workflows: Designing workflows where AI streamlines repetitive tasks while humans steer strategic creativity and design decisions.
- Continuous Human Oversight: Maintaining final decision-making in human hands to ensure design integrity and ethical accountability.

7.3 Ethical Considerations in AI-Powered Design Decisions

As AI integration into design thinking becomes increasingly more common, ethical considerations must emerge to the fore. Those considerations make sure AI-driven tools are used responsibly by minimizing bias in AI algorithms. Of course, this is one of the major ethical concerns: bias in AI algorithms. AI systems are trained with data, and if that data comes along with biases, then this could reflect such biases in the recommendations or decisions it arrives at. Take the example of design thinking. In such a scenario, it will result in software or products that inadvertently favour certain groups at the cost of others. As a result, there will be unequal access or even suboptimal user experiences for such communities. Therefore, teams have to ensure that the data being used to train AI tools is diversified and represents all potential users.

Other ethical issues relate to privacy and data security in design decisions AI. Most AI tools base their work on large datasets containing very sensitive user information. Hence, their collection, storage, and use should be done with regard to current data protection regulation, such as the GDPR. Teams must be transparent with the users on the use of their data, protect user privacy through the entire design process, anonymize where possible, and give proper cybersecurity measures preventing unauthorized access to sensitive information.

Finally, the intangible aspects also come from the employment aspect. AI tools taking more and more tasks in the design and development process may displace more jobs for developers and designers. Even if AI increases productivity, its introduction in teams should not be a reason to reduce a workforce's status. Hence, such training and opportunities for upskilling would help team members adjust to this changespace while continuing to play their vital role in AI-enhanced design thinking (Wilson, 2018).

8. CONCLUSION

The fusion of AI with design thinking marks a significant paradigm shift in software engineering, enabling teams to develop smarter, more user-centric solutions at an accelerated pace. This concluding section recaps the key themes and findings presented throughout the chapter, emphasizing the value and challenges of AI-enhanced design thinking. It reflects on the ongoing transformation of software development methodologies and the role of multidisciplinary collaboration in shaping the future. Ultimately, the conclusion reinforces the notion that while technology provides powerful tools, human-centered thinking remains at the heart of meaningful innovation.

This chapter discusses the integration of AI-driven tools within the design thinking process of software engineering, specifically on how AI contributes to every stage of design thinking-from ideation to prototyping and testing. The main contributions of this study are the overall analysis of how these AI tools such as Stepsize, Cody, Tabnine, Mutable, and Bugasura can make the process of making software easier and better, by automating routine tasks, improving collaboration, and providing data-driven insights on how to create a great design. This way, AI enables developers and designers to pay more attention to creative problem-solving and user-centered innovation.

This discussion also delved into integrating AI with design thinking: barriers in reluctance to adopt, human control, and ethical concerns over bias, privacy, and the option between human-centric and non-human interfaces. It used practical cases studies to present how AI-based software engineering is working wonders in enhancing code quality, speeding up iterations, and facilitating distributed team collaboration. Findings In short, the research reveals that AI is efficient and scalable but must be used responsibly keeping human-centric principles of design thinking at its core.

It has been established that AI is a transformer in the design thinking process, especially in software engineering. This is because AI allows teams to iterate faster, generate more innovative solutions, and ultimately produce high-quality software products through automating repetitive tasks and offering powerful data analysis capabilities. Enhanced real-time insights into user behavior, data-driven ideation, and collaboration among team members are some ways AI enhances design thinking. Even more than that, debugging and code refactoring processes are made much more smooth and efficient by using AI-based tools like Bugasura and Mintify. End. But, beyond technical enhancements, AI also changes how a team approaches creativity, problem-solving, and decision-making. It will enable teams to work at really complex challenges while staying focused on empathy and user needs. To better assimilate AI into design thinking, the approach should find a sweet spot: AI as a collaborator with human designers and developers, not a replacement.

The future of software engineering will eventually be in the continually new integration of AI through the design thinking process to create an opportunity for more innovative, efficient, and user-centric development of software. That means the continued evolution of AI technologies will bring higher improvements in several fields, such as in generative design, which enables AI to autonomously generate multiple design solutions, or AI-driven natural language processing that yields very deep insights into user feedback. In combination with emerging technologies like virtual and augmented reality, AI will eventually transform the team prototype and test software in ways that are even more immersive and accurate in their simulation of user interactions. The ethical implications will become increasingly important as AI becomes more deeply embedded in the workflows of software engineering. Issues of bias in AI tools, user privacy, and the need to maintain a balance between the level of automation by AI and human oversight of the activity will be crucial for making AI-driven software development fair, inclusive, and user-focused. Implementing the right strategies, AI can provide unprecedented innovation in software engineering, with teams designing, developing, and delivering the products. The users continue to respond with altered needs in the digital age.

REFERENCES

Babu, C. S., William, M. P., & Fazil, R. A. (2025). The Role of Chatbots in Educational Leadership: Enhancing Decision-Making and Efficiency Through AI Tools. In Chatbots in Educational Leadership and Management (pp. 291-320). IGI Global Scientific Publishing.

Brown, T. (2009). *Change by Design: How Design Thinking Creates New Alternatives for Business and Society*. HarperBusiness.

Buchanan, R. (1992). Wicked Problems in Design Thinking. *Design Issues*, *8*(2), 5–21. DOI: 10.2307/1511637

Cross, N. (2011). *Design Thinking: Understanding How Designers Think and Work*. Berg Publishers. DOI: 10.5040/9781474293884

Daugherty, P. R., & Wilson, H. J. (2018). *Human + Machine: Reimagining Work in the Age of AI*. Harvard Business Review Press.

Flores, M., & Meseguer, J. E. (2018). AI in Software Engineering: Current Applications and Future Directions. *ACM Computing Surveys*, *51*(4), 1–34.

Gerber, E., & Carroll, M. (2012). The Psychological Experience of Prototyping. *Design Studies*, *33*(1), 64–84. DOI: 10.1016/j.destud.2011.06.005

Kim, J., Sung, Y., & Moon, Y. (2018). Machine Learning-Based Code Generation in Software Development. *Journal of Systems and Software*, *146*, 93–105.

Ray, B., Posnett, D., Filkov, V., & Devanbu, P. (2020). Large-Scale Study of Technical Debt in Open Source Software Projects. *IEEE Transactions on Software Engineering*, *45*(10), 965–982.

Razzouk, R., & Shute, V. (2012). What Is Design Thinking and Why Is It Important? *Review of Educational Research*, *82*(3), 330–348. DOI: 10.3102/0034654312457429

Suresh Babu, C. V., & Adhithya, S. (2023). ChatGPT and Other Generative AI Tools in Education: Transformative Potential and Ethical Considerations. In Keengwe, J. (Ed.), *Creative AI Tools and Ethical Implications in Teaching and Learning* (pp. 135–152). IGI Global., DOI: 10.4018/979-8-3693-0205-7.ch007

Tufano, M., Watson, C., Pantiuchina, J., & Bavota, G. (2019). Empirical Study on the Use of Automated Refactoring Tools in Open Source Projects. *Proceedings of the ACM Joint European Software Engineering Conference and Symposium*, 612-623.

KEY TERMS AND DEFINITIONS

Design Thinking: A user-centered, iterative problem-solving methodology that emphasizes empathy, creativity, and experimentation to develop innovative solutions.

Artificial Intelligence (AI): The simulation of human intelligence in machines, enabling them to perform tasks like learning, reasoning, and problem-solving in software development.

AI-Driven Tools: Software applications that leverage machine learning, natural language processing, or other AI technologies to automate, enhance, or support various phases of software engineering.

Technical Debt: The implied cost of additional rework caused by choosing a quicker, less optimal solution in software development instead of a better, more time-consuming approach.

Prototyping: The process of creating early models or simulations of a product to explore ideas, test concepts, and gather feedback before final development.

Agile Development: A flexible and iterative software development methodology that emphasizes collaboration, customer feedback, and rapid delivery of functional components.

Empathy Mapping: A tool used in design thinking to gain deeper insight into the user's experiences, needs, and emotions, forming the foundation for user-centric solutions.

Code Refactoring: The process of restructuring existing computer code without changing its external behavior to improve its readability, maintainability, and performance.

Debugging: The identification and correction of errors or defects in software code to ensure proper functionality and performance.

Collaboration Tools: Digital platforms or applications that support communication, coordination, and teamwork among distributed software development teams.

Machine Learning: A subset of AI that involves training algorithms to identify patterns and make decisions based on data, often used in predictive and automated software tasks.

Human-Centered Design: An approach to problem-solving that focuses on involving the human perspective in all steps of the design process to ensure usability and relevance.

Chapter 3
FusionFlow:
A Software Development Approach in the Era of Design Thinking and AI

A. D. N. Sarma
https://orcid.org/0000-0003-2093-388X
Jaya Soft, India

ABSTRACT

The chapter begins with a brief introduction to design thinking, AI and its advantages. Outlines how the combination of design thinking approaches with the advantages of AI is relevant to software development. Outline the gaps in the existing software development methodologies. Moreover, explain the need for design thinking and AI in software development process. Besides, explain a conceptual view of FusionFlow, which is a software development methodology. FusionFlow model is formed a fusion of design thinking, tools and techniques of AI and existing software practices. Briefly explain various phases of FusionFlow and explain its key characteristics. Furthermore, provide a mapping between various phases of design thinking and FusionFlow -software development model. Finally, presents the benefits of FusionFlow model.

1. INTRODUCTION

Design Thinking (DT) is a process that concerned with solving complex problems in highly user centric way focuses on human first. Further, DT is based on the methods and processes that designers use, which was evolved from a wide range of different fields including architecture, engineering and business. Besides, DT pro-

DOI: 10.4018/979-8-3693-9531-8.ch003

cess can be applied to any field including but not limited to software development that transforms the way and brings creative way to develop software focusing on innovation and user centric approach. In recent years, the field of Artificial Intelligence (AI) has made major progress and finds its presence in all most all industries including software development from automating code generation to testing and deployment. In today's rapidly evolving digital world, role of DT methodologies together with AI can play a significant role in software development that transform boundaries which leads new possibilities of software development methodologies that overcome business challenges and provide business value.

The broad objective of this chapter is to provide an evolution of software development models, and various types of software development methodologies. In addition, mention gaps in traditional software development. Besides, present evolution of DT and its process. Moreover, present the need for DT and AI in software development. Additionally, provide a conceptual view of new software development process that is based on the fusion of three different disciplines such as DT, AI and existing software development processes. In short, this new software development model is called 'FusionFlow'. Further, explain various phases of the FusionFlow model and its key characteristics. In addition, provide a mapping between phases of DT and FusionFlow: software development model. Moreover, mention various benefits of FusionFlow. Finally, conclude the chapter. This chapter is primarily aimed at business leaders, executives, software practitioners, managers, and developer community to provide a complete view of the FusionFlow – Software Development Model and its benefits.

According to a study by Sreenivasan and Suresh (2024) stated that the two disciplines such as DT and AI work together and how AI technologies can advance the design process in terms of encourage innovation, produce more individualized and user-centric solutions. Further, this study examined the fusion of AI and DT to improve the design by making it more unique and innovative way. Additionally, this study was made clear that there is need to address crucial issues like justice, bias, and ethics when incorporating AI into design processes. Moreover, this study revealed potential future fields of study and cross-disciplinary collaborations influencing AI-infused DT. The design industry could greatly benefit from the combination of DT and AI. Further, responsible AI-driven design results from embracing human-AI collaboration focusing on ethics and user privacy. By proactively and morally incorporating AI, and DT together can transform the design process that improve lives, and contribute to a more inclusive and sustainable future.

This chapter is organized as follows: Section 2 presents evolution of software development, various types of software development methodologies, and gaps in the traditional software development methodologies. Section 3 covers evolution of DT, phases of DT, need for DT in digital software development. Following up,

Section 4 depicts various phases in Software Development Life Cycle (SDLC) related work in the field and. Section 5 presents benefits of FusionFlow model in software development process. Finally, Section 6 concludes the chapter. At the end of the chapter, Key Terms and Definitions are provided.

2. SOFTWARE DEVELOPMENT METHODOLOGIES

2.1 Evolution of Software Development

In 1940s-50s, software development process was manual. In those days, computer programmers used to write code using low level programming, which is known as machine language instructions and deal with hardware. In 1950s-60s, programmers start coding using high level programming languages such as BASIC, COBOL and FORTRAN.

In the past 50 years, software development has evolved significantly, spreads its use in all most all industries and software development teams have evolved with it. In 1970s, Waterfall model was invented by Dr. Winston W. Royce, which was the oldest methodology in the field of software development. In 1980s, iterative model was evolved and it focuses on an initial, basic implementation first and then gradually adds more complexity. The main advantage of this model is continuous improvement. It allows for improvements and changes to be made at each stage of the development process, instead of waiting until the end of the project. Further, parallel development is also possible to plan. In this, each phase is iterative and collaborative. In 1990s, Rapid Application Development (RAD) was evolved and couples of years later Rational Unified Process (RUP) was evolved. The RUP is an iterative software development process and is also popularly called unified modelling. This methodology has divided into four phases such as inception, elaboration, construction, and transition.

From 2000 onward there was a paradigm shift in software development methods that focuses more on to agile nature, customer centric. In 2010, a new concept of DevOps was evolved that brings together both Development (Dev) and IT operations (Ops). The primary goal of DevOps is to bridge the gap between development and operations teams. The benefits of this approach are increased collaboration, accelerate delivery through automation fluid responsiveness, fast feedback, and shorter cycle times. In 2013, Docker was released which changes both development and deployment approaches. In simple terms, Docker is a software platform that use operating system level virtualization to deliver software in packages. These software packages are referred as containers that contain all of the necessary elements to run software in any environment. The Docker platform enables developers to create, collaborate, test, monitor, ship, and run applications within lightweight containers, giving them the power to deliver better code more quickly (Weiss, 2024). Later, it extends to a new methodology called Continuous Integration/Continuous Delivery (CI/CD), which aims to streamline and accelerate the software development lifecycle. The process of CI/CD mainly helps organizations to avoid bugs and code failures while maintaining a continuous cycle of software development and updates.

Figure 1. Evolution of Software development models

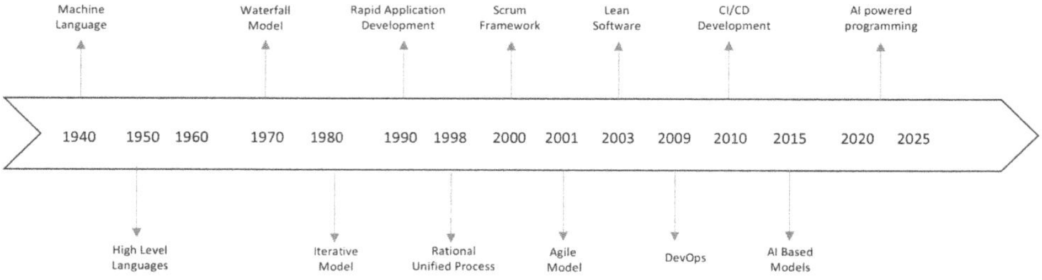

In, 2020s, the software development landscape has undergone substantial changes because of AI technology development and gained widespread and become an integral part to software development. Figure 1 shows the evolution of software development models.

Nowadays, software engineering is a more diverse discipline than ever, with a variety of methodologies, approaches and practices that fulfil different needs of projects. Further, software engineering focuses solely on engineering and is a branch of computer science that deals with the design, development, testing, and maintenance of software applications. Software development is defined as the process of designing and implementing a software solution to satisfy a user, which is relatively less scope as compared to software engineering and is a subset of software engineering. The future of software development processes seams interesting. AI, automation and intersection of DT will play a significant role in paradigm shift of development process and improve customer centric, feedback loops, collaboration, enabling early error detection, auto code remain critical in a world of constant change. According to the study Torkaa and Albayarak (2024), the rise of AI-assisted code-generation tools has significantly transformed software development. The following systems are capable of generating code, such as ChatGPT, OpenAI Codex, GitHub Copilot, and AlphaCode that take advantage of advances in Machine Learning (ML) and Natural Language Processing (NLP) enabled by large language models (LLMs). These tools automatically generate software source code to programmers. In recent years, the shift is moving from manual programming to AI powered programming in software development and this trend will continue for two to three decades and change the total landscape of software development. In coming year, the focus more into optimization of these tools, and to improve their accessibility to make AI based software development more inclusive and equitable.

2.2 Software Development Methodologies

Software development process is a structure approach that describes the processes involved in software development from inception to deployment and maintenance. This software development process is also called SDLC. There are several software development processes available in the literature, and each process has a multiple number of phases, which are different from other and each process has its own advantages and disadvantages. A typical software development process is envisaged in figure 2 and it has six phases.

Figure 2. A typical software development process

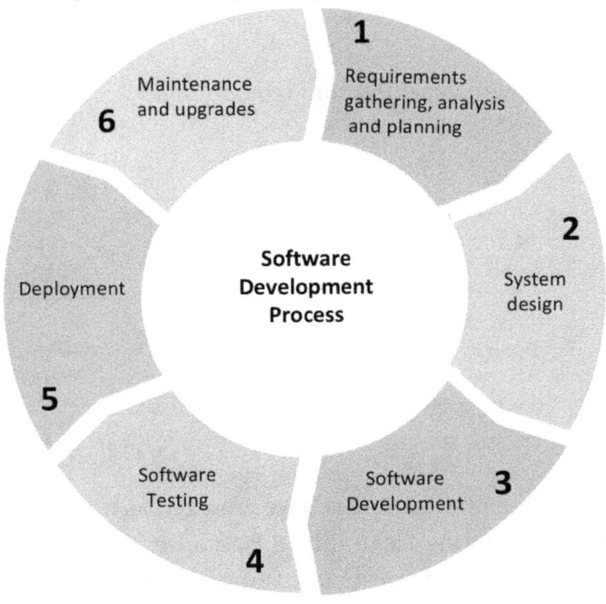

A software development model, in short software model, is a structured representation of the software development process, which provides a framework for planning, structuring, and controlling the process of developing an information system. In generally, a software development model provides a simplified view of a system in a big picture and model comprises of various phases, whereas a software methodology provides a detailed approach of a software model which includes process, procedures and best practices. Thus, software methodology provides a detail for each step of the software model. Moreover, it provides detail guidelines how to perform execute each task with in the phases of the model.

Broadly, software methodologies are classified into two major categories such as traditional and agile based, which is envisaged in figure 3. In traditional software development methodologies consists of various stages or phases. Further, traditional method uses a linear approach where the stages must be competed in sequential order. In summary, the development team works with a predetermined set of phases and complete each stage before proceed into the next stage till the end of the development. Thus, the development process is unidirectional only, which means no feedback from the present stage to its previous stage. This category of approach is highly suitable when all the requirements are available at the beginning of the project and clear. Traditional methods are good choice when there are no changes in the requirements but practically very difficult. The examples of traditional software development methodologies – Waterfall, V-Model, Prince2, Iterative, and Spiral to mention a few.

Figure 3. Types of Software development methodologies

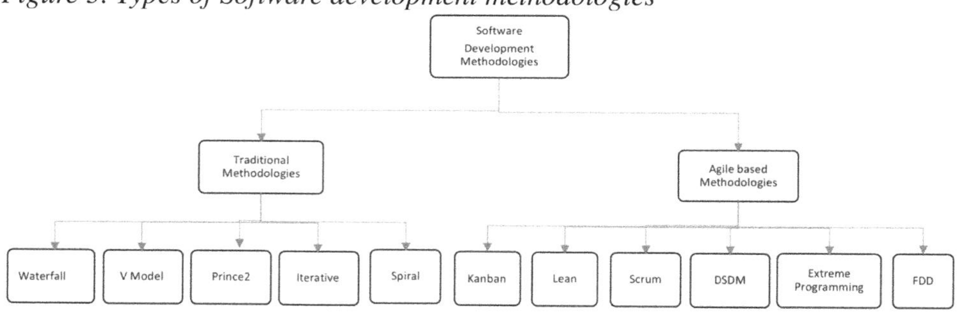

In recent years, Agile methodologies have emerged as prominent contenders in software development, offering flexibility, adaptability, and efficiency in delivering high-quality software within designated timeframes. The most popular Agile methodologies are Kanban, Lean, Scrum, Dynamic System Development Method (DSDM), Extreme Programming (XP), Feature-Driven Development (FDD) to name a few. The FDD method involves five crucial steps spanning the entire development lifecycle that includes development an overall model, build a features list, plan by feature, design by feature and build by feature. The last two steps are iterative. According to a study (Tetteh, 2024), the most common methods of agile development are including DSDM, Scrum, FDD, XP, Kanban, Adaptive Software Development (ASD), Mendix, Lean, and Crystal.

2.2.1 Traditional methodologies

The most common traditional software development models include but not limited to these.

1. **Waterfall Model:** This software model was developed during 1970 which considered as one of the first software development processes. The model is built on linear and sequential processes. Figure 4 (a) shows a typical Waterfall model, the various phases in this model starts from requirements gathering to maintenance. Each phase is defined with a set of deliverables. In this model, requirement changes are difficult to carry out once development begins. As a result, increased time delay and cost in order to carry out the changes.
2. **V-Model:** This model is a refined version of the Waterfall Model with a focus on validation and verification at each phase, which uses a step-by-step procedure to develop software as shown in figure 4 (b). In this model testing activity is parallel, each development activity corresponds to a testing phase this results improved software quality over Waterfall model. Additionally, addressing changing requirements remains difficulty. Further, this model is used for small to medium sized projects where requirements are clearly defined and second testing activities early on and throughout each phase of the development process.

Figure 4. Various types of traditional software models

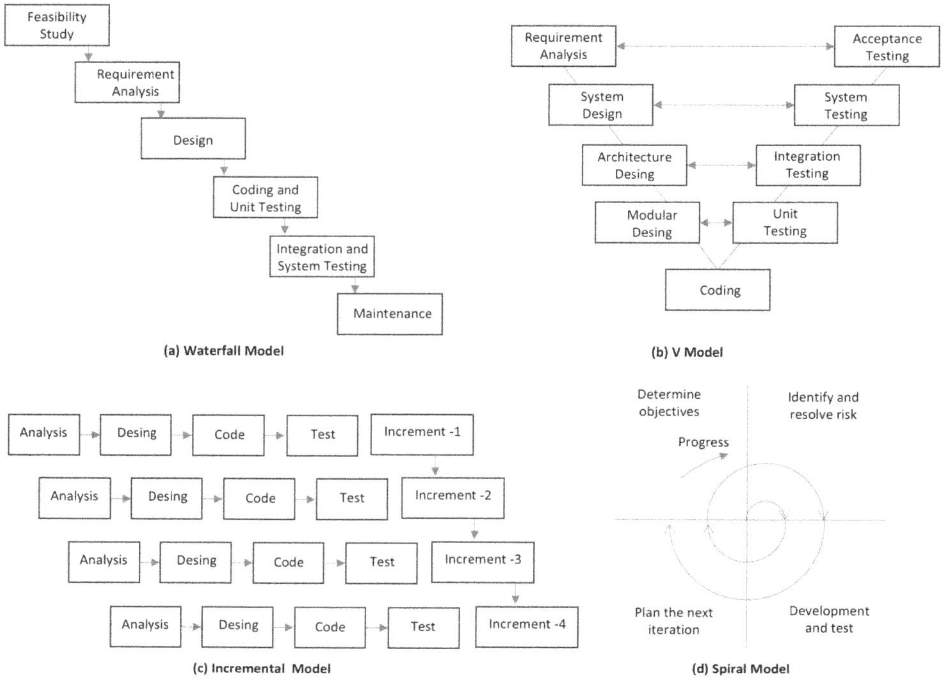

3. **PRINCE2** –PRINCE2 Methodology is a structured project management methodology and is more similar to waterfall model. **PR**ojects **IN** **C**ontrolled **E**nvironments in short **PRINCE**, which is a process-based method for effective project management. It is a de facto standard used by the UK Government, widely recognised and practised in the private sector in the UK and internationally. In PRINCE2, the number 2 stands the second edition that was updated in 1996 of the earlier PRINCE method which was initially announced and developed in 1989.
4. **Incremental Model:** Development and delivery occur in small, incremental segments. The total requirements are breakdown into small number modules. In this model, each module goes through the requirements, design, coding and testing phases, which is shown in figure 4 (c). And each subsequent release of the system adds function to the previous release until all designed functionally has been implemented. This model is most commonly used when there is a possibility of changing the requirements. The client will interact at the end of each increment and provides feedback. So that, it helps to implement client feedback

there by the failure rate of the model is relatively less compared to iterative model where the client will interact only after all iterations of development.

5. **Spiral Model:** The Spiral model is seen as an evolutionary design (Boehm, 1988) in that system is developed from a series of prototypes. Each prototype adds improvements to previous ones. This model combines iterative development with risk analysis. The software project continuously passes through phases or iterations called spirals. Moreover, this model consists of four main phases such as (i) Planning, (ii) Risk Analysis, (iii) Engineering and (iv) Evaluation. A simple spiral model is shown in figure 4 (d) and the number of loops can vary based on the project. Further, each loop of the spiral represents a phase in the software development process. As the number of loops increases then the prototype enables gradual refinement. The main advantage of this model is that the component of risk is included and also customer feedback.

2.2.2 Agile Methodologies

Agile Model: It was evolved in 2001 and is based on iterative and incremental development with a focus on collaboration, user feedback and flexibility. The various agile methodologies are Scrum, Kanban, Extreme Programming. Agile is about adaptability and responsiveness. It breaks down development into smaller, manageable iterations called 'sprints', allowing for regular feedback and adjustments. Over last five years, many organizations are moving to agile methodologies because of its advantages over traditional software development methodologies. In another study, Mishra and Alzoubi (Aug 2023) convey that the use of agile methodology has become widespread in organizations that previously relied on traditional or structured software development methods, such as the waterfall approach. In spite of many advantages of Agile methodologies, a combination approach may be necessary, as Waterfall may be required for certain projects or development phases.

a) **Kanban:** It exhibits many principles characteristic of Agile that includes the capacity to adapt to changes and transparency across the team. Further, it is a flow-based process that emphasizes continuous delivery and visualizes software development workflow using boards. The advantages of this method are: flexibility, focus on continuous delivery, · reduction of wasted work / wasted time and increased productivity are a few.
b) **Lean Software Development:** Lean principles are originated from manufacturing sector. The very objective of this methodology is to maximize value and minimize waste. It is centred around the seven principles such as eliminate waste, amplify learning, defer commitment, deliver as fast as possible, build quality in, respect for people and optimize the whole.

c) **Scrum:** It is a framework within the Agile model that uses sprints, daily stand-ups, and specific roles like scrum master and product owner. It is one of the most popular Agile methodologies. In general, Scrum uses fixed-length sprints, typically this value ranges from two to four weeks long, with defined roles like the Scrum Master and Product Owner. However, Scrum model is flexible to change the length of sprints, which is generally not to small and not to long but the value is decided based on the type of the project and need.

d) **Extreme Programming (XP):** It is one an agile software development framework that aims to produce higher quality software and higher quality of life for the development team. Further, it focuses on technical excellence and customer satisfaction with practices like pair programming and test-driven development. Also, it provides a close collaboration between developers and customers.

e) **DevOps:** It integrates both development and operations to improve overall collaboration and productivity by automating various tasks at each phase of software development as well as workflow. Additionally, it provides continuous feedback to improve the system. Further, it emphasizes automation, continuous integration, and continuous delivery.

2.3 Gaps in the Traditional Software Development Methodologies

Although software development processes are highly matured enough in the modern times, there exists a few gaps with reference to design thinking perspective. The following are the most common gaps found in traditional software development approaches, such as: (i) follow a linear and sequential approaches like Waterfall model, (ii) rigid requirements and mainly focused on functional requirements in logic, where developers write code to solve specific problems, (iii) limited user engagement, (iv) siloed teams and poor performance rigidly follow the processes to ensure quality output (v) missing innovation as well as automation, (vi) focus on creating apps through manual coding, (vii) lack of collaboration and customer feedback (viii) long lead times in software delivery and (ix) difficult to handle change management. Further, the advancements of new technologies such as AI, ML and DL, Big data, 5G, Internet of Thinks (IoT), Blockchain, Augment Reality (AR), and Virtual Reality (VR) are also playing a pivotal role in design and development of software. Here, software refers either a product or solution or a business application that are build using the traditional software methodologies. Thus, the intersection of design principles and new age of technologies together can impact the entire SDLC and even support and maintenance.

1. **Liner and Sequential Process** – Waterfall model is a linear and sequential which means that the various phases in this are linear, and phases are sequential. Further, each phase will take longer duration. So that during these phases' user involvement is minimal and zero involvement even in a few cases. As a result, the products or solutions that are developed during the time interval of individual phased will be disconnect. Generally, software products or solutions are time intrinsic, there is a cost associated for each activity that performed during these phases. In this model, until all the phases are completed the feedback from the user is not available to incorporate changes in the system.
2. **Rigid Requirements:** Gathering of requirements are typically fixed and collected at the beginning of the project development. Incorporating changes to these requirements may require significant effort and time. Further, this mainly impacts other phases software development and the cost associated to make changes in these requirements increases drastically as advancing phase by phase. Further, traditional approach focuses on fulfilling functional requirements in logic by writing coding to solve the problems, which results lack of understanding detail requirements and needs of users.
3. **Limited User Engagement**: In the traditional linear software methodologies primary focusing on the requirement specifications. This results, the study phase of SDLC is confined to gather both technical and functional requirement of the target software to be developed. Further, during requirement elicitation process, less focus or even neglecting the end user experience into consideration. Moreover, while elicitation phase is focused on usability into consideration but not in depth. In most of the software solutions built without fully understanding the needs, behaviours and pain points of the target users into the consideration. As a result, the solutions that are build are not user centric and does not fit to meet the user's expectation.
4. **Siloed Teams and Poor performance**: The software team members such as developers, designers, product and project managers, and other stakeholders work in silos. This results major communication gap among the software team members, which results the overall performance of the project teams. Further, this leads to poor performance of the development process. This can lead to misaligned goals, a lack of collaboration, and incomplete solutions.
5. **Innovation Lacking:** Waterfall methodology is one of the traditional software development methodologies that comprise sets of linear sequential phases such as requirement gathering, design, development, testing, deployment and maintenance. At the end of each phase, a predetermined set deliverables are listed. Thus, this linear sequential model is not only resulting creativity but also missing the focus on innovation. Therefore, the team could not explore innovative approaches to build the end user software.

6. **Slow Feedback Loops**: In both traditional waterfall models and a few agile methodologies, the feedback process between users and stakeholder is slow. It can impact the ability to move quickly from one phase to other phase during the development life cycle. This results longer development to make necessary modification in the development.
7. **Difficult to Handle Changing Requirements** Traditional software development methodologies are based on predefined set of requirements. Thus, any changes in requirements of the system which leads difficulties to address these changes during development phase. But changing requirements are inevitable in the software that needs to address effectively without impacting much on the time lines of the systems development as well as cost.
8. **Lack of Automation and gaps in quality assurance:** Traditional software methodologies are manual and lack of automation not only at phase level but also at activity level within each phase of the model. Staring from study phase to final deployment involves lot of manual process of activities. For example, testing of the development process is performed manual and less automated. Further, this leads gaps between design, development, and quality assurance teams. As a result, quality issues to be notices at later stages to develop the system. leads, leading to difficulties when changes arise during development. Adapting to these changes can be slow and costly.

3. DESIGN THINKING

3.1 Evolution of Design Thinking

The principles of DT has evolved over the past eight decades from an applied scientific methology into a standard framework and process, Further, the roots of DT spans into manufacturing, eductition, health industries and several domains in-cuding software development. The evoluation of desing thinking is shown in figure 5. In1960s is the age of industrail design and focus is in industrial desing and its architecture. Later, the roots of desing thinking is extended as applied scientific methodology to solve issues related to industrial designing. Further, foundations of DT were emerged into multple areas that emphasizing mainly problem-solving and human-centered design aspects.

In 1970, the concept of systems thinking was evolved which leads to development of problem solving frameworks. In 1980s, Stanford founded design program and recognized desing thinking as a methodology that helps to solve problems related to business, technology and society. In 1990s, Stanford's Design Program played a pivotal role in formally recognizing and developing DT as a methodology for addressing complex problems in business, technology, and society. Later, the use of DT has been extended in various fields including but not limited to business strategy, education, healthcare, and manufacturing fields.

Figure 5. Evolution of design thinking

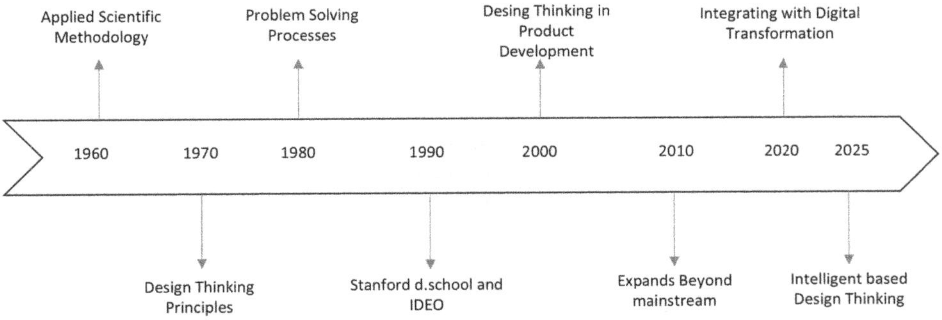

In 2000, DT became an approach in all major industries for sovling problems as well as innovatively. Later, it became a stanard approach for developing products and servcies in software development. In 2020s, the use of desing thinking become a key in digital transforamtion can focusing on User Experince (UX), Customer Experience (CX), Agile practices and Lean startup principles. Early models of desing thinking are confined to human-centered problem solving whereas later models uses prototyping and agile methodologies for solving problmes in software engineering. Further, integration of emerging technologies like AI in desing thinking as well software development. The ongoing evolution of DT continues to address complex, large-scale problems, with an emphasis on user-centered innovation, collaboration, and iteration.

3.2 Desing Thinking Process

The process of DT is continuously evolving and mixing with other methodologies including system design and service design. The principles of DT are applied across diverse filed including software development because of its strong foundation looking at the needs, dreams and behaviours of people—the end users. Figure 6 shows the DT process, which can be divided into five phases or steps such as Empathize, Define, Ideate, Prototype, and Test. In the figure, these steps are represented in sequential to form an overview of the DT phases and these steps are also known as modes. In general, all these steps are not linear but some time in iterative or in parallel. One of the important points is that any one of the DT phases may generate an idea that leads to repeating an earlier stage.

Figure 6. Design thinking process

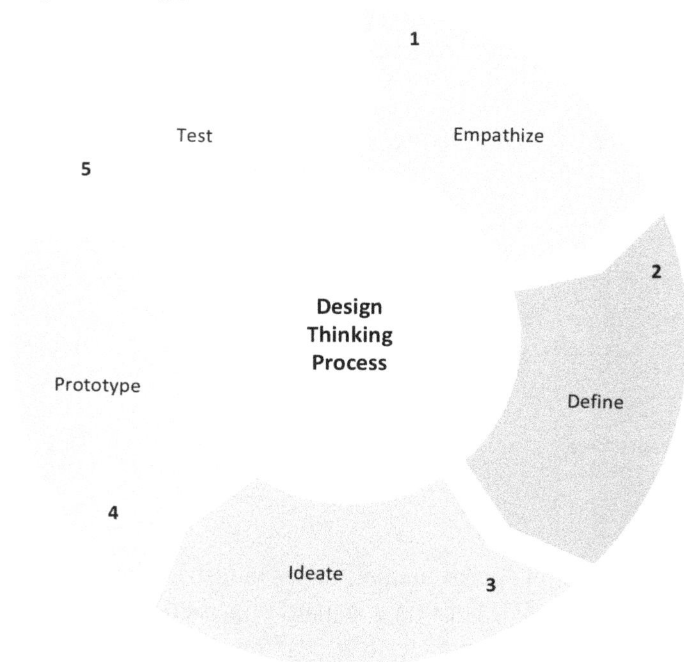

Empathize – It is the first stage of the DT process, in which research is made to understand on the users' needs, pain points and challenges.

Define - The problem is defined based on the users' needs from the first stage. Clearly articulating the problem, based on insights gathered in the empathize stage.

Ideate –Generating multiple ideas and allow creative thinking to solve pain points and challenges of user needs.

Prototype –The focus is to create solution through multiple mock-ups. The output of this stage is a tangible deliverable and get users feedback to refine

Test –Prototype is validated with users and refine the solution as per the feedback collected from the user.

The focus on empathy, creativity, and collaboration remains central, empowering teams to tackle complex challenges with innovative solutions.

3.3 Need for Design Thinking and AI in Software Development

In digital age, there is a need for DT principles in software development due to the following reasons. More particularly, to leverage the benefits of contemporary technologies such as AI, ML, Deep Learning (DL), Bigdata, IoT and 5G to encourages creative solutions and out-of-the-box thinking. These emerging technologies are influencing all most all industries one way or other in terms of its functioning including software development process. At the same time, design thinking has an impact on the software development process because of it is user focused and fosters innovation. Further, ensures the software meets user needs and solves real problems. Similarly, AI can speed up software development, bug fixing, automating tasks, improving code quality, enhancing security and user experiences. Further, influence of AI technology together with DT can transforming the entire software development process from traditional to agile and beyond. Additionally, the complementary features of DT and AI transforms software development and eliminates the redundant processes, speedup the development, improves code quality, improving user centricity and fosters innovation.

a) **User-Centered Approach**: The approach of DT majorly focusing on empathy and a detail understanding of user's requirements. This can ensure that solutions that are developed tailored to fulfil the user needs. This contrasts with traditional software development processes, which may prioritize technical requirements over user experience.
b) **Fostering Innovation**: DT challenges assumptions and encourages exploration of new solutions, fostering a culture of creativity and innovation. It helps teams move beyond conventional solutions to more novel and effective approaches whereas in traditional software development there was no room to focus on innovation.
c) **Rapid Iteration and Prototyping**: The process of DT supports rapid prototyping as well as iterative testing, which enables software teams to quickly validate ideas through prototypes. Further, make changes in these prototypes to address changes in rapid iteration and this process to be continued till to get the final product. This contrasts with the more rigid waterfall model, which lacks such iteration. Further, the concept of protype increases to explain the function of system in simple means and reduces the risk.
d) **Improved Collaboration and Cross Functional Teams**: DT fosters collaboration among designers, developers, product managers, and end-users, ensuring that all perspectives are taken into account during the development process. This collaborative approach not only helps bridge the gap between software team members but also other project teams. This is approach is unlike siloed traditional software development methodologies.
e) **Adaptability**: The process of design thinking's focuses on flexibility makes it easier to incorporate changes during the development process, enabling teams to adjust to shifting requirements or emerging insights without extensive delays or rework.

3.4 A Comparison between SDLC and Design Thinking Process

In spite, SDLC and DT are primarily focused on problem solving approaches, but they differ in focus and process. SDLC is a structure and sequential methodology used for new developing software or modify existing software. It is more technical and process oriented. In comparison, DT is a human-centered, and iterative approach. Both approaches can complement to each other. The following table 1 gives a snapshot of software development and DT approaches.

Table 1. Comparison between software development and design thinking process

Parameter	Software Development Life Cycle	Desing Thinking
Focus	System Development focusing on requirements.	User Centric.
Process	Structure and predetermined phases.	Iterative and Prototype.
Innovation	Innovation is less focused in overall software development cycles.	Innovation is highly focused in design thinning.
Phases	Study → Requirement Gathering→ Design → Implementation → Testing → Maintenance	Empathy → Define → Ideation & Collaboration → Prototype → Testing → Refinement & Iteration
End Goal	Developing a functional software solution.	Developing user centric solution.
User feedback	Slow user feedback.	Faster user feedback.
User involvement	User involvement is less focussed	User involvement is more focussed
Collaboration between teams	Collaboration between team and cross functional teams are less focussed.	Collaboration between team and cross functional teams are highly focussed.
Iteration	Liner and sequential in Waterfall whereas iterative in Agile methodologies.	Continuous iteration based on user feedback and even circular in few cases.

4. FUSIONFLOW - SOFTWARE DEVELOPMENT MODEL

In today's rapidly evolving technological landscape, organizations and software practitioners are increasingly relying on sophisticated software development methodologies that drive innovation, customer centric, collaborative and maintain competitiveness. According to the study by Docherty (2017), the most successful innovative approaches resulting from the DT process that require a visionary leader who supports a democratic approach to decision-making. Further, DT can act as an enabler in the innovation process. Additionally, the integration of AI tools and techniques, in the existing software development processes can result to a new stream of software development which is in sort FusionFlow. FusionFlow is a modern software development, which mainly focusses on user centric, faster, iterative, and focused on business value to the end user that leverages the benefits of DT, AI tolls and techniques and existing software process.

4.1 Conceptual View of FusionFlow

FusionFlow is a modern software development approach that is merging of different disciplines of software development, DT and AI technologies. The term FusionFlow comprises a combination of two words Fusion and Flow, where fusion refers a smooth integration of various methodologies, tools, or discipline such as software development processes, DT principles, and AI technologies. Here, the term fusion means a combination of three disciplines such as traditional software development, DT, and AI technologies that conveys a sense of synergy, where each discipline complements and enhances the others. Additionally, the term flow refers a seamless and adaptive transition between these disciplines, with the emphasis on innovation and efficiency when these different approaches converge. In the context of DT, "flow" could refer to iterative cycles of ideation, prototyping, and testing, while in AI, it may imply the optimizing, real-time decision-making process powered by intelligent algorithms. In simple terms term flow suggests a smooth, continuous, and efficient process.

The FusionFlow is one of the software development approaches for building software. It eliminates the drawbacks of traditional software development and offers several advantages. Further, these modern software development leverages AI tools and techniques, DT principles and the existing software development processes in order to build software solutions or products in ease, faster and more iterative. Figure 7 shows a conceptual view of a FusionFlow software development which is formed from the ideas of three disciplines such as software development, DT and AI technologies.

Figure 7. A conceptual view of FusionFlow: A Software Development Approach

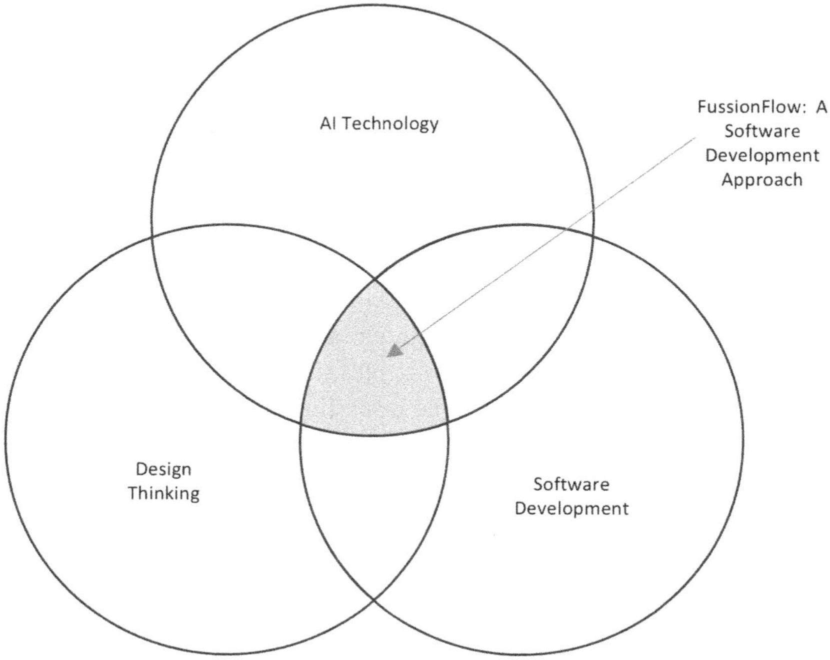

Software Development – Software development process is a structured approach to develop and maintain software products, or solutions or applications. In general, the software development work is divided into smaller, parallel, or sequential steps or phases or sub-processes to build software. This entire process is most commonly known as software SDLC. Broadly, software development process can be divided into two categories like traditional software development and agile software development. Traditional software development includes like waterfall, V-Model, Spiral, Incremental, Iterative and PRINCE2 to mentation a few whereas examples of agile methodologies include RAD, Scrum, Extreme Programming, Lean, and Kanban to list a few.

Design Thinking – It suggests a smooth, continuous, and efficient process. In the context of DT, the term "flow" could refer to iterative cycles of ideation, prototyping, and testing, Additionally, DT is not only a problem-solving approach but also solution approach that brings human-centered design principles at its core. The use of DT as a problem-solving framework has received significance attention dure to its reliance on adductive reasoning and human-centeredness. According to the study of Balzano and Bortoluzzi (2024) focuses on three points. First, study on existing body of work on DT by elucidating the specific effects of abductive reasoning and human-centeredness on the innovation quality of team decisions made in time-sensitive environments. The outcome of this study states that abductive reasoning may adversely affect team innovation quality, whereas a pronounced focus on human-centeredness yielded more favorable outcomes. Second, this study contributes to the decision-making under time constraints that supplements existing theories on the dynamics and speed of decision-making by introducing a perspective that examines the relevance of different reasoning approaches when time is of the essence. Third, this study sheds additional light on the effect of team size on innovation quality. Furthermore, this study reveals that small teams have high innovation quality as compared to large size teams.

AI Technology – Technology is the application of scientific knowledge for practical purposes.

Technology refers to the application of scientific knowledge, tools, techniques, and systems to solve problems, make processes more efficient, and create new possibilities. It allows humans to perform tasks more effectively to accomplish things that were previously impossible or difficult. In simple terms, technology refers to methods, systems, and devices which are the result of scientific knowledge being used for practical purposes whereas a tool is a specific item or software used in project management, while a technique is a broader method or approach applied to perform tasks. In AI, the term "flow" refers the optimized, real-time decision-making process powered by intelligent algorithms. In simple terms, AI is reshaping how software is designed, built and maintained to next generation user needs. AI is transforming the software development by automating processes, enhance productivity and optimize efficiency at each stage of SDLC. Further, it transcends like code generation, bug detection, and automate software testing. Moreover, AI tools can process vast amount of data in real time and provide insights in a short time. Additionally, AI algorithms can predict potential issues before they become critical problems so that the team can proactively address them.

According to study conducted by Sreenivasan and Suresh (2024) the goal is to understand how AI technologies may advance the design process, encourage innovation, and produce more individualized and user-centric solutions. Further, this study intends to shed light on the potential of AI as a catalyst for creativity and the ethical implications of AI-driven design by discovering overlapping ideas and methodologies between DT and AI. According to the research, AI can significantly influence the design process by eliminating tedious processes, improving user-centricity, and stimulating creativity. AI may support designers' decision-making, prototyping, and ideation processes, resulting in more creative and effective design solutions. Addressing bias in AI algorithms and data privacy is imperative to ensure ethical AI integration.

4.2 Major Phases of FusionFlow

The major phase in FusionFlow, a software development approach, is shown in figure 8, this leverages DT approach, AI technology and tools and existing software development process.

Figure 8. Phases in FusionFlow

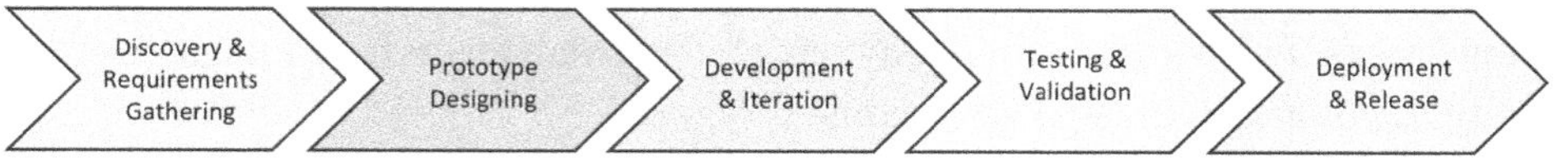

Explanation of Phases:

1. **Discovery and Requirements Gathering -** This phase mainly involves to understand what the stakeholders and users need to build software or modify the existing software. The goal is to collect and refine requirements before significant development begins. The major activities of this phase include identify the stakeholders, establish project goals and objectives, identify specific user problems and difficulties, eliciting detailed requirements and functionalities. Further, maintain a constant communication with stakeholders, ensuring their perspectives are integrated seamlessly. In the last few years, the use of DT in software process has been increased in software engineering. In a study, Parizi et al. (2020) proposes the uses of integration of DT techniques in software requirements engineering activities, which include problem exploration, fostering innovative solutions and integrating into agile methodologies to satisfy stakeholders needs. Additionally, it is mentioned that DT provides the customer needs up-front and helps to empathize with users, examining their behaviours, and producing outcomes focused on users' demand. Despite its many benefits and successful use cases in this scenario there are some of the shortcomings related to its uses in requirements engineering. One of them lies in the difficulty with eliciting other non-functional requirements, besides usability. A qualitative survey conducted by Pinto et al. (2022) with software developers who have had previous experiences with the use of DT suggested that DT process does not include non-functional requirements and usability. Notwithstanding, several studies reported use of DT in software development focused on improving the users' experience, and identifying their needs.
2. **Prototyping Desing**: In this phase is focused to develop initial UI/UX designs and prototypes. The prototypes will provide tangible ideas for stakeholders to evaluate and provide feedback. In Agile, design is often iterative, and prototypes

can evolve into more refined versions over time. Prototypes may be created early on to help clarify ambiguous requirements. Prototypes may be created early development to clarify requirements and gather feedback before full-scale development. This increases the user collaboration and feedback, and also reduces risk in the development.

3. **Development:** This is where the bulk of the work happens, with development happening in small cycles (Sprints in Agile). Each cycle delivers a working product increment, and feedback is immediately integrated into the next iteration. This phase is iterative. There is a bidirectional communication between both development and testing phases. Further, the major activities of this phase include coding and building software components with a spirit of collaboration, collaboration with cross functional teams, and maintain a dynamic development environment. As the number of phases in the FusionFlow model is less as compared to other traditional software development models like Waterfall. Because of the reduced number of phases and the tasks to be performed for each phase also minimal, as it adopts automation, and uses various tools for prototype and automation which results the overall time required for development reduces.
4. **Testing:** After each iteration, testing is carried out to ensure quality and identify issues. Prototypes are tested with stakeholders to validate that the development aligns with their needs. Once the testing is done, the user feedback will be sent back to development state to improve as per the user recommendations. The major activities of this phase are testing and identifying issues in the development process. Further, continuous testing ensures a robust, and functional product is delivered to customer.
5. **Deployment & Release**: The product is released in its initial or refined form to the user base. The feedback received here feeds into future iterations. The major activities include plan for regular, incremental releases of software, allowing for ongoing feedback and improvements, and ensures working software is delivered to customers regularly.
6. **Maintenance & Continuous Improvement**: Post-release, the product undergoes maintenance, bug fixes, and iterative improvements based on ongoing user feedback, much like Agile's principle of continuous delivery and iteration.

4.3 Key Characteristics of FusionFlow

FusionFlow is a software development methodology that refers to the building software applications (or services or products) that leverages existing software process and the principles of DT and AI technology and tools. The key characteristics of FusionFlow is envisaged in figure 9 that prioritizes key characteristics such as user centric, innovation, UI/UX centric, Iterative, flexibility, collaboration, and customer feedback as a major focus. The key characteristics of modern software development refers to a specific feature that has a significant impact on its performance.

Figure 9. Key characteristics of FusionFlow model

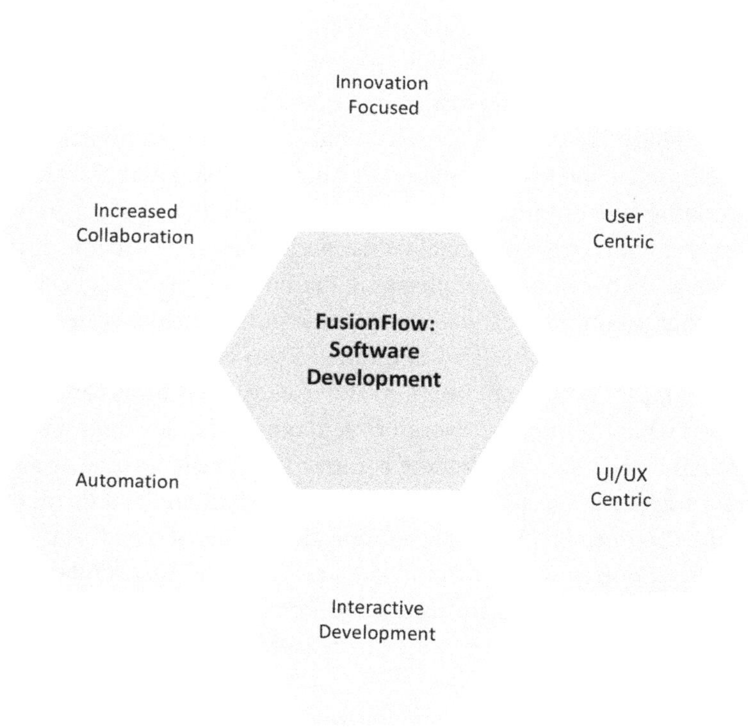

4.3.1 Innovation Focused

In software development innovation refers transforming creative ideas in building new products or modifying existing products or solutions that drive business growth, efficiently, and meet customers. In traditional software development approaches, there was no focus on innovation whereas modern software development methods have focused on innovation not only in user requirements phase but also in all other phase. According to the study of Andersson et al, (2021), it was found that there is a positive relationship between software development and innovation in firms. In this approach the ideas are collected from several individuals to fit to the customer needs to solve their problems. From all the collected ideas the best idea is selected. It is depicted in figure 10.

Figure 10. Innovation through divergent thinking

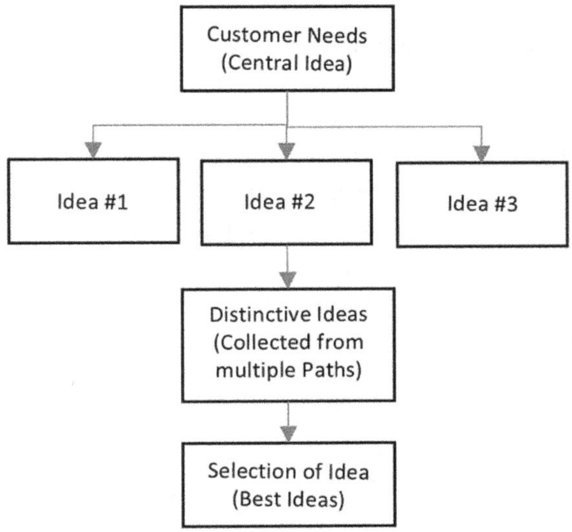

4.3.2 User Centric

The terms user centred design refers a methodology that focuses on the needs and preferences of users during the design process whereas user centric design refers a comprehensive approach at a broader level not only at design process but also focuses on strategy and culture of the organization. DT is centred around the end user and fulfil the needs of users. According to the study of Sreenivasan and Suresh (2024), integrating AI with DT enhances the human-centered approach by fusing data-driven insights with sympathetic comprehension. By using AI to evaluate user data at scale, designers can find subtle trends and preferences that guide their work. By incorporating AI-driven analytics into DT approaches, designers may enhance their decision-making abilities, verify presumptions, and improve solutions by utilizing user input. This collaborative approach guarantees that solutions speak to users' underlying motivations and goals in addition to their explicit demands. By integrating AI's quantitative analysis and DT's qualitative insights, organizations can develop more user-centric, compassionate solutions that provide significant value to end users.

4.3.3 UI/ UX Centric

The importance of understanding end user needs and involving them in the software development process is well known in software engineering. . According to study of Lucena et. al. (2017), Agile Software Development methodologies have incorporated user feedback in different ways. User stories should represent the needs of a user, but often express the views of the Product Owner or the software development team. Several works have investigated integrating User Centered Design into Agile software development to satisfy end user needs. This work proposes a different approach focused on satisfying end user needs employing DT iterative software development. Furthermore, DT often refers to optimal experience, particularly in user-centered design. This positions the software development methodology as being centered on users' needs and experiences, aligning with human-centered design principles. Additionally, the study of Lucena et. al. (2017), IBM's DT brings up-front analysis and user feedback in all the iterations offering a better understanding of what problems need to be solved and what are the best solutions to satisfy the user needs. According to our survey, using a Likert scale varying from very low to very high, 80% of the surveyed reported End-Users had a very high satisfaction rate on the projects delivered. The user experience improvement was related to a productivity boost resulting in time and resources savings and user base growth for the delivered services. With the help of UI/UX, designers and developers create protype using wireframes, or sketches, which is an early, tangible version of a product or service to visualize, test and validate and collect feedback from the user. The advantage of this protype design is that it identifies potential issues if any in the early stage of the development and this in turn reduces the risk of costly errors.

4.3.4 Interactive Development

FusionFlow focuses on developing software in interactive way, where users including stakeholders actively engage with the product during from discovery, prototype design, development and testing phases. In discovery phase, business analysis will collect requirements from the user and validate it from other stakeholders and incorporate feedback. In prototype design both designers and developers create prototypes and validate with the user and feedback into the system. Both development and testing are iterative, which include user feedback for necessary improvements. FusionFlow methodology emphasizes iteration, continuous feedback, and collaboration between designers, developers and users, enabling real-time adjustments and improvements. This approach is not only enhancing interactive development but also ensures user satisfaction of the final product that aligns closely with user needs.

4.3.5 Increased Collaboration

The ability of DT will improve user-centricity, comprehend user wants, and formulate challenges successfully motivates its strategic incorporation into AI systems. This combination speeds development and produces more ethically sound and efficient AI systems by enabling iterative design and fast prototyping. Additionally, cross-functional appeal, inviting collaboration among different roles. The name **FusionFlow** communicates that it is suitable for teams spanning across various disciplines: designers, developers, and AI engineers. In essence, FusionFlow effectively communicates a cutting-edge, holistic approach to software development that blends creativity, user-centered design, and powerful AI tools to create smarter, more efficient, and scalable solutions. Further, AI can make collaboration easer for multiple teams for exchange of ideas, suggestions in terms much simpler way, which provides to build solutions collaboratively.

4.3.6 Automation

Automation is the process refer to use of machines or technology or tools to perform tasks without much intervention of human. This approach tries to streamlines process of software development that eliminates many of the manual tasks, repeated tasks in various phases more particularly in development, and testing. It minimizes the manual operation of task there by saves a lot of time at the same time reduces the errors which results in improve the efficiency of the development process. According to a study Trocin et al. (2023) discusses the proliferation of ML, is part of AI, has gained wide acceptance during the last few years to boost the creative process of design. Further, this study suggested layouts options but also more complex action possibilities like generation of new ideas and prototyping for their visualization. Additionally, AI can automate monotonous design activities. Owing to the automation, designers can now concentrate on more imaginative and strategic aspects of the design, saving them time.

4.4 Mapping between Phases of Desing Thinking and FusionFlow

A mapping between various phases of DT and FusionFlow model is shown in table 2.

Table 2. Mapping between design thinking phases and software development phases of FusionFlow

Desing Thinking	FusionFlow: Software Development
Empathy and Define phase are all about understanding the user's problem and defining the challenge from their perspective.	This correlates with discovery and requirements gathering phase and understanding user needs and
Ideation and Collaboration phase focuses on brainstorming multiple solutions. Teams from various disciplines (designers, developers, and business stakeholders) collaborate.	This phase is about the prototype design, including the architecture, UI/UX design, and technologies to use. It includes either mock-ups, wireframes and/ or prototyping depending on the complexity of the product to be built. It mainly focusses on what the new product or feature will do.
Prototyping and testing- Prototyping involves creating quick, low-fidelity prototypes to test the feasibility of ideas with users.	Development and testing – In this phase, developers write code and testing to ensure it works as expected. User feedback is collected and implemented back in to the system development. Both development, testing and feedback collection are iterative.
Refinement and Iteration - is about continuous improvement based on user feedback, even after prototypes are tested. Additionally, involve continuous user feedback loops to improve the product.	This is similar to deployment and release. Further includes support and maintenance, where software is iteratively updated with bug fixes, new features, and optimizations. Additionally, involve continuous user feedback loops to improve the product.

5. BENEFITS OF FUSIONFLOW SOFTWARE DEVELOPMENT APPROACH

The benefits of FusionFlow - software methodology as follows:

Improved Business Value - According to a survey of Forrester (2018) on Total Economic Impact (TEI) methodology of IBM's DT practice on various sizes of projects whose detail as follows. This survey was conducted on various project sizes ranging from small, minor, major, and enterprise whose duration ranges <6 months, 6-12 months, 12-24 months, > 24 months respectively. According to this study, the project is categorised into minor and major, the minor project is typically built by a single team over 40 weeks and expects $2M in profit, whereas major project is typically built by two teams over 100 weeks and expects $4M in profits. The major projects has two teams over 100 weeks and expects $4M in profits. The team size of minor project has a product manager, 12 developers, four testers, two designers, and 12-person cross-functional team, whereas a major project has two product managers, 24 developers, four testers, four designers, and 18- person cross-functional team. In both types of projects not all team members are fully devoted to the project at all times, depending on project phase. The study showed that DT provides multiple value propositions. A few of these pints are listed in the below paragraph.

- Design solutions that better meet the needs of end users, to delight customers and ultimately increase profits.
- Refine business strategy by identifying and investing in the most impactful user problems to reduce business risk and improve results.
- Energize employees to be more collaborative, do better work, and achieve heightened job satisfaction.
- Discover redundant or wasteful processes to streamline efficiency.

Table 3. Summary of Total Economic Impact of IBM's design thinking practice.

Phase → Detail ↓	Design	Development and Testing cost	Maintenance Cost	Increased Profit from Faster Time-To-Market
Percentage of reduction	75% reduction time required to gather and align on initial requirements	33% reduction time required for project development and testing	50% reduction number of design defects	50% faster time-to-market
Cost reduction for small projects	$196,272 cost savings for a minor project	$222,783 cost savings for a minor project	$76,628 cost savings for a minor project	$182,096 in profit for a minor project
Cost reduction for large projects	$872,325 cost savings For a major project	$1,138,534 cost savings for a major project	$153,255 cost savings for a major project	$1,050,240 in profit for a major project

Improved User Satisfaction – FusionFlow approach improves user satisfaction from beginning to end of the development cycle. Mainly in protype design phase, it allows users feedback, which reduces risk in the development that improves not only user satisfaction but also results a successful outcome. The users can experience the product look and feel from the beginning of the development phase before to begin the design phase and early feedback helps to build right sight from the beginning.

Cost Reduction – The reduction of the cost in software development mainly depends on planning, scope creep, improper requirements gathering, and repeated manual tasks. The FusionFlow provides effective planning is a proactive activity that can be planned from discovery phase to final release phase. The prototype technique minimizes risk associated with complex requirements as wells unclear requirements. As the prototype design is in the second phase, which eliminates major part of the risk that is related to unclear and complex requirements, and provision for user feedback this results optimal use of the resources like time, manpower and cost. Further, it uses automation expensively as compared to other development models because it leverages the workflow automation with the aid of AI techniques and tools. And also uses DevOps, CI/CD practices. All this results, reduction of software development cost.

Enhanced Innovation and business value – In this method users bring come with new approaches by adapting suitable new techniques that helps to solve user problems not only in the prototype phase but also in design as well as in other phases too. Thus, the FusionFlow model provides user centric, innovation and also offers lot of business value in terms of reduced development time, reduced testing time by automation which results financial value; customer satisfaction in terms of user centric, improved user feedback as customer value. Further, improves the organizational efficiency and retains organizational innovation to foster further development and expansion of new products and services.

Reduced Development Lead Time – The lead time of the overall development reduces relatively with respect to traditional software approaches because it uses automation for repeated tasks such as testing of the application to name a few. Further, the number of phases is minimal as compared to traditional development methodologies, this results reduction of task to be performed as a result reduces the overall development time. Besides, the FusionFlow model uses various tools of DT and AI for prototype and automation of various day to day activities.

6 CONCLUSION

In this chapter, we explored the FusionFlow - A software development approach that focusing on its lesser number of phases, iterative nature, focus on user centric, innovation, collaboration, automation, and the continuous delivery of value. In digital era, software development will continue to adapt to the changing needs, optimize its processes and overcomes challenges of the ever-evolving technology world. The approach of DT and use of AI tools and techniques together can provide a valuable contribution to software development processes and improves innovation, faster development and building user centric solution. The conglomeration of DT, AI tools and techniques and existing software methodologies can result to new stream of software development process in the ear of AI which is coined as “FusionFlow”. Presented a conceptual view of FusionFlow model and its major phases. Further, explained its working. Further, mentioned the key characteristics of the FusionFlow. The FusionFlow software development model offers several benefits and overcome the limitations of the traditional software development model. Finally, presented various benefits of the FusionFlow software development model.

REFERENCES

Andersson, M., Kusetogullari, A., & Wernberg, J. (2021). *Software development and innovation: Exploring the software shift in innovation in Swedish firms*, Technological Forecasting and Social Change, Volume 167, 2021, 120695, ISSN 0040-1625, https://doi.org/DOI: 10.1016/j.techfore.2021.120695

Balzano, M., & Bortoluzzi, G. (2024). Time is running out: How design thinking shapes team innovation under time constraints. *European Management Journal*. Advance online publication. DOI: 10.1016/j.emj.2024.08.003

Boehm, B. (1988). A Spiral Model of Software Development and Enhancement. *IEEE Computer, 21*(5), 61–72. DOI: 10.1109/2.59

Docherty, C. (2017). Perspectives on Design Thinking for Social Innovation. *The Design Journal, 20*(6), 719–724. DOI: 10.1080/14606925.2017.1372005

Forrester. (February, 2018). *The Total Economic Impact™ of IBM's Design Thinking Practice*. Retrieved January 15, 2025, from https://www.ibm.com/design/thinking/static/Enterprise-Design-Thinking-Report-8ab1e9e1622899654844a5fe1d760ed5.pdf

Lucena, P., Braz, A., Chicoria, A., & Tizzei, L. (2017). IBM Design Thinking Software Development Framework. In Silva da Silva, T., Estácio, B., Kroll, J., & Mantovani Fontana, R. (Eds.), *Agile Methods. WBMA 2016. Communications in Computer and Information Science* (Vol. 680). Springer., DOI: 10.1007/978-3-319-55907-0_9

Mishra, A., & Alzoubi, Y. I. (2023, August). Structured software development versus agile software development: A comparative analysis. *International Journal of System Assurance Engineering and Management, 14*(4), 1504–1522. DOI: 10.1007/s13198-023-01958-5

Parizi, R. B., Silva, M. M., Couto, I., Trindade, K., Plautz, M., Marczak, S., Conte, T. U., & Candello, H. (2020). *Design Thinking in Software Requirements: What Techniques to Use? A Proposal for a Recommendation Tool*. Conferencia Iberoamericana de Software Engineering.

Pinto, F. A., Brandão, A. A., & Siqueira, F. L. (2022). *Design Thinking and Non-Functional Requirements Elicitation*: A Survey. Workshop em Engenharia de Requisitos. *PRINCE2 Methodology. (n.d.)*. Retrieved January 21, 2025, from https://www.prince2.com/uk/prince2-methodology

Sreenivasan, A., & Suresh, M. (2024). Design thinking and artificial intelligence: A systematic literature review exploring synergies. International Journal of Innovation Studies.

Tetteh, S. G. (2024). Empirical Study of Agile Software Development Methodologies: A Comparative Analysis. *Asian Journal of Research in Computer Science*, *17*(5), 30–42. DOI: 10.9734/ajrcos/2024/v17i5436

Torka, S., & Albayrak, S. (2024). Optimizing AI-Assisted Code Generation. https://doi.org//arXiv.2412.10953DOI: 10.48550

Trocin, C., Stige, Å., & Mikalef, P. (2023). *Machine Learning (ML) diffusion in the design process: A study of Norwegian design consultancies. Technological Forecasting and Social Change,* 194. *Technological Forecasting and Social Change*, *122724*, 122724. Advance online publication. DOI: 10.1016/j.techfore.2023.122724

Weiss, T. R. (Sep 30, 2024). Exploring Docker for DevOps: What It Is and How It Works. Retrieved January 21, 2025, from https://www.docker.com/blog/docker-for-devops/

KEY TERMS AND DEFINITIONS

5G: The fifth-generation of cellular network technology.

Agile Model: A software development model fallows iterative and incremental development.

AlphaCode: The first AI code generation system, which was a part of DeepMind's mission to solve intelligence that writes computer programs.

Big data: A collection of structured, unstructured, and semi-structured data that keeps growing over time.

Blockchain: a decentralized and distributed ledger technology that facilitates the process of recording transactions and tracking assets across a business network.

ChatGPT: A generative AI chatbot developed by OpenAI. GPT stands for Generative Pre-training Transformer.

Crystal: An agile methodology for software development.

DevOps: A combination of both software development (Dev) and IT Operations (Ops).

Empathize: Empathize is the first stage of the design thinking process.

FusionFlow: A modern software development model, which leverages the principles of design thinking, AI and existing software process.

GitHub Copilot: A code completion and automatic programming tool developed by GitHub and OpenAI.

Ideate: One of the phases in design thinking process where designers come up with ideas on how to solve specific user challenges.

Incremental Model: A software development models where requirements are divided into multiple standalone modules called increments.

Iterative Model: A software development approach that breaks down the overall development into smaller, called iterations.

Kanban: A visual method for managing workflow at the individual, team, and even organizational level.

Lean Model: A software development model emphasizes optimizing efficiency and minimizing waste.

Likert Scale: A scale named after its inventor, Rensis Likert, which is used to measure people's opinions, attitudes, perceptions or behaviours quantitatively.

Mendix: A cloud-based low-code application development platform uses visual drag-and-drop elements.

OpenAI Codex: An artificial intelligence model developed by OpenAI.

Prototype: A simulation of how a real software product will look, work, and feel.

Scrum: A framework for getting work done within agile.

Spiral Model: A software development model that is a combination of waterfall and iterative development process with a risk analysis.

TEI: Total Economic Impact that access cost benefit analysis.

V-Model: A software development process modal, which has both verification and validation.

Chapter 4
Empathy-Driven Development:
Integrating Design Thinking Into Next-Gen Software Engineering

Muhammad Usman Tariq
https://orcid.org/0000-0002-7605-3040
Abu Dhabi University, UAE & University College Cork, Ireland

ABSTRACT

This chapter examines how design thinking-based empathy-focused principles are changing software engineering procedures. This chapter explores how empathy can be used to bridge technical rigor with human-cantered insights in order to create software that is focused on users. From conception to post-launch developers can create experiences that speak to users' needs by integrating empathy into every aspect of the software lifecycle. This enhances functionality and builds user trust. The chapter explores particular tactics to help teams strike a balance between engineering precision and creativity including iterative feedback loops collaborative prototyping and sympathetic user testing. It also explores how empathy is changing in response to new technologies that require a greater awareness of varied user experiences such as artificial intelligence (AI) and the Internet of Things (IoT).

INTRODUCTION

Software engineering has undergone a radical change with empathy-driven development, which combines technological innovation with human-centered design. In the quickly changing digital world of today, software is more than just effectively resolving issues. Rather, the focus is on developing solutions that appeal to the users.

DOI: 10.4018/979-8-3693-9531-8.ch004

Because of this change, design thinking—a method that places a high priority on comprehending the wants, feelings, and experiences of users during the software development process—has begun to incorporate empathy. Empathy-driven development begins with the user and grows around them, producing software that not only works but also engages, empowers, and delights. This contrasts with traditional development methodologies, which frequently concentrate on the technical feasibility or economic viability of solutions (Dul, 2022). In software engineering, empathy is putting oneself in the users' position to fully comprehend their challenges, aspirations, and ambitions. Empathy is the capacity to profoundly comprehend and share another person's feelings. As a method of problem-solving, design thinking emphasizes empathy by advising developers and designers to understand user requirements before trying to come up with a solution. Design thinking promotes the investigation of user viewpoints by cultivating an atmosphere of empathy, which leads to more significant and successful advancements in software engineering. According to this concept, empathy encompasses more than just recognizing functional demands; it also includes comprehending the psychological and emotional factors that affect user behavior (Eghdam, 2024). The creation of user interfaces (UI) and user experiences (UX) is a crucial illustration of empathy-driven development. Functionality—making sure buttons function, websites load, and databases connect—may be the focus of traditional software development. An empathy-driven approach, on the other hand, puts more emphasis on how people feel when interacting with the system. Take, for example, a program made to help senior citizens manage their health information. An empathetic developer could consider the nervousness an older person experiences while figuring out complicated menus or understanding medical jargon. In addition to making sure the software functions well, the developer would try to make the UI simpler, provide user-friendly navigation, and include reassuring cues that lessen cognitive strain (Dul, 2022). This produces an experience that not only meets the intended technical objectives but also considers the user's emotional and cognitive reality. Beyond UI and UX, empathy-driven development has significant ramifications for software engineering. Teams that adopt an empathic mindset start posing new queries throughout the development process, such as: What annoyances may the user experience? In what ways may this program simplify their life, both practically and emotionally? By probing deeper into user behavior, motives, and expectations, these questions open the door to more interesting and fulfilling software experiences. This strategy has already had a big influence in industries like healthcare, education, and finance, where users' emotional reactions to software may be just as important as its functionality (Adhikari Egodawele et al., 2022). For example, healthcare applications are made to not only give patients accurate information but also to ease their worry and promote treatment compliance. A supportive message or a nonjudgmental interface emphasizing progress over perfection might be features of a fitness app that understands the user's body issues. An empathy-driven approach to instructional software may go beyond just delivering knowledge and thinking about ways to keep students interested, lessen irritation, and provide a sense of accomplishment—especially for those who find it difficult to learn using conventional techniques. Because of these empathy-based design choices, user pleasure is greatly increased, and the software becomes not just useful but also appealing and influential (Eghdam, 2024). On a deeper level, software developers are forced to reconsider the function of technology itself by empathy-driven development. Building systems that satisfy fundamental needs is no longer enough; engineers now need to think about how their work impacts people's lives. A balance between emotional intelligence and technical rigor is necessary for this mental change. Building systems that provide users with a sense of understanding, value, and support is just as vital as creating systems that are scalable, safe, and stable. This frequently entails going beyond the user persona and having direct discussions with users, testing with a variety of demographics, and revising designs in response to actual input rather than conjecture (Adhikari Egodawele et al., 2022; Tariq, 2024). Adding a collaborative element to software engineering, empathy-driven development encourages interdisciplinary teams in which users, developers, and designers collaborate throughout the development process. To create a more integrated development process where user insights may directly feed technical choices, design thinking promotes the dismantling of barriers between these responsibilities. This degree of cooperation works especially well in agile settings where success depends on constant input and iteration. Teams may remain attentive to user demands and continually modify their solutions to get more individualized and efficient results by integrating empathy into agile approaches (Gao et al., 2023). Nevertheless, there are difficulties in incorporating empathy into software engineering. It may be challenging for certain firms to adopt empathy as it takes time, money, and a culture change. Spending more time learning about users' emotional landscapes may seem like a luxury in high-pressure settings with limited deadlines and resources. Converting qualitative, affective insights into tangible, implementable design decisions is another difficulty. Emotional pleasure is a subjective concept that is more challenging to assess than established measurements like performance and dependability. Therefore, in addition to standard usability tests, empathy-driven development necessitates new forms of testing and feedback systems, such as emotional mapping or user journey evaluations (Apasrawirote et al., 2022).

The variety of user experiences is another important factor. If developers and designers just consider their own viewpoints or those of a uniform user base, empathy-driven development runs the danger of being overly limited. Development teams must aggressively seek out other perspectives and experiences, especially from underrepresented or marginalized user groups, to really sympathize. If this isn't done, software may be created that, despite good intentions, alienates or excludes groups. A financial management software, for instance, might not connect with users who are experiencing financial instability if it assumes that all of its users have steady incomes. As a result, the app may unintentionally make matters worse rather than better (Gao et al., 2023). Furthermore, there are situations where using empathy-driven concepts in software development conflicts with commercial objectives, especially when scalability and profitability take precedence above user delight. There could be conflict between the need to produce emotionally compelling experiences and the demands to cut expenses or deliver features fast. Nonetheless, businesses like Apple, Amazon, and Netflix that have adopted empathy-driven development have shown that putting customer delight first may result in sustained commercial success. These businesses succeed in part because they put the user experience first, realizing that a strong emotional bond with the product encourages consumer happiness and loyalty, both of which improve the bottom line (Mazumder & Garg, 2021). Thus, empathy-driven development is a paradigm change in software engineering that places equal weight on the technical functionality and the user's emotional and cognitive experience. Software engineers may develop solutions that are not just dependable and effective but also highly sensitive to the wants, requirements, and emotions of their customers by incorporating empathy into design thinking. By strengthening the bonds between people and technology, this human-centered approach has the potential to transform industries, improve user satisfaction, and spur innovation. Empathy will be a crucial component of next-generation software development as it continues to be acknowledged as a major force behind user-centered design. This will guarantee that technology not only fulfills functional requirements but also improves the human experience in general (Apasrawirote et al., 2022; Tariq, 2025).

Purpose of the Chapter

The purpose of this chapter is to investigate how data analytics and high order predictive techniques allow for understanding and forecasting of consumer behavior. As a how to read guide for anyone interested in the intersection of data driven insights and consumer psychology, it is a must read. This chapter introduces readers to the foundational knowledge, practical tools and real world applications of analyzing data to enable them to apply analytics to use it for strategic decision making in all areas of business. It provides a fresh angle of how design thinking can be combined and applied with empathy driven development to help bridge the gap between technological precision and human centric ideas, building a much stronger connection with the consumer. The methodologies of collecting and analysing data, the advanced modelling techniques, the ethical considerations, and the new technologies that are going to shape how consumer behaviour prediction can be anticipated are discussed in this book for readers. Also, the research proposal presented here highlights the importance of ethical practices and the merit of the consumer oriented innovation for the businesses to stay competitive.

This chapter is structured as an Introduction to the importance of data analytics for predicting consumer behaviour, as well as the inclusion of the empathy and design thinking approach. It explains the evolution of empathetic methods and the effect they have on analytics in the Background section. The first part (Fundamentals of Data Analytics) is about core concepts, processes, and the role of data quality, while the second part (Tools and Techniques) discusses the traditional methods such as surveys, the digital approaches like web scraping, and advanced method such as predictive modelling. Success Stories, Case Studies, Ethical Considerations provide application in multiple industries, and also talk about privacy, consent, data security, and bias. Finally, the Future Trends chapter discusses the following emerging technologies: AI and IoT; and finally, a Conclusion presents the key insights and anticipates future innovations.

BACKGROUND

This section helps establish an important ground for understanding how empathy driven methods and design thinking have evolved to shape our modern software and system design. The paper explores — and what it means that these approaches have become so critical to the shaping of predictive analytics and consumer engagement strategies. In this chapter, readers will learn how empathy enhances user centric innovation by bridging the technical precision with human needs and the stage to a deeper dive into data driven approaches in the rest of the chapter. The way software development teams comprehend and satisfy customer demands is being revolutionized by the integration of empathy into requirements engineering. Gathering functional specifications is usually the main goal of traditional requirements engineering, which makes sure the software will complete jobs quickly and achieve predetermined business goals. Empathy-based requirements engineering, on the other hand, adopts a more human-centered methodology with the goal of comprehending the experiential and emotional dimensions of the user's software interaction. In addition to meeting functional demands, teams may create solutions that offer a more fulfilling and significant user experience by understanding the user's frustrations, goals, and motivations (Peláez et al., 2024). Empathy mapping is a crucial method for integrating empathy into requirements in engineering. Finding out what the user thinks, feels, sees, and hears when using the program is part of this approach, which aims to provide a comprehensive picture of the user. Development teams might find hidden demands and pain areas that might not be apparent using conventional requirement-gathering techniques by putting themselves in the user's shoes and visualizing their experience. While a development team is working on a mental health app, for example, empathy mapping may show that users experience anxiety or vulnerability when inputting sensitive personal data. By considering these feelings, features like private, secure login processes or the use of soothing, comforting language across the user interface may be developed to make the app seem more reliable and encouraging (Tariq, 2025). Another empathy-based technique that can improve the requirements of engineering is the user persona. Personas are made-up characters designed to symbolize various user types that may utilize the program. Development teams may make more inclusive design decisions by using these personas to gain a deeper understanding of the varied demands and behaviors of users. Empathy-driven requirements engineering incorporate emotional motives, anxieties, and motivations in addition to basic demographic information. When creating an educational platform, for instance, one persona may stand in for a student who is easily demoralized by failure, which would prompt the team to give priority to features that offer prompt feedback and support. The team may create requirements that address users' psychological demands in addition to their functional ones by understanding the emotional experience of this persona (Peláez et al., 2024).

Using direct user interaction methods, such observation and interviews, is another tactic. While focus groups or surveys may be used in traditional requirements engineering to get user input, empathy-driven techniques frequently include more in-depth, qualitative interaction. To uncover instances of annoyance, perplexity, or joy, developers may study people in their natural settings as they engage with existing software solutions. Subtle emotional clues that may be missed by quantitative data are revealed by this direct observation. For example, while creating a project management application, seeing a user having trouble organizing tasks may indicate that the issue is not only one of functioning but also of feeling overburdened. Designing a solution based on empathy-based analysis might result in a simpler user experience, either by providing visual assistance to lessen cognitive load or segmenting activities into smaller, more manageable segments (Seufert, 2024). Several case studies demonstrate the effective use of empathy in requirements engineering. The strategy used by Airbnb to rebuild their site is a noteworthy example. The business first concentrated on offering useful tools for making hotel reservations, but they quickly saw that the user experience encompassed much more than just finding a place to stay. Airbnb found that emotions of trust, connection, and hospitality drove both hosts and guests through empathy-driven research, which included user interviews and house visits. Features like thorough host profiles, validated evaluations, and a messaging system that promoted in-person encounters were developed because of this realization (Peláez et al., 2024). As a result, Airbnb's platform evolved from a simple booking tool to a reliable location where individuals could build deep connections, greatly enhancing the company's success. The creation of Slack, the well-known team communication application, is another strong argument. The creators of Slack were initially concerned with finding practical solutions to issues like facilitating quicker team communication. However, they discovered a deeper user need for a tool that enhanced productivity and made work more pleasurable through empathy-driven research. The development team behind Slack came to the realization that customers were frustrated by inflexible, excessively formal communication solutions that didn't mimic how people spoke. Understanding this annoyance, they incorporated entertaining features like emoticons, GIFs, and humorous notifications into the design of Slack (Seufert, 2024).

By meeting both practical and emotional demands, these features significantly increased user happiness and assisted Slack in developing a devoted user base, even though they were not necessarily required for operation. Importantly, there are difficulties with empathy-based requirements engineering. Prioritizing emotional and experienced aspects in addition to technical ones takes time, money, and a change in development teams' culture. Taking the time to fully comprehend user emotions may seem like a luxury in hectic, deadline-driven workplaces. Furthermore, because not all emotional experiences are the same, it might be difficult to balance the demands of varied users. One user's comfort level may irritate another, which might result in disagreements over needs prioritization. To guarantee that users' emotional requirements are satisfied without sacrificing the software's overall functioning, empathy-based techniques necessitate ongoing development, user testing, and feedback loops. Development teams may produce software that better fits the emotional and cognitive experiences of users by using empathy-driven requirements engineering methodologies. Developers may learn more about what consumers need and desire by using techniques like empathy mapping, personas, and direct user interaction. Examples like Airbnb and Slack show how empathy can spur more significant advancements, producing software that not only works well but also emotionally connects with users. Empathy has the power to completely transform the collection, analysis, and resolution of user needs as it is increasingly included into software development processes (Seufert, 2024).

Ideation and Innovation: Brainstorming Beyond Boundaries

Effective ideation and innovation processes are essential for businesses looking to remain competitive in a time of swift technological breakthroughs and constant change. Teams may explore ideas beyond conventional bounds with the help of advanced ideation tools like mind mapping and collaborative brainstorming, which promote creativity and lead to ground-breaking software solutions. By using these strategies, businesses may access the combined knowledge of a diverse workforce, producing innovative ideas that have the potential to upend markets and transform user experiences (Arif & Jawab, 2024). Mind mapping is a potent technique that encourages unrestricted association and mental exploration by graphically representing concepts and their relationships. It enables people and groups to begin with a main idea and then delve into a variety of related subjects, forming a network of related concepts. This method not only aids in thought organization but also in seeing trends and possible answers that might not be immediately obvious when using linear thinking. To generate ideas for a new project management application, for example, a software development team may employ mind mapping. Team members can explore areas like work assignment, time tracking, communication tools, and software integration after beginning with the fundamental concept of "project management." The team can identify links between ideas thanks to this visual depiction, which encourages creative solutions like a real-time collaboration tool that lets team members update project progress instantaneously, promoting accountability and transparency. Another sophisticated ideation method is collaborative brainstorming, which combines several viewpoints to provide a wealth of ideas. Collaborative brainstorming promotes equitable participation and gives all voices a chance to be heard, in contrast to conventional brainstorming sessions that could be hampered by the dominance of a few outspoken individuals. Engagement and creativity may be increased by using strategies like round-robin brainstorming, in which team members each provide an idea in turn, or the "brainwriting" approach, in which participants jot down ideas and distribute them for additional elaboration. The creation of the well-known productivity app Trello serves as a real-world illustration of effective group brainstorming. The designers of Trello held lengthy brainstorming meetings with engineers, designers, and users before beginning to create the program (Arif & Jawab, 2024). They collected feedback from a range of stakeholders by creating an open atmosphere, which eventually resulted in the development of an easy-to-use interface that graphically depicts tasks as cards on a board. This strategy addressed actual customer pain issues and made the program user-friendly, producing a solution that appealed to a broad market (Arif & Jawab, 2024).

When these ideation methods are critically examined, their advantages and disadvantages are revealed. Though useful for visualizing concepts, mind mapping can become cumbersome when too many branches are included, which could cause confusion instead of clarity. Additionally, mind mapping's non-linear structure may be difficult for certain people, which may prevent those who prefer more organized methods from participating. Facilitators must steer the mind mapping process to keep it controlled and focused while promoting unrestricted idea sharing to lessen these problems. Conversely, collaborative brainstorming is excellent at producing a wide variety of ideas and encouraging collaboration. But it can also be prone to groupthink, in which the need for unity prevents people from critically analyzing ideas. Less outspoken team members may hesitate to express their thoughts, which can lead to lost chances for creativity. Organizations might use tactics like anonymous idea submissions or hiring a facilitator to get more reticent individuals to speak up to overcome these obstacles (Tariq, 2024). These methods guarantee that all ideas are given equal weight by preserving a balance between teamwork and critical examination. Beyond the methods themselves, real-world instances of innovative software solutions resulting from ideation demonstrate the effectiveness of these strategies. Spotify is one such example, which transformed music streaming by investigating consumer preferences and experiences through group brainstorming sessions. Spotify's staff saw the demand for customized playlists by actively interacting with consumers and holding ideation workshops. Features like "Discover Weekly" and "Daily Mix," which examine listening patterns and select music based on personal preferences, were created because of this realization. In addition to differentiating Spotify from rivals, this creative strategy encouraged strong customer loyalty and engagement (Arif & Jawab, 2024).

Slack, a communication tool that revolutionized business collaboration, is another notable example. The Slack team used collaborative brainstorming and mind mapping to examine the intricacies of team communication as it was being developed. They found a weakness in the current tools, which had trouble staying organized and being easily accessible, by concentrating on user experiences and pain areas. This insight led to the development of threaded conversations and channels, which helped teams effectively handle discussions. The result was a platform that improved communication and teamwork, which accelerated Slack's growth in several sectors (Tariq, 2025). To sum up, firms looking to spur creativity and develop ground-breaking software solutions must employ sophisticated ideation strategies like mind mapping and group brainstorming. By cultivating a collaborative culture and promoting a range of viewpoints, these strategies allow groups to investigate concepts beyond traditional limits. Useful examples like Slack and Spotify show how successful ideation can result in game-changing solutions that connect with consumers and upend markets. Organizations must, however, be aware of the possible drawbacks of these strategies and make sure they combine innovation with critical analysis. In the end, teams may unleash their full creative potential and propel the next wave of innovation in software development by utilizing the power of empathy, cooperation, and organized brainstorming.

Prototyping for Purpose: Rapid Iteration in the Digital Age

The capacity to rapidly prototype and develop software solutions has become crucial for satisfying user demands and maintaining competitiveness in today's fast-paced digital environment. Development teams may produce early iterations of software solutions, test them with users, and make the required modifications in response to feedback thanks to rapid prototyping. By allowing teams to experiment with many concepts and features before settling on a final product, this iterative design method not only improves user engagement but also stimulates creativity. Numerous frameworks and tools have been developed to speed up prototyping, promoting user-centric design and a continuous improvement in culture. Figma, a web-based design platform that enables teams to collaborate and generate interactive prototypes, is one of the most popular tools for fast prototyping. Multiple stakeholders, including as designers, developers, and product managers, may collaborate easily using Figma's real-time collaboration tools, offering immediate feedback and ideas. Teams may swiftly modify designs in response to user feedback or team insights thanks to this instant communication, which can greatly cut down on the amount of time spent on revisions. For example, designers may use Figma to create a clickable prototype that mimics the user experience while creating a mobile application. Before writing a single line of code, stakeholders may test navigation flows and get usability feedback. Organizations may promote a user-centered design process and save time and money by using Figma (Sithipolvanichgul et al., 2024).

InVision, which specializes in turning static designs into interactive prototypes, is another useful tool for quick prototyping. Designers may submit their visual designs to InVision's user-friendly interface and link them together to create a smooth user experience. This is very helpful when doing usability studies with actual users or demonstrating the possible user experience to stakeholders. A team working on an e-commerce site, for instance, can use InVision to prototype the shopping cart feature so that consumers can test the user interface and give input on how intuitive it is. The team can see problems and make data-driven choices to enhance the design by watching consumers as they interact with the prototype. Effective user interaction simulation provided by InVision helps to guarantee that the finished product meets user expectations and raises satisfaction (Brosig et al., 2022). Frameworks such as Design Sprint provide an organized method for fast prototyping that goes beyond technologies. The Design Sprint is a five-day approach created by Google Ventures that aids teams in validating concepts and designing solutions through user testing and fast prototyping. This approach, which leads teams through phases of comprehending the issue, outlining potential solutions, selecting the best concepts, prototyping, and user testing, places a strong emphasis on teamwork and intense concentration. Teams are forced by the Design Sprint's time limits to prioritize tasks and make choices fast, which results in prototypes that are more targeted and efficient. A firm that wants to develop a new health tracking software, for example, may utilize a Design Sprint to test several feature concepts and identify user needs in a single week (Arif & Jawab, 2024). To guide subsequent versions based on actual input, the team would have a prototype ready for user testing by the end of the sprint.

Tools and frameworks that support iterative design cycles are essential for promoting user-centric innovation and ongoing improvement. Development teams may obtain priceless insights into user preferences, habits, and pain spots by routinely testing prototypes with real users. Real-time alterations are made possible by this repeated feedback loop, which results in a final output that is more polished. For instance, Instagram, a well-known social networking site, constantly improves its functionality and user experience through iterative design cycles (Sithipolvanichgul et al., 2024).

To guide subsequent versions based on actual input, the team would have a prototype ready for user testing by the end of the sprint. Tools and frameworks that support iterative design cycles are essential for promoting user-centric innovation and ongoing improvement. Development teams may obtain priceless insights into user preferences, habits, and pain spots by routinely testing prototypes with real users. Real-time alterations are made possible by this repeated feedback loop, which results in a final output that is more polished. For instance, Instagram, a well-known social networking site, constantly improves its functionality and user experience through iterative design cycles (Brosig et al., 2022). The ride-sharing business Uber, for example, uses fast prototyping to test new features like fare splitting and in-app chat. Uber may improve these features based on actual usage scenarios by developing them and getting user input, making sure they improve the user experience overall and offer value. Iterative design cycles and quick prototyping provide benefits, but there may also be drawbacks that businesses need to consider. One major worry is the possibility of scope creep, in which the original project specifications change and grow as the prototype is being developed. This may result in strained resources and longer than anticipated schedules. Teams must fight this by keeping lines of communication open on project priorities and goals, setting limits on what features are essential and what are extras that might detract from the core aims (Sithipolvanichgul et al., 2024).

Effectively combining user testing feedback presents another difficulty. It can be challenging for teams to identify which insights are most useful for promoting changes because of the wide range of viewpoints and preferences that may surface during user interactions with prototypes. Teams may prioritize actionable findings and make sure that the most important concerns are addressed in later iterations by using an organized method of gathering feedback, such as surveys or focus groups (Brosig et al., 2022). Iterative design cycles and fast prototyping are essential in today's software development environment because they help businesses provide user-centric solutions quickly. Prototypes may be swiftly developed and tested using tools like Figma and InVision and frameworks like Design Sprint, guaranteeing that the finished product satisfies user requirements and expectations. Organizations may unleash creativity and bring about significant change in their software solutions by adopting a culture of experimentation and continuous improvement. In a market that is becoming more and more competitive, development teams may employ fast prototyping to remain ahead of the curve and provide outstanding user experiences while navigating the difficulties of scope creep and feedback synthesis.

Empathetic User Testing: Feedback Loops that Drive Excellence

Empathetic user testing is a vital technique that improves product quality and spurs creativity in the ever-evolving world of software development. Development teams may produce solutions that genuinely connect with consumers and successfully meet their requirements and preferences by incorporating user feedback into the product lifecycle. This strategy not only improves user experiences but also increases loyalty and satisfaction. Real-world applications combined with techniques for integrating user feedback at different phases of development show how sympathetic user testing may result in notable enhancements in product quality (Martins et al., 2023). Implementing a continuous feedback loop, which entails gathering insights at every stage of the software lifecycle, from initial design to post-launch review, is one efficient method for incorporating user feedback. The course of development may be greatly impacted by early user input in the design phase. Focus groups, user interviews, surveys, and other methods assist teams in obtaining both qualitative and quantitative information that guides design choices. For instance, to understand the workflows and pain points of potential users, such as physicians and patients, a development team may interview them when creating a new healthcare application. Early collection of this data helps the team produce a user-centric design that meets certain requirements and lowers the possibility of later, expensive adjustments (Chen & Zhang, 2023).

Using usability testing in the prototype stage is another crucial tactic. This gives teams the opportunity to see actual users engage with their prototypes, giving them important information about how well the design works in real-world scenarios. By providing remote user testing, where users may offer feedback from their own devices, tools like User Testing and Lookback make this process easier. These tools may be used, for example, by a team creating a new e-learning platform to evaluate how users access materials and move through courses. Before the finished product is released, the team can find areas for improvement by examining user interactions and getting input on how well features work. This iterative process guarantees that the result closely matches customer expectations and improves the user experience in general (Tang et al., 2022). Long-term product success also depends on putting in place a mechanism for continuing input beyond launch. Constant feedback features, such feedback buttons or in-app surveys, let users express their thoughts and quickly report problems. Future improvements and upgrades can be influenced by this real-time input. For instance, Asana, a project management application, uses user forums and in-app prompts to aggressively solicit customer input. This promotes user involvement and a feeling of community by allowing the team to rank features and fixes according to user feedback. Asana exhibits its dedication to satisfying customer requirements and promoting product innovation by keeping lines of communication open (Martins et al., 2023).

Empathetic user testing's practical applications show how it affects product quality and creativity in a range of sectors. The revamp of the Airbnb platform serves as a noteworthy illustration. Airbnb carried out in-depth user testing and research to comprehend consumers' experiences after realizing that they had trouble locating appropriate lodging. New features including enhanced search filters and tailored suggestions were added because of this procedure. Airbnb greatly improved the user experience by incorporating customer feedback into the redesign process, which raised bookings and user happiness (Chen & Zhang, 2023). Like this, Intuit, a financial technology business, used sympathetic user testing to enhance their TurboTax program. To find problems with the tax preparation process, the team performed usability testing and user interviews. The software's interface was significantly altered because of feedback from actual users, which included improved navigation and more understandable instructions. In addition to improving product usability, this dedication to user-centered design strengthened client loyalty and trust, which eventually resulted in greater retention rates throughout tax season (Martins et al., 2023). A critical evaluation of these tactics reveals the advantages and possible drawbacks of using sympathetic user testing. Integrating user feedback into the software lifecycle promotes a culture of cooperation and ongoing development, which is one of its main advantages. Teams may get a better grasp of users' requirements and produce more creative and practical solutions by actively incorporating users. Additionally, by lowering the possibility of creating features that consumers will not find appealing, this approach lowers the need for expensive redesigns and improves the overall quality of the product (Tang et al., 2022). However, organizing and synthesizing user input properly may cause difficulties for enterprises. Finding useful insights might be challenging due to the enormous amount of feedback that is gathered. Teams should set precise standards for ranking feedback according to user impact and viability to solve this problem. Teams can classify and rank insights for more action by using a methodical approach to feedback analysis, such as affinity diagramming or theme coding. Making sure a variety of users are represented in testing is another difficulty. Focusing on a small group of people might lead to a product that doesn't satisfy the demands of a larger market. Teams should aim for diversity by involving users with different backgrounds, skills, and experiences to counteract this. This variety enhances the feedback process and results in a more thorough comprehension of user requirements (Arif & Jawab, 2024). By incorporating user feedback into the software development process at every stage, empathic user testing is a crucial technique that promotes excellence in software development. Teams may produce products that truly connect with people by implementing tactics like usability testing, continuous feedback loops, and continuous feedback methods. Real-world examples of the concrete advantages of sympathetic user testing on product quality and innovation include the redesign of Airbnb and enhancements to TurboTax. Organizations may improve their software solutions and increase user happiness and long-term success by emphasizing user input and cultivating a collaborative culture. Adopting sympathetic user testing will be essential to maintaining competitiveness and providing outstanding user experiences as the digital world changes (Tang et al., 2022).

Balancing Creativity with Engineering Rigor

The equality of art and structure in software production is a crucial yet not always easy task. It becomes even more important when the organization is trying to adopt design thinking alongside the conventional engineering approaches. Especially relevant in this context are such concepts as 'user orientation, empathy' and 'prototyping' which originate from 'design thinking' movement that is significantly different from traditional engineering approach based on its structuring and methodically. On the other hand, engineering precision, reliability, and scalability may work against flexibility, exploration, and innovation inherent in design thinking. Thus, understanding of how to implement these two approaches can help to achieve the benefits of each method while avoiding weaknesses inherent in the other (Virnandes et al., 2024). Design thinking, at times, starts with emulating with the fact that the users must be understood before a solution can be offered to him. This shift towards the end user is not only good for business, but for technological development as well because often it challenges the teams to look beyond the technicalities of how problem could be solved and deal with how it should be solved. For instance, in the formative stages of the iPhone, Apple successfully worked on how the user would engage with the object, their aim was to make the phone as easy to use as possible. This put Ray into features such as the touch screen and natural user interfaces that were not standard on phones at that time. Nevertheless, transforming such creative visions into engineering solutions was a very substantial challenge in skeptical engineering since the underlying technology needed to satisfy the envisioned user interaction with reliability, performance, and scalability. This example shows that creativity should be followed by the engineering constraints to translate innovative ideas into practical devices (Chen, Ye, & Huang, 2023). Adopting design thinking in engineering foundational practice may prove hard in organizations that are used to a rigid sequential model such as the waterfall model. This means that since design thinking is cyclical and requires continuous improvement through continuous construction and testing of ideas, it can easily be done by people. On the other hand, engineering paradigms are somewhat more rigid in a sequential series of stages of development, testing and implementation. The binary between UX and engineering schooling and practice is well complemented by the agile approach because it is based on flexibility and cyclic progression. It shows that in agility teams can work creatively and with high technical skills at the same time and change solutions quickly depending on the given user's needs. That said, there are tensions to be addressed when introducing or implementing design thinking within software teams. As mentioned earlier, there can be many benefits to design thinking when used with this type of team. The engineering-oriented professionals may also consider design thinking as too 'soft' or not sufficiently problem-oriented and as not taking technical solvability into account. This skepticism is especially common due to the perception that design thinking only focuses on the feel or look of the design or some emotions that a user will go through while using a certain product as opposed to the restraints of engineering (Virnandes et al., 2024). To this effect, there is a need to show how design thinking can support engineering initiatives as indicated below. For example, the use of design thinking at the beginning of a project can eliminate confusion in the middle stages of development when many resources have already been dedicated to a given direction which does not meet the needs of users. By actively involving the users and testing and redesigning along the way more than once it is possible to minimize the chances of creating solutions that do not meet the exact needs or requirements of the users. The steadiness of the Engineer2Designer system allows for cross- function traineeships, in which engineers and designers can learn about each other's disciplines first-hand and develop respect for one another's work. An example of this is Google and its Material Design; while it was developed by Google, it was the result of collaboration between the companies in house designers and outside partners. The framework combines design and engineering approaches to achieve the aesthetics of the user interface and to make sure that it works across the product properly, while not sacrificing aesthetic concerns to technical concerns. In blending design and engineering the typical Google approach of done well, Google has produced an aesthetically pleasing product that is also technically sound (Chen, Ye, & Huang, 2023). Therefore, the integration of design thinking with the engineering conventional principles entails the strike between the dart and the target. To combat resistance in design thinking within software teams, it must be shown how it can make user centered innovation even better while preserving technical quality. Through cooperation and going for the more flexible processes, teams can achieve a balance to support creative and innovative process with more strict engineering principles to improve quality and user experience in software products (Virnandes et al., 2024).

Design Thinking in the Age of AI and IoT

Consider design thinking emphasis on empathy; the practice has a new relevance in an age when devices known as the Internet of Things (IoT) and artificial intelligence (AI) pervade our lives. This is why making user experiences the center stage as these technologies get integrated into our daily lives is more important. Empathy–driven principles means that no matter the type of project virtual or actual always ensure that the human being is the nucleus in AI and IoT. Design thinking involves continually trying to understand users' needs and behaviours and their difficulties, so we arrive at the creation of not only technologically new solutions, but meaningful and usable ones (Daradkeh et al., 2023). Some of these challenges are well-captured in the context of AI development, referring to as empathy-driven design thinking where the issues such as bias inherent in the algorithms, or low trust by users in the decision-making capabilities of AI can be handled. Empathy makes it easier for the teams to see the problems facing the users, or the issues of mistrust in the system. For example, in the context of applying AI in health care, design thinking enables the creation of an AI system that extracts, from patients' data, both clinically relevant knowledge and patient-centric understanding. This implies that physicians should explain the AI recommendations clearly and in layman language to enable the patient to make informed decision. If there is no such empathy, the users may feel themselves treated distant or may not even trust an AI involvement in the decision-making processes, no matter how advanced the tool is (Wang, Shi, & Qu, 2024).

The Internet of Things is another area in which design thinking is extremely important. Making devices that are IoT connected to speak to each other and making them easy to use is important as these devices get integrated into homes and businesses. Adherence to thinking principles enable the creation of interfaces which are easier to use, and it allows the technology to meet its intended use. Consider the smart home ecosystem: everything from thermostats to security cameras will need to be integrated as if they were all, well, one neat system." (Daradkeh et al., 2023). They can easily become awkward to operate, again with an interface that is a) credibly farm from optimal or b) cobbled together from poorly integrated components. But at the heart of it, the proposed design thinking approach will enable developers to pay attention to how users truly live and navigate their space and so create IoT devices that are easier to operate. This might include functional interfaces between multiple devices and more generally, making users aware of the status of their system, and originating not only for functionality but for the user's feelings of security and satisfaction (Arif & Jawab, 2024). Quite possibly one of the most stimulating examples of empathy-driven design in AI is the creation of self-driving automobiles. Many companies like Waymo have been able to apply design thinking when in the process of finding out how the public feels when they are using self-driving cars. Some of the ways in which it was mentioned that the car's autonomy has been made safer include The current ways that people react when in a car that is able to drive on its own have been adjusted to make it feel safer and more natural for the users. For example, "gazebo" or a screen with what the car 'sees on the road decreases anxiety, as users feel they are in charge. This empathetic approach pulls the conversion from fear based to trust based, illustrating how important user experience is in such systems of Artificial Intelligence (Wang, Shi, & Qu, 2024).

Likewise, Nest's learning thermostat is an excellent example of how an approach to product design, such as design thinking can define success in the sphere of IoT products. Nest designers discovered that most users are inconvenienced by old fashioned thermostat models, especially when programming their heating and cooling systems. Through the key principles of empathy Nest was able to develop a device that adapts to the user's daily routine compellingly little interaction. The problem of controlling a heater is utilized by the thermostat, but it also satisfies the user's need for warmth with corresponding savings and no need to fiddle with the settings (Daradkeh et al., 2023). There are however some difficulties concerning the Integration of design thinking AI and IoT projects and they include? This may be summarized by the conflict between design and use, or between fancy and function. That is, in many emerging technology projects, it is possible that technical capability will push the envelope beyond what users are ready to accept. Design thinking reduces the risk in this area by encouraging a step-by-step gradual approach that is initiated by the user. The fourth issue is the ethical aspect—empathy-based values must also consider general aspects of AI and IoT, for example, privacy or absence of work because of the growing automation. In this case, design thinking can assist due to promotion of openness as well as user values and perceptions regarding new technologies are integrated in the process (Leso et al., 2024; Wang, Shi, & Qu, 2024).

Empathy as a Success Factor in Agile and Lean Development

Closely associated with these methodologies are the concepts of Agile and Lean development; empathy is also essential to determine how best to proceed with improvement while relying on adaptability and collaboration. Though Agile and Lean practices are fast and efficient ways of delivering value, design thinking, being user-centric, brings this to another level. Learning design thinking with Agile and Lean creates an insurance that whilst technical and processes benefits of these methodologies are being supplied, so are the gains adding value to the needs of the users (Leso et al., 2024). In Agile development, teams operate in cycles, providing and incorporating small amounts of content to a product with frequent feedback from those who will use it. Design thinking supplements this by the integration of empathy into the process to ensure that before teams begin to build solutions, they need to understand the user's problems, challenges and expectations. This alignment also guarantees that the Agile principle of ''responding to change over following a plan' encompasses beyond internal project changes and competently includes the feedback from the user as the major influence for change. For example, in Agile software development, employing ideas derived from empathy-based design to conduct user testing and feedback often means that the Agile teams will be able to make the right product updates to result in highly enhanced user satisfaction which often is not considered in functional specification approaches (de Noronha, Ferraro, & Silva, 2022).

It is easy to therefore deduce that lean development, with its core principle of making efficient use of all available resources, also stands to gain from the practice of empathy. Sometimes waste in development does not occur as most people expect it through involving ineffective activities, but through creating features or products that people do not need. That is, the application of empathy enables Lean teams to understand which of the features within the product are valuable for users and thus avoids delivering those features that users do not want or need. This makes the development process less complex and ragged but at the same time guarantees the fact that the product offers due value to the target market (Yang et al., 2023). Slack is one of the companies that integrated Lean into its practices: they asked users about their problems and designed their platform to help solve those problems. This empathetic approach was used by Slack to eschew on adding unnecessary frills and to instead focus on smooth and easy to use communication tools. Empathy also improves work cooperativeness and flexibility in Agile teams, thus making the teams' environments to be more effective allowing consolidation of different perspectives and knowledge of the team. During the Agile working process, the team members are to provide data by developers, designers and other members of the team (Leso et al., 2023).

This fosters good relations in certain teams by making each worker to be aware of the other, and the problem that they encounter in their line of duty. This is important in Agile since frequent communication is needed to sustain the rate of implemented work. It is much easier to solve problems, or at least understand that it is impossible to please either the technical team or the users completely, when team members can put themselves in each other's shoes. For example, when a designer writes a specification for a feature they are working on with a developer, the feeling of empathy will help one understand that while creating an aesthetic feature, some certain constraints of the developer must be taken into consideration before the feature is adopted fully (de Noronha, Ferraro, & Silva, 2022). Furthermore, empathy ensures flexibility in Agile since it reminds teams about users and how they may be changing in their preferences or behavior. This results in frequent course correction, which is an inherent characteristic of agility, all of which is done with the user at the forefront as mercy/empathy enshrines. For instance, in the development of the Spotify, the team mainly relied on user-centered insights within the application. Originally, it began as a music streaming site but evolved after understanding users' wants and needs through feedback that included elements such as custom playlists based on user mood, music for workouts and other activities that helped the user base find value beyond only internet music streaming (Yang et al., 2023).

These incorporated into the business have been made Spotify adaptable in the marketplaces making it gain a competitive edge. Still, incorporating empathy within the settings of Agile and Lean working models has some considerations. The first challenge is the prevention of empathy from becoming a rate limiting step to the number of iterations in Agile or compromising the lean efficiency objectives. It is often feared that taking time to do user research or feedback will impair the spirit of constant iteration. In order to counter this, the teams have to employ a lightweight approach to inclusion of empathy, which may be in the form of brief user interviews, or usability tests that take not more than 15 minutes, or simple surveys that could render the valuable information without posing more challenges to the workflow (Leso et al., 2023). Therefore, understanding the needs and feelings of other people is a critical success factor in Agile and Lean developing which relates to design thinking to guarantee the focus on users. Engaging collaboration increased mutual understanding, and ensuing flexibility – all these made it possible for Agile teams to better manage change and provide users with what they need. Empathy also enhances Lean processes through the minimization of wastes, particularly by directing the attention to the actual areas the user cares most about. For example, Slack and Spotify inspire empathy-based strategies as enhanced techniques to increase product success in fast-paced settings for speed, efficiency, and focus on consumers (de Noronha, Ferraro, & Silva, 2022).

TEACHING EMPATHY-DRIVEN SOFTWARE ENGINEERING

Teaching empathy driven software engineering is gradually assuming significance due to the ever-rising significance of user-oriented design and innovation. Introducing design thinking puts the future software engineers in a position whereby they feel and know what the user requires, faces, or even feels at any one time. The cultivation of these principles into the educational setting entails a transformation from strict technical skills education to what could be summed up as incorporating human centered design, along with the appropriate programming and engineering knowledge (Seufert, 2024). Implementing empathy-centered approaches across such settings can enable pre-service engineers to cultivate the right mental approach when designing solutions that positively address users' needs. As one of the most efficient educational methodologies, thinking workshops and real-life situation-based activities must be applied as guidelines for teaching principles of empathy-driven software engineering. In design thinking, there is a focus on leading with empathy, which will mean that students start out with understanding the user. For instance, in a software engineering class a set of students can be given an assignment of providing a solution to a definite category of users: people with disabilities. All these show that apart from interviews, user observation and prototyping, students get to understand how to tackle user problems with the software. The above hands on, experience based-learning methods help improve on the students' empathy to the users for which they will design (Yawised et al., 2022; Brown, 2023).

The next strong practice is cross-disciplinary collaboration as an element of software engineering curricula. Unfortunately, most software engineers find themselves working in a cocoon that concerns only technical processes. But in the real world, successful software development involves designers, product managers and users as well. It means that developing projects which students must complete in teams with members from different disciplines may help educators foster empathy. For example, a project may comprise engineering students interning with psychology or design students to design and create an application to help those with mental issues (Leso, 2022). By now, a software engineer can learn how the various societal views and paradigms help in the development of not only a software product that will enable societal functionality but also software products which are social products that are able to sense our common emotions. Also, empathy-related case studies could offer possible and successful class examples to the students. Evaluating other people's success stories facilitates identifying connection between theory and practice. For instance, Airbnb is regarded as a company that successfully implemented the concept of empathy in the product offering process (Dul, 2021; Norman, 2023). Both the founders of Airbnb and its successors knew their first appearances with the platform as hosts and guests themselves, which made it easier for them to invent solutions for real inconveniences. When explaining design thinking to students, teachers should use examples such as Airbnb; in this way, they will be able to explain to students that true software solutions that change users' lives are created by focusing on empathy. Because of the realization that empathy forms part of learning among engineering students, academia and industry have embraced the principles to bring out these changes in training (Yawised et al., 2022). The pioneer in this setting is Stanford University's school, where existing courses are centered on empathy in design thinking. They have played a critical role in fashioning the attitude of engineers, entrepreneurs and designers that develop persona friendly technologies in the technology market. Likewise, the Empathy Lab at Google drives user needs by inviting engineers and designers to create a safe environment that uses virtual reality such as role play scenarios to envision and understand the users' difficulties. The above success stories demonstrate that empathy is the key to not only better software but also more innovative and easier to use products (Leso, 2022).

Although teaching empathy driven software engineering is not without these challenges it is apparent they should do so for the next generation of engineers. Another task that will also be rather time-consuming is changing the old approach to classify the software development as a function that has nothing to do with emotions or social aspects. It will perturb some students and educators to put as much value in empathy as they do in coding abilities. Nevertheless, due to a short period of an empathy-based approach, there is more and more evidence that proves its effectiveness in both academic and business spheres. At the present, institutions should strive to incorporate empathy as one of the competencies and crime fighting techniques in software engineering as a fundamental ability like technical skill (Dul, 2021). Thus, dedicated to nurturing empathy in software engineering, it is essential to develop fresh approaches that would foster the act of learning under the role of users. design thinking, interdisciplinary collaboration, and systems thinking into education institution can redirect empathic engineering abilities to create more effective software solutions, that fit users' needs. Empathy in the software development needs to be driven as successful leaders like Stanford University and Google show the ability of engineers who are trained to think emphatically to deliver user-centered products that take the market, transforming business. Given the increasing trend of emphasis on human-centered design, questions of empathy will become increasingly pertinent, as such concepts are reflected in the teaching of software engineering (Seufert, 2024).

CONCLUSION

Empathy driven software development is not just a theoretical framework, it is a transformative approach to how technology engages with the human. Empathy is the ability for developers to concentrate on creating user centric solutions that cater to emotional of cognitive and social needs, as opposed to just functional requirements. Empathy sits at the heart of the process; by putting the user at the center of the design and development, where technology is both technically precise as well as meaningful. It's not surprising that the need for empathy in software design has grown as technologies like Artificial Intelligence (AI), Internet of Things (IoT) and machine learning are emerging. These systems are more and more part of our everyday life and require more personalized, thoughtful, emotionally intelligent interactions. Empathy driven methodologies are used to ensure the user diversity is respected by these technologies, accessibility needs are addressed, and inclusion is promoted in the systems. Microsoft's Xbox Adaptive Controller and other user-centred advancements in AI are real world examples showing how empathy can enable groundbreaking innovation and trust and satisfaction.

Empathy finds its way to confronting the ethical aspects in a fast-changing technological landscape. Developers struggle with how to achieve the balance between user privacy and emotionally intelligent design. Empathy is a proactive stance to promote transparency, inclusion and responsible innovation. New systems are not allowed to exploit or alienate users, but rather to empower them with systems that are both accessible and trustworthy. Looking forward, the work of integrating empathy into design thinking will help innovation in the future. Virtual and augmented reality applications hold great promise for improved user understanding and rapid, agile and lean development cycles that support empathic principles. The trick is to build empathy in a sustainable way into the organizational cultures so that it is no longer relegated to a secondary consideration, but rather a critical success factor. In short, empathetic software development is not an optional add-on, it is a must for software development in the future. It takes software and transforms it into tools that users resonate with, responding to their needs through means outside of the obvious. The more technology spreads, the more and more eyes will be on empathy, making the call for engineers and designers to create systems that are effective but also human centric, ethical and deeply impactful.

REFERENCES

Adhikari Egodawele, M. H., Sedera, D., & Bui, V. (2022). A systematic review of digital transformation literature (2013–2021) and the development of an overarching a-priori model to guide future research.

Apasrawirote, D., Yawised, K., & Muneesawang, P. (2022). Digital marketing capability: The mystery of business capabilities. *Marketing Intelligence & Planning*, *40*(4), 477–496. DOI: 10.1108/MIP-11-2021-0399

Arif, J., & Jawab, F. (2024). Application of fsQCA method in operations. In *Intersecting Entrepreneurship* (p. 291). Internationalization, and Green Innovation.

Brosig, C., Bley, K., Strahringer, S., & Westner, M. (2022). The missing piece-calibration of qualitative data for qualitative comparative analyses in IS research. In *ECIS*.

Brown, T. (2023). *Change by design: How design thinking creates new alternatives for business and society*. Harper Business.

Chen, M., Wang, H., Liang, Y., & Zhang, G. (2023). Net and configurational effects of determinants on cloud computing adoption by SMEs under cloud promotion policy using PLS-SEM and fsQCA. *Journal of Innovation & Knowledge*, *8*(3), 100388. DOI: 10.1016/j.jik.2023.100388

Chen, M., Ye, Y., & Huang, X. (2023). The metaverse in supply chain knowledge sharing and resilience contexts: An empirical investigation of factors affecting adoption and acceptance. *Journal of Innovation & Knowledge*, *8*(1), 100446. DOI: 10.1016/j.jik.2023.100446

Daradkeh, F. M., Hassan, T. H., Palei, T., Helal, M. Y., Mabrouk, S., Saleh, M. I., & Elshawarbi, N. N. (2023). Enhancing digital presence for maximizing customer value in fast-food restaurants. *Sustainability (Basel)*, *15*(7), 5690. DOI: 10.3390/su15075690

de Noronha, M. E. S., Ferraro, D. M. J., & Silva, R. D. S. V. (2022). Bibliometric analysis on the orchestration of dynamic capabilities. *International Journal of Innovation: IJI Journal*, *10*(4), 610–637.

Dul, J. (2021). Advances in necessary condition analysis. Downloaded on Jan, 21, 2022.

Dul, J. (2022). Problematic applications of necessary condition analysis (NCA) in tourism and hospitality research. *Tourism Management, 93*, 104616. DOI: 10.1016/j.tourman.2022.104616

Eghdam, T. (2024). *Future of youth hockey culture.*

Gao, J., Zhang, W., Guan, T., Feng, Q., & Mardani, A. (2023). Influence of digital transformation on the servitization level of manufacturing SMEs from static and dynamic perspectives. *International Journal of Information Management, 73*, 102645. DOI: 10.1016/j.ijinfomgt.2023.102645

Graham, J. R. (2024). Identifying primary school teachers' perceptions of the maker mindset in Indonesian international schools (Doctoral dissertation, Murdoch University).

Kar, A. K., He, W., Payton, F. C., Grover, V., Al-Busaidi, A. S., & Dwivedi, Y. K. (2024). How could quantum computing shape information systems research–An editorial perspective and future research directions. *International Journal of Information Management*, •••, 102776.

Leso, B. H. (2022). Unlocking the digital organization: A view of the digital transformation capabilities. [Doctoral dissertation, Universidade Federal do Rio Grande do Sul]

Leso, B. H., Cortimiglia, M. N., & Ghezzi, A. (2023). The contribution of organizational culture, structure, and leadership factors in the digital transformation of SMEs: A mixed-methods approach. *Cognition Technology and Work, 25*(1), 151–179. DOI: 10.1007/s10111-022-00714-2 PMID: 36118918

Leso, B. H., Cortimiglia, M. N., Ghezzi, A., & Minatogawa, V. (2024). Exploring digital transformation capability via a blended perspective of dynamic capabilities and digital maturity: A pattern matching approach. *Review of Managerial Science, 18*(4), 1149–1187. DOI: 10.1007/s11846-023-00692-3

Martins, C. E. H., de Souza, R. C., da Costa Júnior, J. F., & de Sousa Neto, M. V. (2023). Criação de um sistema de medição de desempenho para uma empresa de prevenção a fraudes. *Gestão e Projetos: GeP, 14*(1), 133–165. DOI: 10.5585/gep.v14i1.23265

Mazumder, S., & Garg, S. (2021). Decoding digital transformational outsourcing: The role of service providers' capabilities. *International Journal of Information Management, 58*, 102295. DOI: 10.1016/j.ijinfomgt.2020.102295

Norman, D. A. (2023). *The design of everyday things: Revised and expanded edition.* Basic Books.

Peláez, K. M. L., Cuello, M. A. J., Díaz, V. C. B., & Armijos, M. R. R. (2024). Estrategias innovadoras para el manejo sostenible de los laboratorios clínicos. *Journal of Science and Research*, *9*(2), 173–203.

Seufert, S. (2024). Impact of IT investments on a company: Towards an approach for managing the IT business value (Doctoral dissertation, Duisburg, Essen, Universität Duisburg-Essen, 2024).

Sithipolvanichgul, J., Dhir, A., Talwar, S., Srivastava, P., & Kaur, P. (2024). Knowledge arbitrage: What are the risks, and do they matter? *Journal of Knowledge Management*, *28*(10), 2818–2842. DOI: 10.1108/JKM-05-2023-0411

Tang, M. C., Huang, C. H., & Chiang, F. H. (2022). Examining the development trajectory of IT outsourcing: A main path analysis. In *PACIS* (p. 76).

Tariq, M. U. (2024). Navigating the Personalization Pathway: Implementing Adaptive Learning Technologies in Higher Education. In Minh Tung, T. (Ed.), *Adaptive Learning Technologies for Higher Education* (pp. 265–291). IGI Global., DOI: 10.4018/979-8-3693-3641-0.ch012

Tariq, M. U. (2024). Leveraging AI for Entrepreneurial Innovation in Healthcare. In Özsungur, F. (Ed.), *Generating Entrepreneurial Ideas With AI* (pp. 192–216). IGI Global., DOI: 10.4018/979-8-3693-3498-0.ch009

Tariq, M. U. (2024). Streamlining Operations Insights and Innovations From the Gulf Cooperation Council (GCC). In Ayed, T., Ali, I., Abdelhamid, H., & Mohamed, A. (Eds.), *Utilizing Case Studies in Business Education* (pp. 188–216). IGI Global., DOI: 10.4018/979-8-3693-3779-0.ch010

Tariq, M. U. (2025). Breaking Boundaries: Computational Thinking in Educational Policy Leadership Management. In Agboola, B., & Thompson, C. (Eds.), *Navigating Leadership and Policy Management in Education* (pp. 77–102). IGI Global., DOI: 10.4018/979-8-3693-9215-7.ch003

Tariq, M. U. (2025). Strategic Integration of Technological Advances in Modern Business Practices. In Sedky, A. (Ed.), *Building Business Knowledge for Complex Modern Business Environments* (pp. 95–120). IGI Global., DOI: 10.4018/979-8-3693-6447-5.ch004

Tariq, M. U. (2025). Empowering Learning Through Networked and Connected Education: Case Studies in Digital Engagement. In Gierhart, A. (Ed.), *Cases on Enhancing P-16 Student Engagement With Digital Technologies* (pp. 169–198). IGI Global Scientific Publishing., DOI: 10.4018/979-8-3693-5633-3.ch007

Virnandes, S. R., Shen, J., & Vlahu-Gjorgievska, E. (2024). Shaping trust in public service: A convergent mixed-methods investigation of digital government transformation.

Wang, Y., Shi, J., & Qu, G. (2024). Research on collaborative innovation cooperation strategies of manufacturing digital ecosystem from the perspective of multiple stakeholders. *Computers & Industrial Engineering*, *190*, 110003. DOI: 10.1016/j.cie.2024.110003

Yang, Z., Chang, J., Huang, L., & Mardani, A. (2023). Digital transformation solutions of entrepreneurial SMEs based on an information error-driven T-spherical fuzzy cloud algorithm. *International Journal of Information Management*, *69*, 102384. DOI: 10.1016/j.ijinfomgt.2021.102384

Yawised, K., Apasrawirote, D., & Boonparn, C. (2022). From traditional business shifted towards transformation: The emerging business opportunities and challenges in the 'Metaverse' era. *Incbaa*, *162*, 175.

KEY TERMS AND DEFINITIONS

Empathy-Driven Development: A development approach that places understanding and addressing user emotions and experiences at the forefront of software engineering processes.

Design Thinking: A problem-solving framework that emphasizes creativity, empathy, and user-centric insights to guide the development of solutions.

Iterative Feedback Loop: A cyclical process of collecting, analysing, and incorporating user feedback to continually refine a product during its development.

Prototyping: The creation of preliminary versions of software to test and gather feedback for iterative improvement.

Agile Development: A methodology focused on iterative progress, collaboration, and adaptability in software engineering, aligning well with empathy-driven practices.

Chapter 5
The Democratization of Software Development and Design Thinking:
Governing Design Quality in Citizen Software Development

Maaike Stoops
https://orcid.org/0009-0003-5139-1806
LINKIT B.V., The Netherlands

Pablo Alfonso Aguilar Calderón
https://orcid.org/0000-0002-4939-0383
Universidad Autónoma de Sinaloa, Mexico

Óscar Manuel Peña Bañuelos
https://orcid.org/0009-0007-1241-9051
Universidad Autónoma de Sinaloa, Mexico

ABSTRACT

The ongoing democratization of software development, fueled by the proliferation of low-code/no-code platforms and AI-assisted tools, is fundamentally transforming the technological landscape by enabling non-technical citizen developers to create functional applications with minimal coding expertise. As organizations increasingly adopt these accessible development approaches to accelerate digital transformation, critical questions emerge regarding the potential erosion of established design principles, including user-centered methodologies and rigorous usability testing. This chapter systematically examines both the opportunities and challenges presented by this democratization movement, analyzing its impact on

DOI: 10.4018/979-8-3693-9531-8.ch005

software quality, maintainability, and user experience. The discussion culminates in practical recommendations for balancing accessibility with excellence, ensuring that democratized software ecosystems produce solutions that are not only rapidly deployable but also robust, scalable, and genuinely user-centric in an increasingly competitive digital economy

1. INTRODUCTION

In today's fast-evolving technological environment software development is becoming increasingly accessible to a wider audience. The rise of low-code and no-code platforms, combined with artificial intelligence (AI) integration, has allowed individuals with little formal training—referred to as "citizen developers" (Kirvan, P. et al., 2023)—to design and create software solutions. A practice previously reserved for specialists. As a result, almost anyone can now develop and deploy working software. This process of making a technology or practice available to anyone is known as democratization. In this case we are talking about the democratization of software development.

With the rise of citizen developers, the dynamics of the software development process and the roles within development teams change. Software development teams traditionally include multidisciplinary roles like developers, testers, a scrum master, and product designers. However, now that citizen developers can develop and deploy full software applications, employees from different parts of organizations are empowered to make software solutions. As described by Redhat in 2018 low-code platforms not only make software development more attainable, but also speed up the time in which working software can be developed. As a result, organizations that practice low-code development tend to follow fewer formal processes. Compared to traditional software development, I have also experienced that low-code development teams often have fewer and less formalized roles and responsibilities. Teams might lack a product designer, as low-code platforms provide many User Interface elements out of the box (Rokis & Kirikova, 2023).

Besides a shift in roles, the process of software development also changes. Traditionally software development teams used the Waterfall method, where the scope, budget and timeline are fixed upfront. To make software development more iterative, teams are trained to work through Agile frameworks and methodologies. However, since one person can fulfill different the roles in the team, the agility of software development reaches a new level. When one person can execute multiple, if not all, roles within the software development team, there is less inherit focus on methodologies and alignment. Such citizen developer can design, develop, test and deploy new functionality in a matter of hours or days rather than weeks or months. But as the speed of software development increases there is a considerable risk that teams no longer spend time on doing user research, as these practices are perceived to slow down the, increasingly fast, development work. So, the speed of development could reduce the active involvement of users and design professionals in the software design and development process. As citizen developers might lack a design background, software development could suffer from professional oversight. As a result, the application of Design Thinking practices is likely to decrease while speed and agility increase.

Design Thinking has long served as a foundational methodology within the field of software development, fostering the creation of solutions that are both functionally effective and user-centric. By placing human needs, behaviors, and experiences at the core of the design process, Design Thinking enhances the desirability, usability, and overall impact of software products. Its application ensures that technological solutions remain aligned with real-world user expectations and challenges. However, when the principles of Design Thinking are overlooked or inconsistently applied, software systems risk becoming less intuitive, accessible, or meaningful to their intended users. In recent years, the growing movement of citizen development—which empowers non-professional developers to create software using low-code or no-code platforms—has introduced new dynamics into the software engineering landscape. While this democratization of development expands access and participation, it also raises critical questions regarding quality assurance and human-centered design.

One of the central inquiries this chapter addresses is whether it is reasonable or feasible to expect citizen developers to adopt and implement Design Thinking methodologies in their practices. Through this lens, the chapter examines the broader implications of citizen-led development on software quality, analyzing the potential tensions between ease of creation and adherence to established design and usability standards. It considers how the absence—or presence—of Design Thinking in this context influences the effectiveness, inclusivity, and long-term sustainability of software solutions developed outside traditional engineering environments.

This chapter is structured to provide a comprehensive investigation into the evolving relationship between Design Thinking and contemporary software development practices—particularly in the context of agile methodologies and citizen development. Section 2 presents a critical literature review to examine the current integration of Design Thinking within agile software development frameworks. It highlights the anticipated roles and responsibilities of both end users and professional designers throughout the iterative design process, emphasizing the value of multidisciplinary collaboration in achieving human-centered software solutions. Section 3 details the methodological approach adopted to assess the potential risks associated with diminishing user and designer involvement in the design and development phases. This section lays the foundation for understanding how the erosion of stakeholder participation can adversely affect usability, accessibility, and solution relevance. Section 4 expands the discussion by analyzing the role of emerging technologies—particularly Artificial Intelligence (AI)—in mitigating these challenges. It explores the extent to which AI-powered tools and platforms may support or substitute certain aspects of design governance, user engagement, and decision-making within software projects. Following this, Section 5 engages in a reflective discussion on the implications of the findings for both practitioners and researchers. It addresses the practical limitations and ethical considerations of delegating design authority to automated or minimally guided processes. Finally, Section 6 concludes that while technological augmentation and process refinement may enhance the quality of software developed by citizen developers, such approaches remain insufficient to fully replace the contributions of a multidisciplinary team. The inclusion of trained designers and user experience experts remains a critical factor in preserving the integrity, inclusivity, and long-term sustainability of software systems.

2. LITERATURE REVIEW

To fully appreciate the current trends in user-centered design and the role of citizen developers in software creation, it is important to first understand how software development has become increasingly accessible over time. The following section provides a brief historical overview of the key technological and social changes that enabled the widespread participation in software development, setting the stage for the emergence of design thinking practices among non-professional developers.

The software development landscape has evolved significantly over the past few decades, transitioning from an exclusive, resource-intensive practice to a widely accessible and collaborative discipline. Understanding this historical transformation is essential for contextualizing the emergence of new paradigms such as citizen development and their relationship to methodologies like Design Thinking. In the early stages of computing, the development and deployment of software were activities largely confined to well-resourced institutions, such as large corporations and government agencies. High development costs, coupled with the limited availability of specialized expertise, rendered software engineering an exclusive endeavor. Only organizations with significant financial and technical capacity could afford to build and maintain custom software solutions. This exclusivity began to shift during the 1990s with the advent and expansion of the open-source movement. As articulated by the Open Source Initiative (2009), open standards and free-to-use development frameworks began to reshape the landscape. Not-for-profit organizations played a pivotal role in fostering this change by developing programming languages, libraries, and platforms that were made freely available to the global developer community. In exchange, individual developers and contributors engaged in a reciprocal model of knowledge sharing—building upon these resources and reinvesting their enhancements and insights back into the community. This virtuous cycle of collaborative innovation significantly reduced the barriers to entry for aspiring developers. Simultaneously, the widespread adoption of the internet and the mainstreaming of personal computing—particularly from the late 1990s onward—further democratized access to development tools and knowledge (Couldry, 2012). The convergence of open-source philosophy, increased connectivity, and affordable hardware catalyzed a shift from centralized software creation to more distributed and participatory modes of development.

Statista estimated in October 2024 that the number of internet users globally is currently 5.52 billion, which accounts for 67.5% of the global population. As a result, more people use software every day, and the need for good software products grows. Concurrently more people are able to develop software. In the last 5 years, the number of global software developers increased 20% to an expected 28.7 million in 2024. In 2030 this number is expected to be 45 million, an increase of over 50% from where we are today.

Until recently, developers needed a high level of technical expertise. But with emerging technologies, the technical expertise of a software developer is becoming less of a bottleneck to build software. Low-code, and no-code platforms like Mendix, OutSystems, Appian and Microsoft PowerApps have gained popularity (Matvitskyy, et al., 2024), enabling people with limited technical expertise to take on the role of developers. By providing a visual interface to build software based on pre-defined components, developers are enabled to 'drag and drop' a software application, rather than writing lines of code. Developers can, for example, place a button and define what happens when a user clicks it through a graphical user interface.

Besides low-code and no-code technology, Artificial Intelligence is playing an increasingly significant role in software development. Developers can already use AI to check or write code, but now enables non-developers to build software. Microsoft's GitHub, worlds largest code repository, released Spark as recently as October 2024. This AI-powered tool allows people to build small, working applications with prompts. By prompting to build, for example, a tool to track bookings for your upcoming holiday, it will write the code for such software including its interface and logic. Both open-source frameworks, and low-code or no-code platforms increasingly integrate AI to support their developers' communities. AI helps testing and debugging software, ensuring best practices and adherence to industry standards. Mendix, a top low-code platforms according to Gartner's magic quadrant, predicts that by 2028 GenAI will reduce the cost of software development by 30% compared to 2023.

So, tools now lower complexity and improve software development. Where software development was previously reserved for people with official education, anyone tech savvy with a device and access to the internet can now publish small websites and applications. Consequently, the profile of the developer is transitioning from a highly skilled professional to what is now known as a "citizen developer". These citizen developers often build small software solutions for the problems around them. A common example is a web designer bringing their designs to life using no-code tools, bypassing the need for extensive programming knowledge. But different roles within organizations can now build software. Roles like marketers, lab researchers, and warehouse managers can now also build applications specific to their tasks. Take a lab researcher who can automatically run checks on the research data of their team. Because software users can now develop software, these developers assume responsibilities designing, building, implementing, and maintaining software. Previously, users gave input on functional requirements and software developers them. Now user are developers, and the development practice shifts towards domain experts creating solutions tailored to their specific fields.

Now that software development is more attainable, more people can become software developers. Software development also happens much faster. Redhat, a prominent provider of enterprise open-source solutions, stated already in 2019 that low-code and digital automation platforms enabled software development to go up to 90% faster then traditional writing of software code. With the rise of AI accelerators, this speed is set to increase further. Agile is already prominent within software development, but software is built faster its agility is expected to grow further.

a. Agility in Software Development

In the early stages of software engineering, development processes were predominantly guided by the Waterfall model, a linear and sequential methodology wherein the technical and functional specifications were defined comprehensively at the outset. As noted by Făgără an et al. (2021), this rigid structure often resulted in software products that failed to meet users' evolving expectations, lacked technical feasibility in rapidly changing environments, or became economically unviable as market conditions shifted during the development lifecycle. To illustrate the limitations of this approach, consider a hypothetical case: a team begins developing a food delivery application in late 2019 using traditional programming tools and a feature-rich design. Given the extensive scope and the sequential development process, the application is not ready for launch until late 2020. During this period, the COVID-19 pandemic rapidly altered global behaviors, prompting dramatic shifts in consumer needs and expectations. By the time the application reaches completion, many of its initially prioritized functionalities may have lost relevance due to the emergence of competing platforms offering more responsive and user-centered features.

A practical example further underscores this challenge. During the pandemic, the author participated in the development of a mobile application that allowed customers to place orders directly from their table at restaurants. In the Netherlands, numerous similar applications were rapidly introduced in 2020 to support restaurant operations amidst staff shortages and social distancing regulations. While the development team prioritized complex payment system integrations as essential to the product's initial release, competing applications gained early traction by offering simpler, yet more immediately valuable features aligned with user preferences. This case exemplifies the critical need for agile, user-centered design methodologies, such as Design Thinking, which allow for continuous feedback, iterative development, and adaptability in the face of changing user needs and technological landscapes.

The Waterfall methodology uses a linear process similar to traditional project management, where the scope, timeline, and budget are defined upfront (Sherman, 2015). However, in software development projects, this approach often led to failures. For instance, in the case of a food delivery application, the scope of a project frequently shifts over time. These shifts may arise from external changes, such as the COVID-19 pandemic. But even without external changes, organizations noticed drawbacks in defining the full scope at the project's outset. During implementation, software teams face unforeseen factors, such as overlooked technical requirements or user feedback revealing needs different from initial assumptions. Teams realized Waterfall's rigid upfront planning failed to match software development's dynamic nature. As a reaction, Agile methodologies grew in popularity (Larman, 2004). Agile aimed to make software development iterative and enabled teams to adjust quickly to new insights. Instead of following long-term plans and releasing software only after extended timelines, Agile teams deliver functional software to users much faster. By releasing software every few weeks, teams frequently test functionality with stakeholders. Additionally, Agile improves stakeholder feedback throughout the development cycle. The focus shifted to execution and collaboration rather than processes and contracts.

The release of the Agile Manifesto in 2001 marked the formal rise of Agile methodologies, transforming how teams worked. Dam and Siang (2022) describe that Design Thinking also gained recognition for embedding user-centered principles into solution design. Agile's iterative approach introduced a new way of validating software with real users through short development cycles. In a 2-4 week Agile sprint cycle, new functionality is showcased regularly. This process fosters continuous improvement through real user insights. By combining Design Thinking with Agile, organizations can gather user insights while designing and developing software solutions. As software development grew and iterative approaches gained importance, Agile became popular. Design Thinking provided tools to integrate user insights. Combining the two methodologies offers organizations a structured way to enhance user-centricity in software. However, organizations often face challenges combining Agile with Design Thinking. Agile emphasizes delivering small, functional increments quickly, while Design Thinking requires upfront investment in understanding users' needs with a holistic view of the product context. This difference in pace may lead teams to prioritize speed over user research. This contradiction causes tension in current development projects. But how will that evolve in 5 years? With 45 million global software developers delivering increasingly faster software, and additional unofficial developers, the speed of production and agility will grow exponentially. How can we apply Design Thinking effectively in such compressed processes?

b. Strengths and Risks of Integrating Design Thinking and Agile

Agile software development methodologies and frameworks aim to introduce iteration and flexibility into the software development process. Frameworks like SAFe (Scaled Agile Framework) offer structured approaches to deliver "best value and quality for people and society in the shortest sustainable lead time." While SAFe emphasizes delivering value, it often does not specify how user-centered quality is embedded into the development cycle.

Design Thinking complements Agile by providing a structured approach to understanding and validating user needs. As described by the Interaction Design Foundation, Design Thinking helps teams redefine problems and create innovative solutions that deliver value through steps like Empathize, Define, Ideate, Prototype, and Test. Together, Agile and Design Thinking form a powerful combination: Agile's iterative cycles enable frequent software validation, while Design Thinking ensures a focus on user-centered design. Both Design Thinking and Agile methodologies are iterative. Design Thinking helps teams understand value, while Agile focuses on delivering and validating that value efficiently. New insights gained while validating developed software can be flexibly incorporated into Design Thinking activities.

Consider again the development of a food delivery application. Using a traditional Waterfall approach, a team might spend a year designing, developing, and implementing the application without user feedback until the end. Even if initial research followed Design Thinking principles, new assumptions about user needs could go unchallenged for months. The team might find that users initially considered certain challenges important, but functionality to address them no longer aligns with actual usage patterns. Only when users start using the software can their responses to its design be evaluated. By continuously testing the application throughout development, Design Thinking ensures the product aligns better with user needs.

Agile focuses on releasing software functionality with short lead times, allowing actual use to be tested throughout development. This enables teams to continuously validate the user value of their solutions. Combining this with the steps of Design Thinking—Empathize, Define, Ideate, Prototype, and Test—helps teams understand user challenges and find innovative, valuable solutions for application features. However, gaining the right insights requires actively applying Design Thinking within Agile practices. For example, Agile best practices suggest showcasing working software at the end of each sprint. While new functionality is presented to stakeholders, I often encounter situations where only a limited number of stakeholders are involved—typically budget holders—while users or other partners only see the software when it is finished. This limits feedback on the software's desirability.

In one project, an organization implemented a software solution for case managers to track client records. After release, the team realized it did not fit how case managers worked. Managers saved information in Microsoft Word during the day and later copied it to the software, resulting in errors and inefficiencies. Developers using traditional coding languages often recognize that user experience (UX) design is compromised in projects due to pressure and limited resources (Rodriquez et al., 2022). Agile teams under pressure to produce working software often prioritize speed over deep user research, leading to surface-level understanding. Solutions may fail to address root problems or sacrifice user experience for delivery speed. Without considering the full user experience, functionality is implemented in ways that make solutions less attractive to users.

Table 1 lists the strengths of combining Agile and Design Thinking as well as the risks that Agile aspects are prioritized over Design Thinking best-practices.

Table 1. Strengths of combining Design Thinking and Agile and risks if Design Thinking is neglected.

	Strengths	Risks
User-Centric Focus	Design Thinking ensures that Agile teams consistently focus on user needs by embedding empathy and real user feedback into development cycles.	Agile teams may deprioritize deep user research due to time constraints, leading to a superficial understanding of user needs.
Iterative Process	Both frameworks are iterative, allowing Agile teams to integrate continuous user feedback gathered through Design Thinking to refine solutions.	Agile's rapid release cycles can result in rushed decisions, sacrificing Design Thinking Activities for speed and short-term deliverables.
Continuous Validation	Agile's short release cycles enable regular testing of user value, while Design Thinking provides the structure to define and validate that value effectively.	Continuous output pressure may prevent Agile teams from thoroughly testing design assumptions, leading to misaligned product features.

continued on following page

Table 1. Continued

	Strengths	Risks
Innovation	Design Thinking's ideation and prototyping stages foster creative problem-solving, while Agile supports flexible implementation and quick adaptation of innovative ideas.	Teams may default to incremental changes without fully exploring innovative ideas, stifling innovation if Design Thinking is not fully utilized.
Reduced Risk of (user) Assumptions	Frequent Agile releases allow assumptions from initial research to be tested and corrected early, reducing reliance on initial findings.	Without periodic engagement with users and a broad range of stakeholders (versus just budget holders), Agile teams may make incorrect assumptions about user and stakeholder needs.
Functional Scope Definition	Design Thinking enables reframing of problems based on new insights, which Agile can incorporate efficiently through iterative updates.	Agile teams may hesitate to shift scope based on Design Thinking insights due to the pressure of maintaining sprint commitments.
Cross-Functional Collaboration	Agile's collaborative structure benefits from the multidisciplinary input encouraged in Design Thinking, enriching the understanding of user needs.	Agile teams often lack dedicated design expertise, resulting in an incomplete adoption of Design Thinking practices and potential skill gaps.
Enhanced User Satisfaction	Combining Agile's iterative validation with Design Thinking's user-centred approach increases the likelihood of delivering valuable, relevant products.	Rushed implementations or inadequate design iterations may lead to a disjointed user experience, failing to meet user expectations.
Stakeholder Alignment	Frequent Agile reviews, informed by Design Thinking insights, keep stakeholders updated and aligned on product direction and user value.	Repeated demos to the same stakeholders (without users) risk reinforcing internal biases rather than reflecting true user perspectives.

While Agile's focus on incremental delivery complements Design Thinking's iterative nature, risks remain. Teams may prioritize speed over depth, overlooking empathy or innovative ideas. Without experienced designers leading prototyping and user research, teams may fail to fully adopt Design Thinking, resulting in shallow user understanding or missed opportunities for innovation. By balancing Agile's rapid delivery with Design Thinking's user focus, teams can create innovative, impactful software. However, failing to rigorously apply Design Thinking within Agile cycles, risks undermining solution quality. Some risks are even more profound as Design Thinking itself, has undergone democratization. Since its popularization in the 1990s, professionals from business leaders to software developers have applied its principles, often without formal training.

c. Democratization of Design Thinking

Design Thinking traces its roots to practices in architecture, industrial design, and engineering in the 1960s (Dam & Siang, 2022). With the growth of industrially produced products, there was a need to formalize the design process, moving away from aesthetics toward systematic and holistic problem-solving.

In the 1980s, design methodologies adopted a more human-focused approach. Users began to play a significant role as principles of psychology, human factors, and ergonomics were integrated. From the 1990s onwards, institutions like Stanford and IDEO helped form Design Thinking into a teachable methodology with defined processes and toolboxes. Initially, organizations adopted Design Thinking not to replace professional designers but to foster awareness about design principles and user-centered design. Over the decades, many trainings, books, and models helped business leaders, entrepreneurs, and developers practice Design Thinking. As more organizations emerged, competition grew, and user-centered solutions were found to result in higher sales.

In the early 21st century, Design Thinking was often applied by non-trained designers using methodologies for user research and tools like the Business Model Canvas. These practitioners often lacked skills in user research, holistic product context mapping, and graphic design. Today, many tools make Design Thinking accessible to non-designers. For example, Miro is used for brainstorming by over 60 million people across roles like product management, engineering, IT, UX, marketing, and sales. Canva, with over 170 million users, explicitly targets non-designers.

With the increasing popularity of these tools, designing and developing software in cross-functional teams has become easier. Currently, Agile frameworks like Scrum ensure teams collaborated effectively, producing high-quality software. These methodologies organized communication between stakeholders, developers, analysts, and designers, ensuring both product and process met standards. With the rise of citizen development, developers take on more roles in software development. Resulting in less need for rigid processes or strict quality governance.

Current Agile development teams already risk losing focus on applying Design Thinking best practices like user research and concept development structurally and qualitatively. Additionally, technology allows a single citizen developer to build software even faster. The agility of software development will only increase as software can now be built in days rather than months. Will Design Thinking best practices remain relevant at this level of agility?

3. METHODOLOGY

To investigate the democratization of software development and its implications for the application of Design Thinking, this study employs a qualitative, exploratory research design. The methodology combines a comprehensive literature review, an evaluation of existing tools and frameworks, and a thematic analysis to explore the integration of Design Thinking in citizen development contexts.

a. Literature Review

The foundation of this research is a comprehensive review of relevant academic and professional literature. Sources include peer-reviewed journal articles, industry white papers, and case studies related to low-code/no-code development platforms, Agile software methodologies, and Design Thinking principles. The review aims to identify prevailing trends, conceptual frameworks, gaps in the current body of knowledge, and areas where Design Thinking is either enabled or constrained by citizen development practices. This review informs the theoretical grounding of the chapter and supports the contextualization of key findings.

b. Evaluation of Tools and Frameworks

To assess the practical implementation of Design Thinking in citizen development environments, an in-depth analysis of widely used design systems and low-code/no-code platforms is conducted. The evaluation focuses on the following criteria:

- Usability: The ease with which non-technical users can adopt and navigate the tools.
- Adaptability: The extent to which tools support iterative development and customization.
- Alignment with Design Thinking Principles: How well the platforms facilitate empathy, ideation, prototyping, and user feedback loops.

Examples of tools considered include platforms such as Figma, Webflow, Microsoft Power Apps, and Mendix.

c. Thematic Analysis

A qualitative thematic analysis is employed to interpret patterns and insights emerging from the literature and tool evaluations. This analysis focuses on the following dimensions:

- Opportunities for citizen developers to engage in human-centered design.
- Risks associated with reduced involvement of trained designers in the development lifecycle.
- Strategies for embedding Design Thinking principles into democratized software development processes.

This analytical approach enables the identification of core themes regarding the interaction between citizen development and Design Thinking practices, particularly in relation to the quality and inclusiveness of software outcomes.

d. Limitations and Recommendations for Future Research

While the methodology adopted provides a robust conceptual and practical understanding of the research topic, the absence of empirical data (e.g., interviews or case studies) represents a limitation. Future studies could benefit from collecting primary data through qualitative interviews with citizen developers, professional designers, and product teams, or from conducting case-based research that evaluates real-world implementation scenarios.

4. FINDINGS

One of the primary motivations behind the rise of Design Thinking was to involve real users and their insights while designing products and services (Han, 2022). Until the 2000s, most design decisions relied heavily on assumptions from stakeholders and business requirements or a small number of power users. As a result, products often lacked the functionality or usability to bring real value to users because they did not solve actual problems, fit users' workflows, or structure functionalities in a useful way.

Design Thinking provides structure and tools to involve users throughout the design process. By actively engaging users during the phases of Empathize, Define, Ideate, Prototype, and Test, users influence outcomes and ensure products better meet their needs. Although defined in five phases, the process is not linear but iterative. Each activity or insight can lead back to earlier phases or propel the process forward. According to the Hasso Plattner Institute of Design at Stanford University (2010), it is common for teams in the Prototype phase to realize aspects of the problem remain unexplored, requiring additional empathizing to refine their understanding.

In many cases, it is recommended to revisit earlier phases of Design Thinking to gather more insights. Nevertheless, starting in later phases puts teams on a solution-focused track too early. When users are only involved during the Test phase, such as in a showcase, it may reveal useful feedback on what does or does not meet their needs. However, if earlier phases were skipped, there is a high likelihood that significant parts of the solution do not align with user needs or workflows. When these insights are gathered late in the development cycle, teams may already have spent considerable time on solutions that users find less valuable.

Even though citizen developers invest less time than teams, they experience the same feeling of wasted effort. With less governance over quality, it may be difficult for a single developer to revisit and rebuild software. This phenomenon, known as the sunk cost fallacy, describes a "greater tendency to continue an endeavor once an investment in money, effort, or time has been made" (Arkes & Blumer, 1985).

There is a real risk that when a citizen developer spends too much time on a solution, they will resist letting go of it. Skipping the early phases of Design Thinking and gathering insights only after significant development time makes it harder for developers to abandon their work. As a result, the software may be less valuable to users because critical insights from early phases were overlooked, and even improvements identified during testing may be compromised by the time already invested.

Table 2 gives an overview of the different phases of Design Thinking and the risks on the software quality if the phases are poorly or not executed.

Table 2. Risks if Design Thinking phases are poorly executed.

Phase	Description	Risks if Not Executed Properly
1. Empathize	Understand the users' needs, challenges, and behaviours through research and observation.	- Misalignment with user needs- - Development of irrelevant features - Poor user adoption and satisfaction
2. Define	Clearly articulate the problem statement based on insights from the empathize phase.	- Ambiguous requirements - Miscommunication among stakeholders - Wrong prioritization of tasks
3. Ideate	Generate a wide range of creative solutions to the defined problem.	- Limited or unimaginative solutions - Failure to explore innovative ideas - Suboptimal design and functionality
4. Prototype	Create low-fidelity or high-fidelity prototypes to test and validate concepts quickly.	- Overinvestment in flawed ideas - Inability to identify usability issues early - Increased development costs
5. Test	Evaluate the solution with users, gather feedback, and refine the solution iteratively.	- Undetected usability issues - Poor user experience - Increased post-launch fixes and technical debt

Because of the decreasing team size and increasing autonomy of a citizen developer, citizen development results in a lack of trained designers in the design and development process. One citizen developer can design, develop, and implement an application without needing to be a professional designer. As this person does not need to follow strict processes or organizational standards, they may not involve trained designers. Where designers are trained to follow a process for quality outcomes, citizen developers often lack the experience and skills to do so. Even if citizen developers have knowledge and experience about the value of involving users and trained professionals, they may prioritize speed over that value.

Design Thinking has made software development more user-focused and effective. However, with the rise of citizen developers, there is a high risk of skipping key steps in the process, especially the early ones like understanding user needs and defining the problem. This can lead to solutions that fail to meet user needs, wasted time, and reluctance to fix flawed work because of sunk costs. To avoid these issues, all Design Thinking steps must be followed, even in small projects. Involving users early and throughout the process helps create software that works better, meets real needs, and avoids wasted effort.

a. Governing Design Thinking Best Practices Through a Shift-left approach

Involving users and design professionals is key to creating effective software, but with agile practices and smaller development teams, especially in citizen development, speed is often prioritized over Design Thinking phases.

An important aspect of Design Thinking is investigating the problem instead of immediately developing a solution. Citizen developers often create applications for familiar user groups, leading to a high understanding of the problem but also potential blindness to certain aspects. For example, an application for hospital nursing staff might fail if their workflow is not researched. Since nurses are less likely to use laptops or mobile devices, a poorly designed application could increase administrative overhead and reduce patient care time.

The most obvious solution might be ensuring every software project includes a designer and follows Design Thinking best practices. However, with the increased agility of software projects, speed often takes priority. To mitigate the risks from table 2, organizations can embed Design Thinking into citizen development processes without direct involvement of designers or users during early stages. Table 3 outlines practical ways to integrate users and design professionals into Design Thinking. These artifacts help citizen developers implement elements of Design Thinking even without executing every phase fully. Designers can shift to a facilitative role, creating reusable frameworks and validating best practices within workflows.

Table 3. Ways to support developers in implementing Design Thinking best-practices.

Phase of Design Thinking Process	Ways to mitigate Risks
Empathize	Use user personas created by professionals based on historical data, industry trends, and customer research to help non-designers simulate user perspectives. Professionals create a framework for empathy research, including templates for surveys, interview guides, and empathy maps, to ensure teams gather structured insights.
Define	Establish guidelines for defining problem statements, including criteria for alignment with business goals and user needs; provide templates and examples of well-defined problems and persona-based scenarios.
Ideate	Supply empathy maps and journey mapping templates. Develop best practices for ideation sessions, such as structured brainstorming techniques (e.g., "How Might We" prompts) and tools for collaborative sketching; set standards for idea evaluation criteria.
Prototype	Provide heuristics-based checklists and usability standards for non-designers to evaluate prototypes, ensuring alignment with expected user experience quality. Create a design system or component library that includes standardized UI elements, layout guidelines, and interaction patterns to maintain consistency and usability.
Test	Supply predefined personas and usage scenarios for testing sessions, so feedback reflects likely user interactions and helps identify realistic improvements. Define testing protocols, including guidelines for usability testing, feedback forms, and success metrics; offer tools to structure feedback and identify actionable insights.

This same "shift-left" approach of enabling developers to move responsibilities already occurs for security and testing (Jackson, 2021). By automating security tasks and integrating them into the development and deployment pipeline, developers are enabled to implement security best-practices without being security experts. Enhanced tooling is critical to achieving this in Design Thinking, particularly for low-code and no-code platforms. Resources like personas, templates, and guidelines empower citizen developers to adopt user-centric practices. While similar tools are widely available online, organizations must standardize them for key personas and journeys to guide citizen developers effectively. This way they can steer citizen developers without needing to be a professional on the Design Thinking process. Over time, they can adapt based on feedback, updating shared interaction patterns and UI elements across projects.

Complementary training programs in empathy-building, journey mapping, and prototyping are essential for effective tool use. Ideally, training should be embedded within workflows to enhance developers' understanding of Design Thinking principles. Designers must adapt their roles to these accelerated environments. Instead of primarily creating solutions, they should facilitate frameworks, maintain shared repositories of personas, templates, and scenarios, and mentor developers to improve design literacy. While many organizations already have frameworks and libraries, these are often tailored for other designers, innovators, or product managers. For citizen developers, templates and tools should be accessible and fit their workflows.

Tooling could also validate design best practices throughout the development cycle, enabling continuous feedback loops for all developed software. Adopting this approach requires a combination of tooling, frameworks, training, and mentorship for citizen developers to apply Design Thinking effectively. Automating validation processes, such as design quality checks, will also help grow citizen developers' design capabilities over time, increase their understanding of best practices and improve the quality of their solutions.

Embedding Design Thinking in citizen development requires an organizational and cultural shift. Centralized tools must make design resources accessible to all developers, supported by reusable personas, templates, and guidelines. Collaboration between designers and citizen developers should ensure the process remains inclusive and comprehensive. Besides the availability of resources, it is also crucial to get stakeholder buy-in. Management of organizations should actively promote user-centered design as a means of driving innovation and reducing costs. Design advocates across departments can help embed Design Thinking and facilitate cultural acceptance. Highlighting the successes of citizen developers who implement user-centered solutions can further drive adoption.

Redefining designers' roles and embedding user-centered practices into fast workflows strikes a balance between speed and quality. Setting up a library of artifacts and building awareness requires time and resources, but organizations can start with existing tools or those offering the most value. For example, sharing available user journeys with guides and training can help developers integrate them into tools and validate solutions against those journeys. In the nursing staff example, this approach might have helped the developer recognize the app's potential negative impact on workflow. This approach is expected to improve the delivery of innovative, high-quality software solutions, even in fast-paced environments. Measuring the effect is essential to ensure applications deliver higher value for stakeholders without compromising low-code development speed.

b. Changing Role for Designers

The evolving role of designers in organizations that embrace citizen development is essential for maintaining quality, consistency, and user-centered innovation in environments where software design and development are democratizing. Designers bridge user needs and technical solutions, ensuring products are functional, intuitive, and bring real value to users. Without professional designers, the speed and agility of citizen development may lead to fragmented user experiences, poorly conceived solutions, or ethical oversights.

Since citizen developers often lack formal training in design or user research, designers fill a vital gap by embedding structured Design Thinking into the development process. This enables citizen developers to solve problems without becoming design experts. Professional designers ensure user empathy, creativity, and iterative testing remain central to workflows, preventing solutions from becoming technical responses that fail to address user pain points. Some organizations have embraced this model by leveraging design systems that democratize design principles and make them accessible to non-designers. For example, companies like Google and IBM have pioneered this approach:

Google's Material Design offers a comprehensive design system with guidelines, components, and tools. Although not yet tailored to citizen development, it enables teams to create consistent and intuitive user interfaces without requiring deep design expertise. Material Design incorporates accessibility, responsiveness, and usability, allowing developers to deliver high-quality solutions while adhering to best practices.

IBM's Carbon Design System provides a similar framework tailored to enterprise applications. By standardizing typography, color schemes, and interactive patterns, IBM ensures non-designers can produce cohesive and professional interfaces. Carbon Design System integrates with development tools, helping developers implement its components seamlessly. These systems illustrate how organizations equip non-designers with tools to maintain design consistency and quality. However, design systems address only certain aspects of quality. While they ensure consistency and visual quality, they do not govern whether solutions are intuitive and valuable for users. Systems spanning Design Thinking phases are needed to elevate design quality governance. These design systems underscore the continuing importance of professional designers. Design systems, along with other templates and frameworks, must be developed by professional designers and refined continuously to evolve with user feedback, organizational strategies, trends, and competition. To accomplish this, organizations require new designer roles. Titles such as UX/UI Designer, Interaction Designer, Service Designer, and Product Designer have overlapping responsibilities and are often used interchangeably as found in the job descriptions by the Interaction Design Foundation (2024). Similarly, UX Strategists focus more on solution-specific strategies rather than broader frameworks to support others. Designers still lead the execution of Design Thinking phases for each solution rather than enabling others. A new role would combine aspects of Service Design, Facilitation, UX Architecture, Design Strategy, Program Management, and Direction. The shift would focus on supporting developers rather than other designers. These designers would establish frameworks, maintain tools, educate developers, and monitor design quality.

If done well, this new role ensures democratization does not compromise user satisfaction, accessibility, or ethical standards. With accelerating software development reshaping workflows, designers serve as guardians of innovation and user value, guiding non-designers to align their work with organizational goals and user expectations.

c. Opportunities and Challenges of embed Design Thinking in Citizen Development for Organizations

Citizen development, combined with Design Thinking, allows organizations to solve problems and create software solutions by involving non-technical employees. This approach helps organizations innovate faster, fill skill gaps, and focus on user needs. It opens up new possibilities for businesses, governments, schools, research institutes, and startups to develop practical, effective solutions. Some of these opportunities include:

Corporates:

- Leverage employees' creativity and proximity to challenges for faster problem-solving.
- Accelerate innovation by removing bottlenecks in traditional IT processes.
- Address talent shortages by empowering non-technical staff to develop software solutions.
- Create new roles (e.g., design mentors) to guide innovation and ensure alignment with business objectives.

Entrepreneurs and Startups

- Lower barriers to entry, enabling rapid, cost-effective development of solutions.
- Democratize innovation for niche, user-focused markets.
- Iterate quickly on feedback, enhancing competitiveness and market adaptability.

Governments

- Enhance agility and engagement in public service delivery.
- Democratize civic innovation by involving citizens in solution development.
- Increase transparency and public satisfaction with user-focused applications.

Software Providers

- Develop low-code platforms integrated with design thinking for user-centric solutions.

- Expand services by offering training and resources for citizen developers.
- Build ecosystems that integrate seamlessly with existing enterprise tools.

Research Institutes

- Speed up proof-of-concept testing and innovation cycles.
- Increase the impact of research by enabling rapid prototyping and collaboration.
- Expand engagement with non-technical stakeholders in the research process.

However, organizations need to manage risks like security, quality, and compliance to make the most of these opportunities. It can be a challenge to govern citizen development and its compliance with security, technology and design standards. This could potentially lead to poorly designed solutions that harm scalability and usability, or in an organization having very fragmented solutions with different design standards. Besides quality issues, there could also be resistance from the organization to move to this way of working. Especially from traditional IT teams that do not feel responsible for design quality. Citizen development, when paired with Design Thinking, has the potential to transform how organizations approach innovation, problem-solving, and user engagement. By managing risks like security, compliance, and quality, organizations can find a balance between encouraging creativity and maintaining control. Clear rules, proper training, and teamwork are key to making this approach work. With the right support, organizations can take full advantage of citizen development to drive practical solutions and real progress across different industries.

d. The Role of AI and Emerging Technologies

As with any contemporary discourse on software development, it is essential to acknowledge the transformative potential of artificial intelligence (AI). Just as AI has facilitated the authorship of this chapter by supporting a domain expert in synthesizing and articulating complex ideas, it is also poised to play a pivotal role in empowering citizen developers to engage meaningfully in the software design process.

One can envision the emergence of AI-powered development platforms that guide non-technical users through the principles and phases of Design Thinking. In such a system, a citizen developer might simply articulate the problem they aim to address, while the platform—leveraging natural language processing, contextual inference, and conversational interfaces—provides real-time guidance throughout the design and development workflow. Whether explicitly recognized or embedded seamlessly into the process, Design Thinking methodologies could be effectively integrated into the creation of digital solutions.

By incorporating AI into this workflow, such platforms hold the potential to ensure that resulting software products are not only functionally robust and secure, but also aligned with genuine user needs and pain points, thus preserving the human-centered values at the core of Design Thinking. This integration represents a significant step toward the democratization of software development, where high-quality, user-oriented solutions can be crafted by individuals regardless of their formal design or engineering background.

Table 4 gives a summary of examples on how AI could enhance the application of Design Thinking within the different phases of the Design Thinking process:

Table 4. Possible AI enhancements to support citizen developments in applying Design Thinking best-practices.

Phase	Possible AI-Enhancements
Empathize	- Generate user journeys based on knowledge of the personas and company or industry processes. - Simulate insights based on provided user personas and journeys using historical data, trends, and contextual input. - Perform real-time sentiment analysis on user feedback from surveys, social media, and customer support.
Define	- Assist in framing clear, focused problem statements aligned with user needs and business objectives. - Provide templates and examples for problem definition. - Challenge developed work against defined problem statements.
Ideate	- Function as a creative collaborator by proposing solutions informed by best practices and past implementations. - Simulate brainstorming sessions and provide prompts to expand on ideas, e.g., fostering accountability through visibility features. - Suggest features based on personas, journeys, user feedback and industry best-practices.
Prototype	- Auto-generate initial prototypes using low-code or no-code components. - Validate alignment with usability standards, accessibility guidelines, and organizational branding. - Provide real-time feedback on design decisions, e.g., flagging confusing elements or suggesting better layouts.
Test	- Simulate user interactions to identify potential pain points and suggest improvements. - Enable remote usability testing by gathering and analysing real user feedback. - Highlight actionable insights for iterative improvements, such as repositioning underused features.

AI has significant potential to enhance Design Thinking within software development. AI-powered tooling combined with designer-provided templates, standards, and best practices can enable citizen developers to create user-focused solutions. Over time, AI's ability to learn from each project can refine its recommendations and tools, fostering continuous improvement and embedding empathy, innovation, and validation. Similarly, AR and VR technologies can innovate product design, testing, and refinement. By enabling citizen developers to create immersive environments for testing prototypes, gathering user feedback, and refining designs, these technologies add a new dimension to the iterative process. Citizen developers can create virtual mock-ups, experiment rapidly with user interfaces, and visualize data in ways traditional 2D tools cannot. As these technologies mature and become more accessible, barriers to building complex, interactive experiences will lower, enabling more people to build transformative products. However, while AI and emerging technologies improve software development, their integration comes with notable risks requiring responsible implementation. One concern is overreliance on AI, potentially leading to decreased critical thinking around empathy and creative problem-solving. Citizen developers might depend entirely on AI-generated outputs, including design suggestions, without the ability to make qualitative decisions.

Another challenge is the potential for AI systems to perpetuate bias, relying heavily on data that reflects source material biases. In the context of Design Thinking, this may result in flawed personas, limited ideation, or problem definitions failing to represent diverse user groups. For instance, an AI trained on data from Western markets may overlook users in developing countries, perpetuating inequities and reinforcing stereotypes. Addressing these risks requires diverse stakeholder involvement in data selection and algorithm design. Regular audits of data and algorithms can help uncover and correct biases, enhancing fairness and accuracy in AI-generated insights. To mitigate these challenges, design professionals must oversee the process, providing guidelines and ensuring AI-generated insights are critically evaluated. Training programs should equip developers with skills to interpret and assess AI outputs, fostering a balance between human judgment and AI assistance.

Environmental sustainability is another pressing concern. Training large AI models and running inference processes demand significant computational resources, contributing to carbon emissions. As AI becomes integral to citizen development, its cumulative environmental impact may increase. Organizations must optimize AI systems for energy efficiency and prioritize renewable energy sources. To address these challenges, organizations need a clear plan for integrating AI into citizen development responsibly. AI should support, not replace, human expertise, with design professionals overseeing creative and ethical aspects. Citizen developers need proper training to critically evaluate AI-generated outputs. AI tools should include features to detect and reduce bias, with regular data and algorithm checks. Transparent systems explaining AI recommendations can build trust and accountability. Processes should address mistakes and negative impacts, ensuring ethical oversight and inclusivity.

By setting ethical guidelines emphasizing privacy, fairness, and sustainability, organizations can maximize AI's potential in citizen development. Training and workshops reinforce these values, promoting responsible, people-focused innovation. With the right approach, organizations can ensure AI drives inclusive, sustainable, and user-centered solutions.

e. Teamwork Makes the Dream Work

The shift-left approach, especially when supported with AI, suggests that citizen developers can and should execute the whole software design, development and deploy process alone. However, collaboration between software developers, designers, and other professionals remains a cornerstone of successful software development. Each role within a team brings unique perspectives and expertise, creating a holistic approach to solving problems. Designers, for example, contribute insights into user needs, aesthetic principles, and interaction design, ensuring that the final product is not only functional but also intuitive and engaging. Developers, on the other hand, focus on building robust, scalable systems, while product managers and other stakeholders ensure alignment with business goals and market demands. Small teams often lack the creative tension and diverse perspectives that often lead to innovative solutions.

Hill et al. (2014) describe the importance of creative abrasion in the book Collective Genius. The productive tension that arises when diverse perspectives clash constructively, leading to innovative solutions. When developers and designers work together, their differing priorities—such as technical feasibility versus user experience—can create healthy debate. This friction challenges assumptions, pushes boundaries, and forces teams to think more critically, often leading to breakthrough ideas. Beyond developers and designers, involving stakeholders like marketers or end-users adds further dimensions to the discussion, ensuring that the product is viable, desirable, and usable. Without this collaborative tension, the process risks becoming insular, leading to solutions that may lack depth or fail to meet the needs of diverse user groups.

5. DISCUSSION

The democratization of software development is fundamentally reshaping the industry, as low-code/no-code platforms and AI-driven tools empower a growing number of citizen developers. This shift brings significant opportunities for innovation and inclusivity in creating software solutions. However, given the rapid pace of change, all research and insights on the topic risk becoming outdated quickly.

The dynamic nature of technological innovation complicates any definitive conclusions about its long-term impact. Tools and platforms evolve rapidly, with new advancements frequently emerging, making it challenging to establish stable practices or frameworks. As we are in the midst of this transformation, the implications for software quality, team dynamics, and design thinking processes remain fluid. Consequently, any insights presented here should be viewed as provisional and subject to refinement as the technological environment continues to evolve.

During the preparation of this chapter in December 2024, Microsoft CEO Satya Nadella shared his vision of AI agents replacing traditional software. Although such trends may take years to reach widespread adoption, the pace of innovation is accelerating, with successive changes happening more rapidly. For instance, the term "citizen developer" saw a decline in usage a few years ago, as many low- and no-code platforms failed to truly empower non-technical users. Now, this trend is reversing, with platforms increasingly targeting non-trained software developers. This demonstrates the difficulty of making long-term predictions in this field. However, by focusing on organizational mindset shifts and redefining roles for professional developers, the proposed paradigm is expected to help organizations enhance the design quality of their digital deliverables, even as technology continues to evolve. While this study identifies critical shifts and proposes strategies to address emerging challenges, it is important to acknowledge that its findings have not been thoroughly validated with the target groups most affected by these changes. Although the author is active in this environment and has discussed these insights with fellow designers and citizen developers, no structured research has been conducted to confirm their validity. Key stakeholders, including citizen developers, design professionals, and organizational leaders, must be involved more systematically to confirm the practical applicability of the proposed frameworks and strategies. Primary research, such as interviews, case studies, and surveys, would provide valuable insights into the real-world adoption of these practices and the barriers faced in implementing them.

Given the rapid pace of technological change and the preliminary nature of these findings, further research is essential. Future studies should involve empirical data collection to validate the effectiveness of the proposed frameworks and tools. Direct engagement with citizen developers, professional designers, and other stakeholders would provide deeper insights into the practical challenges and opportunities associated with democratized development. Additionally, longitudinal studies could track how the integration of design thinking evolves as citizen development becomes more prevalent. Such research would offer a more comprehensive understanding of whether democratization ultimately enhances or diminishes the quality of software solutions and the user experiences they deliver.

6. CONCLUSION

The intersection of citizen development, Design Thinking, and emerging technologies such as artificial intelligence is transforming the way software is conceived and created. This convergence is democratizing innovation by extending development capabilities beyond traditional engineering teams to include non-technical users. As a result, individuals and organizations are increasingly empowered to solve complex problems, co-create value, and deliver user-centered digital solutions.

By combining accessible development platforms with design-led methodologies, this shift enables rapid prototyping, iterative experimentation, and agile delivery cycles. These changes foster greater inclusivity and responsiveness in digital systems, potentially increasing both user satisfaction and solution relevance across industries. However, while the use of AI-enhanced development tools supports citizen developers in improving the functional quality of their applications, these tools cannot replace the unique contributions of trained design professionals.

Professional designers possess the skills to navigate complex user needs, manage competing priorities, and cultivate the creative tension essential for innovation. Without their guidance, there is a risk that citizen developers—often operating independently—may over-rely on standardized tools and predefined frameworks. Such overdependence can stifle creativity, reinforce initial assumptions, and limit the diversity of perspectives that are critical to high-impact design. Moreover, the absence of collaborative discussion and multidisciplinary input undermines the essence of Design Thinking. Effective design is not merely a product of functional implementation, but of dynamic interaction, critical questioning, and a deep understanding of human experience. These elements are difficult to replicate through automation alone.

To preserve the integrity of design while expanding development access, organizations must adopt a balanced model. Tools, platforms, and templates should be complemented by mentorship, training, and strategic involvement from professional designers. This is not a matter of displacing design teams but of scaling design culture—ensuring that citizen developers internalize Design Thinking principles and apply them consistently in their work.

Ultimately, empowering citizen developers with the right mindset, methodologies, and support structures will help ensure that digital innovation prioritizes not just speed and scalability, but also empathy, inclusivity, and long-term value. In doing so, organizations can transform citizen development from a trend into a sustainable, human-centered engine of digital transformation.

REFERENCES

Arkes, H. R., & Blumer, C. (1985). The psychology of sunk cost. *Organizational Behavior and Human Decision Processes, 35*(1), 124–140. DOI: 10.1016/0749-5978(85)90049-4

Berman, M. (2024, December 20). Microsoft CEO's shocking prediction: "Agents will replace all software" [Video]. YouTube. https://www.youtube.com/watch?v=uGOLYz2pgr8

Canva. (2024, January 24). Celebrating Canva's growth in the US. https://www.canva.com/newsroom/news/canva-us-growth/

Carbon Design System. (n.d.). IBM products. https://ibm-products.carbondesignsystem.com/?path=/story/overview-welcome–overview&globals=viewport:basic

Contrary. (2023, September 21). Miro. https://research.contrary.com/company/miro

Couldry, N. (2012). *Media, society, world: Social theory and digital media practice*. Polity Press.

Dam, R. F., & Siang, T. Y. (2022). The history of design thinking. Interaction Design Foundation. https://www.interaction-design.org/literature/article/design-thinking-get-a-quick-overview-of-the-history

Design Thinking. (n.d.). Interaction Design Foundation. https://www.interaction-design.org/literature/topics/design-thinking

Execute your development needs with a Magic Quadrant™ Low-Code Leader. (2024, October 21). Mendix. https://www.mendix.com/blog/gartner-mq-lcap-2024/

Făgără an, C., Popa, O., Pisla, A., & Cristea, C. (2021). Agile, waterfall and iterative approach in information technology projects. *IOP Conference Series. Materials Science and Engineering, 1169*(1), 012025. DOI: 10.1088/1757-899X/1169/1/012025

GitHub Spark. (2024, October 19). GitHub Next. https://githubnext.com/projects/github-spark

Han, E. (2022, January 18). What is design thinking & why is it important? Harvard Business School Online. https://online.hbs.edu/blog/post/what-is-design-thinking

Hill, L. A., Brandeau, G., Truelove, E., & Lineback, K. (2014). *Collective genius: The art and practice of leading innovation*. Harvard Business Review Press.

Jackson, M. (2021, May 5). Shift left - Moving security to the development phase - The case of secrets detection in code repositories. GitGuardian. https://blog.gitguardian.com/shift-left-moving-security-to-the-development-phase-the-case-of-secrets-detection-in-code-repositories/

Kirvan, P., Liptak, J., & Horwitz, L. (2023, December). What is citizen development. TechTarget. https://www.techtarget.com/searchsoftwarequality/definition/citizen-development

Larman, C. (2004). *Agile and iterative development: A manager's guide*. Addison-Wesley.

Manifesto for Agile Software Development. (2001). https://agilemanifesto.org/

Material Design. (n.d.). Material Design 3. https://m3.material.io/

Matvitskyy, O., Davis, K., & Jain, A. (2024, October 16). Magic Quadrant for enterprise low-code application platforms. Gartner. https://www.gartner.com/doc/reprints?id=1-2J42UZEC&ct=241017&st=sb

Open Source Initiative. (2009, September 19). History of the OSI. https://opensource.org/history

Red Hat. (2018, February). Intelligent process automation and the emergence of digital automation platforms. https://www.redhat.com/rhdc/managed-files/mi-451-research-intelligent-process-automation-analyst-paper-f11434-201802.pdf

Rodriguez, A., Gardey, J., Grigera, J., Rossi, G., & Garrido, A. (2022). UX debt in an agile development process: Evidence and characterization. *Research Square*. DOI: 10.21203/rs.3.rs-2190539/v1

Rokis, K., & Kirikova, M. (2023). Exploring low-code development: A comprehensive literature review. *Complex Systems Informatics and Modeling Quarterly*, *36*(36), 68–86. DOI: 10.7250/csimq.2023-36.04

Scaled Agile, Inc. (2023, May 4). SAFe Lean-Agile principles. https://scaledagileframework.com/safe-lean-agile-principles/

Sherman, R. (2015). *Business intelligence guidebook*. Morgan Kaufmann.

Soegaard, M. (2024, November 29). What does a UX strategist do? Interaction Design Foundation. https://www.interaction-design.org/literature/article/what-does-a-ux-strategist-do

Stanford University Hasso Plattner Institute of Design. (2010, January 1). An introduction to design thinking: Process guide. https://web.stanford.edu/~mshanks/MichaelShanks/files/509554.pdf

Statista. (2024, November 26). Number of software developers worldwide in 2018 to 2024. https://www.statista.com/statistics/627312/worldwide-developer-population/

Statista. (2024, November 4). Number of internet and social media users worldwide as of October 2024. https://www.statista.com/statistics/617136/digital-population-worldwide/

Teo, Y. S., & Newhook, J. (2024, October 4). UX roles: The ultimate guide – Who does what and which one you should go for? Interaction Design Foundation. https://www.interaction-design.org/literature/article/ux-roles-ultimate-guide

KEY TERMS AND DEFINITIONS

Agile: An iterative and incremental set of principles for software development in which requirements and solutions evolve through the collaborative effort of self-organizing and cross-functional teams, alongside their customers or end users.

Artificial Intelligence (AI): The simulation and emulation of human intelligence in machines that are programmed to think and learn in a manner similar to humans. AI applications include areas such as natural language processing, machine learning, and robotics.

Citizen Development: A practice where non-technical employees utilize no-code or low-code platforms to create and develop applications that specifically meet the needs and requirements of their respective department or business unit.

Democratization: The process of making technology and tools accessible and usable for a larger portion of the population, thereby reducing the barriers to entry for non-experts and enabling wider participation and innovation.

Design Thinking: An iterative and user-centred process that seeks to understand the user, challenge existing assumptions, and redefine problems to create and develop innovative solutions that are then prototyped and tested.

Open Source: The open-source model is a decentralized software development model that encourages open collaboration. Source code is made freely available for possible modification and redistribution.

No-Code/Low-Code Platforms: Development platforms that enable users to create and build applications through graphical user interfaces and configuration settings instead of traditional hand-coded programming, thereby simplifying the development process.

SAFe (Scaled Agile Framework): A knowledge base of proven, integrated principles and practices designed for achieving business agility at scale, utilizing methodologies from Lean, Agile, and DevOps.

Scrum: An Agile framework for developing, delivering, and sustaining complex products through iterative progress, characterized by collaboration, accountability, and incremental improvement.

Shift Left: A practice of addressing tasks or challenges earlier in the process, often through automation, tools, or frameworks. Applied here to integrate design thinking and user feedback earlier in software development.

UX Designer: A UX (User Experience) designer focuses on creating seamless, intuitive, and user-friendly digital or physical products by understanding user needs, behaviours, and preferences. They use research, design principles, and iterative testing to enhance usability, accessibility, and overall satisfaction in user interactions.

Waterfall: A traditional, linear approach to software development where all requirements are defined upfront, and development follows sequential phases like design, implementation, and testing.

Chapter 6
Legal Design Thinking in Software Engineering:
A Review of User-Centered Innovations in Legal Technology

Pablo Alfonso Aguilar Calderón
https://orcid.org/0000-0002-4939-0383
Universidad Autónoma de Sinaloa, Mexico

Pedro Alfonso Aguilar-Calderón
https://orcid.org/0000-0003-3881-909X
Universidad Autónoma de Sinaloa, Mexico

José Alfonso Aguilar-Calderón
https://orcid.org/0000-0003-2048-9600
Universidad Autónoma de Sinaloa, Mexico

Aníbal Zaldívar-Colado
https://orcid.org/0000-0002-6622-6630
Universidad Autónoma de Sinaloa, Mexico

Dominik Morales-Silva
https://orcid.org/0009-0002-9401-7235
Universidad Autónoma de Sinaloa, Mexico

Oscar Manuel Peña-Bañuelos
https://orcid.org/0009-0007-1241-9051
Universidad Autónoma de Sinaloa, Mexico

Carolina Tripp-Barba
https://orcid.org/0000-0002-4811-0247
Universidad Autónoma de Sinaloa, Mexico

ABSTRACT

The integration of Legal Design Thinking into software engineering represents a transformative shift in the development of legal technology. By applying user-centered design principles, this approach enhances legal accessibility, operational efficiency, and client satisfaction. This chapter systematically reviews the core tenets of Legal

DOI: 10.4018/979-8-3693-9531-8.ch006

Design Thinking, including empathy, ideation, prototyping, and testing, and examines its role in improving legal services through software applications. Additionally, this work explores the challenges of integrating Legal Design Thinking into software development, particularly concerning technical constraints, ethical considerations, and regulatory compliance. Future opportunities, such as advancements in AI, automation, and interdisciplinary collaboration, are discussed as potential pathways for further innovation in the legal sector. This chapter aims to provide valuable insights for legal practitioners, software engineers, and policymakers in the evolving landscape of legal technology and user-centered innovation.

INTRODUCTION

The convergence of law and technology has fostered the development of innovative strategies designed to enhance the accessibility, efficiency, and overall user-friendliness of legal systems. One such strategy is Legal Design Thinking (LDT), an approach grounded in the core principles of design thinking but specifically adapted to navigate the distinct complexities inherent in the legal domain. As digital transformation continues to redefine various industries, the legal sector has not remained untouched by these changes. LDT has surfaced as a revolutionary methodology aimed at improving user experiences, optimizing procedural workflows, and expanding access to justice.

This chapter offers a comprehensive exploration of the fundamental principles underpinning Legal Design Thinking, detailing its application within the legal field. It also examines existing software solutions that embody and operationalize the LDT approach, highlighting their role in reshaping the landscape of legal technology. Furthermore, the chapter delves into the myriad challenges and opportunities associated with integrating LDT with software engineering, offering a nuanced analysis of its potential for driving systemic change in legal practices.

Through an in-depth review of the current body of literature, supported by case studies and real-world software applications, this work evaluates the tangible impact of LDT on the evolution of legal technology. It identifies both the obstacles faced in its implementation and the opportunities for further development, offering insights into how LDT can be optimized to foster more efficient, equitable, and accessible legal systems. Finally, this chapter proposes several potential avenues for future research, aimed at advancing the integration of LDT with emerging technological innovations and addressing the evolving demands of the legal profession.

This review is structured around four core areas of analysis, each aimed at providing a comprehensive understanding of the scope and implications of Legal Design Thinking within contemporary legal innovation:

- ***The Foundational Principles of Legal Design Thinking.*** The chapter begins by elucidating the conceptual underpinnings of Legal Design Thinking, emphasizing its roots in the broader Design Thinking methodology. Special attention is given to its fundamental components: empathy, ideation, prototyping, and iterative testing. These principles are not merely abstract notions, but actionable frameworks that inform the design of legal services and tools centered around human experiences. The section discusses how empathy enables a deeper understanding of users' needs, ideation fosters creative problem-solving, prototyping facilitates the visualization of legal solutions, and iterative testing ensures refinement through continuous feedback loops.
- ***Application of Legal Design Thinking in the Legal Field.*** Building on its foundational elements, the chapter explores the real-world application of Legal Design Thinking in diverse legal contexts. It demonstrates how this approach is employed to improve client engagement by making legal language more accessible and interactions more intuitive. It also analyzes how LDT contributes to democratizing access to justice by designing systems that are inclusive and responsive to marginalized populations. Moreover, it evaluates how legal practices and institutions are enhancing operational efficiency through human-centered service redesign and the reengineering of legal workflows.
- ***Software Solutions that Embody Legal Design Thinking.*** A key aspect of this review is the identification and analysis of existing software platforms that operationalize Legal Design Thinking principles. This section presents a selection of case studies showcasing innovative applications—ranging from automated document generators and legal chatbots to client-facing legal navigation tools. These examples illustrate how design thinking enhances usability, reduces cognitive overload for users, and streamlines legal processes, thereby making legal systems more approachable and transparent.
- ***Challenges and Opportunities in Integrating Design Thinking with Software Engineering.*** The chapter addresses the complexities involved in bridging Legal Design Thinking with software development. It critically examines technical barriers, such as the translation of abstract legal reasoning into concrete technological artifacts and discusses the implications of user interface design in multilingual and multicultural contexts. Additionally, ethical and regulatory dimensions are explored, including concerns related to privacy, algorithmic fairness, and legal accountability. Despite these challenges, the section highlights substantial opportunities for interdisciplinary collaboration and innovation, particularly when LDT principles are embedded within agile software development processes.

Collectively, these thematic areas provide a structured and in-depth understanding of how Legal Design Thinking functions as both a philosophical orientation and a practical methodology. The chapter ultimately argues for its increasing relevance in the face of rapid technological change and evolving demands for justice system reform. Through a comprehensive analysis, this chapter contributes to the growing body of research on human-centered legal innovation, offering insights for legal practitioners, software engineers, and policymakers involved in the development of legal technology. Design Thinking fosters a problem-solving culture that prioritizes user needs, collaboration, and innovation. By integrating Design Thinking into software engineering and LegalTech, organizations can develop more effective, user-friendly solutions. As technology continues to evolve, the adoption of Design Thinking methodologies will remain essential for addressing emerging challenges in digital transformation.

The remainder of the chapter is structured as follows: Section 2 presents the fundamentals of the Design Thinking methodology and its application in Legal environment. Section 3 introduces the review method. Section 4 analyzes the results, and Section 5 presents the conclusions and future work.

FUNDAMENTALS OF DESIGN THINKING AND PRINCIPLES OF LEGAL DESIGN THINKING

The fundamentals of Design Thinking provide the foundation for a human-centered approach to problem-solving, emphasizing empathy, creativity, and iterative testing to develop innovative solutions. This methodology has gained widespread recognition for its applicability across various industries, including the legal field. When applied to legal contexts, Design Thinking evolves into Legal Design Thinking (LDT), a specialized adaptation that addresses the unique challenges and complexities of law and legal processes. LDT not only retains the core principles of Design Thinking but also incorporates a deep understanding of legal frameworks, user needs, and the intricacies of the legal profession. This section explores the foundational elements of Design Thinking, followed by a detailed examination of how these principles are reimagined and implemented within the context of legal systems. By doing so, it highlights the transformative potential of LDT in creating more accessible, user-friendly, and efficient legal solutions.

Design Thinking

Design Thinking has emerged as a pivotal methodology for fostering innovation across various domains, including business, healthcare, education, and technology. Rooted in problem-solving principles, Design Thinking emphasizes human-centered design, iterative development, and interdisciplinary collaboration to generate creative solutions to complex challenges (Brown, 2009; Liedtka, 2015). This subsection explores the core principles of Design Thinking, its stages, and its application in software engineering and legal technology. This approach is guided by fundamental principles that distinguish it from traditional problem-solving approaches. These principles ensure that solutions address real user needs, incorporate iterative feedback, and foster a culture of experimentation (Brown, 2009; Plattner et al., 2011). The key principles are detailed next.

- Empathy. Understanding users' needs, emotions, and challenges is essential to creating meaningful solutions (Brown, 2009).
- Collaboration. Interdisciplinary teams enhance the ideation process by bringing diverse perspectives to problem-solving (Liedtka, 2015).
- Experimentation. Rapid prototyping and iterative testing allow for continuous refinement and user-driven innovation (Plattner et al., 2011).
- Bias Toward Action. Design Thinking emphasizes hands-on problem-solving rather than lengthy theoretical discussions (Brown, 2009).
- User-Centered Focus. The process ensures that final solutions are functional, accessible, and aligned with real-world user needs (Liedtka, 2015).

The Design Thinking Process (DTP) is commonly structured into five key phases (Cahui, Quispe, Condori, & Chapi 2022), these are detailed next:

- Empathize. Conduct research to understand user needs, pain points, and behaviors.
- Define. Synthesize insights from the research phase to frame the problem clearly.
- Ideate. Brainstorm multiple solutions, encouraging creativity and divergent thinking.
- Prototype. Develop tangible representations of ideas to explore possible solutions.
- Test. Gather user feedback, refine prototypes, and improve the final solution iteratively.

Design Thinking fosters a problem-solving culture that prioritizes user needs, collaboration, and innovation. As technology continues to evolve, the adoption of Design Thinking methodologies will remain essential for addressing emerging challenges in digital transformation.

Legal Design Thinking

Legal Design Thinking is an interdisciplinary methodology that adapts the principles of Design Thinking to address the complex challenges of the legal domain. Rooted in human-centered design, LDT emphasizes the importance of empathy, collaboration, and iterative development in creating solutions that are not only functional but also intuitive, accessible, and responsive to the needs of users. It seeks to bridge the gap between the traditionally formal, complex, and often inaccessible legal system and the evolving demands of modern society for more transparent, efficient, and user-friendly legal services (Hagan, 2017).

At its core, LDT is grounded in four primary stages: empathy, ideation, prototyping, and testing. In the empathy phase, practitioners immerse themselves in understanding the needs, experiences, and pain points of legal system users, such as clients, legal professionals, or underserved populations. This phase emphasizes the collection of qualitative insights through interviews, observations, and direct interactions, ensuring that solutions are tailored to meet the specific needs of the individuals they are intended to serve. The ideation phase fosters creative brainstorming, where diverse perspectives come together to generate multiple possible solutions to identified problems. In the legal context, this can involve exploring new ways of structuring legal information, streamlining legal processes, or creating tools that make legal services more accessible. Once ideas are generated, they move into the prototyping phase, where concepts are translated into tangible, low-fidelity representations of the solution be it a digital tool, a new process, or a service offering. These prototypes are tested and refined through feedback loops, allowing for adjustments to be made before full-scale implementation.

One of the defining features of LDT is its iterative nature. Solutions are continually tested, refined, and improved based on feedback from end-users and stakeholders. This iterative approach ensures that the outcome is not only functional but also effective in addressing the real-world challenges faced by legal professionals and users alike. Additionally, LDT incorporates a focus on accessibility and inclusion, ensuring that solutions are designed with the goal of democratizing access to justice, making legal services more affordable and comprehensible, and increasing engagement with the legal system. Legal Design Thinking aims to transform the legal industry by providing tools and frameworks that are both legally sound and user-centered, thus promoting a more innovative, efficient, and equitable legal system. By embracing this approach, legal professionals can develop solutions that are better suited to the evolving needs of society while maintaining the integrity and rigor of the legal profession. In this regard, there is agreement with Romero (2022), who warns that resistance to change in the legal field may result in competitive disadvantages compared to those who embrace innovative approaches. *Legal Design* emerges as a strategic tool for legal professionals seeking to enhance the skills demanded by innovation and technological transformation in the legal sector.

Application of Legal Design Thinking in Software Engineering

Legal Design Thinking finds application across various domains in the legal sector, from improving client interactions to streamlining internal processes. When integrated with software engineering, this approach leads to the development of tools that enhance efficiency, accessibility, and compliance.

1. Client Engagement: By adopting a user-centered approach, legal services become more accessible and transparent. Simplifying legal documents and contracts enhances client comprehension and trust.
2. Access to Justice: Legal Design Thinking plays a pivotal role in democratizing access to legal services, particularly for marginalized communities. Tools designed with empathy help bridge the gap between complex legal systems and laypersons.
3. Operational Efficiency: Law firms and legal departments leverage design thinking to improve internal workflows. This includes automating routine tasks, enhancing collaboration, and optimizing resource allocation.

METHOD

For the development of this chapter, a qualitative and exploratory research approach was adopted, grounded in a structured review of the existing body of scholarly literature, supported by the examination of real-world practices and documented case studies. The investigation was guided by a set of fundamental research questions, which provided the conceptual framework for the inquiry: (1) What is Design Thinking, and what are its foundational principles? (2) What constitutes Legal Design Thinking (LDT), and how does it diverge or extend from the traditional Design Thinking methodology? (3) How is Legal Design Thinking being applied in the field of software engineering, particularly in the development of LegalTech solutions?

To address these guiding questions, a state-of-the-art literature review was conducted, focusing on peer-reviewed journal articles, book chapters, conference proceedings, and grey literature published within the last two decades, with particular emphasis on the most recent contributions from the past five years. Academic databases such as Scopus, Web of Science, IEEE Xplore, SpringerLink, and Google Scholar were consulted using targeted keywords such as "Design Thinking," "Legal Design Thinking," "LegalTech," "user-centered legal design," and "human-centered software engineering." The selection criteria prioritized works that provided conceptual clarity, methodological rigor, and relevance to the intersection of law, design, and technology.

In the second phase, the research incorporated a descriptive analysis of software applications that explicitly integrate Legal Design Thinking principles. These solutions were identified through industry reports, white papers, open-source repositories, and professional networks in the legal innovation domain. The chapter describes the extent to which they embody user-centered and iterative design methodologies.

In addition, the study includes an analytical synthesis of documented case studies that illustrate the practical implementation of Legal Design Thinking in various legal settings. These cases were selected to represent a diverse range of contexts, including law firms, courts, legal clinics, and public sector initiatives. Each case was analyzed in terms of its objectives, stakeholders, processes, outcomes, and lessons learned, with the aim of identifying both the success factors and the persistent challenges in adopting LDT within legal systems.

Finally, the findings from the literature review, software analysis, and case study examination were triangulated to generate critical insights into the potential and limitations of Legal Design Thinking. This multi-pronged methodological approach enabled a holistic understanding of the field and informed the concluding discussion, which proposes avenues for future research and interdisciplinary collaboration in the design and development of legal technologies.

ANALYSIS

The analysis section of this chapter provides a comprehensive examination of the multifaceted dimensions of Legal Design Thinking (LDT) and its impact on the legal field, emphasizing both its theoretical foundations and practical applications.

This section is structured into four critical subsections, each shedding light on a unique aspect of LDT and its integration within the legal and technological landscapes. The first part delves into the core principles of LDT, tracing its origins in the human-centered approach of design thinking. It highlights the importance of empathy, ideation, prototyping, and iterative testing in addressing the complex challenges within the legal system. By unpacking these foundational elements, this section aims to demonstrate how LDT fosters a deep understanding of user needs and promotes innovative problem-solving in the legal context. The second part explores how LDT has been applied in real-world legal settings, with a particular focus on its transformative role in enhancing client engagement, democratizing access to justice, and streamlining operational efficiency. This analysis illustrates how LDT has the potential to reshape traditional legal practices, making legal services more accessible and responsive to diverse user needs. The third section shifts attention to existing software solutions that integrate the principles of LDT, showcasing cutting-edge platforms and tools that leverage user-centered design to simplify complex legal processes. These solutions not only optimize user experiences but also demonstrate how technology can be harnessed to drive greater transparency and efficiency in legal systems. Finally, the fourth subsection addresses the challenges and opportunities that arise when attempting to integrate LDT with software engineering. It considers a range of technical, ethical, and regulatory considerations that must be navigated to successfully merge legal expertise with technological innovation. By examining these challenges, the section aims to provide a balanced perspective on the potential hurdles in LDT's implementation while also highlighting the vast opportunities for growth and improvement. Together, these subsections provide a holistic analysis of the impact of LDT on the legal sector, offering valuable insights into its potential to transform legal practice through the intersection of design thinking and technology.

The Principles of Legal Design Thinking, Detailing Its Foundation in Empathy, Ideation, Prototyping, and Iterative Testing

Legal Design Thinking is grounded in the core principles of design thinking: empathy, ideation, prototyping, and iterative testing (Roberts, 2024). These principles are adapted to the legal context to create solutions that prioritize user needs and experiences.

- Empathy: LDT begins with understanding the needs, pain points, and behaviors of legal system users, including clients, lawyers, and policymakers. This empathetic approach ensures that solutions are tailored to real-world problems.
- Ideation: Creative brainstorming sessions generate innovative ideas for addressing legal challenges. This phase encourages collaboration between legal experts, designers, and technologists.

- Prototyping: Rapid prototyping allows for the creation of tangible solutions, such as user-friendly contracts, accessible legal documents, or intuitive software interfaces.
- Iterative Testing: Continuous feedback and refinement ensure that solutions are effective, user-friendly, and legally sound.

By applying these principles, LDT bridges the gap between legal complexity and user accessibility, making legal systems more inclusive and efficient.

The Application of Legal Design Thinking in the Legal Field, Highlighting Its Role in Improving Client Engagement, Democratizing Access to Justice, and Enhancing Operational Efficiency

LDT has been successfully applied in various areas of the legal field, demonstrating its potential to improve client engagement, democratize access to justice, and enhance operational efficiency.

- Improving Client Engagement: LDT has been used to redesign legal documents, such as contracts and privacy policies, into visually appealing, easy-to-understand formats. For example, visual contracts with interactive elements have been shown to increase client comprehension and satisfaction (Barton & Berger-Walliser, 2018).
- Democratizing Access to Justice: LDT has been instrumental in creating platforms that simplify legal processes for non-experts. For instance, online dispute resolution systems and self-help legal tools empower individuals to navigate legal challenges without professional assistance.
- Enhancing Operational Efficiency: By streamlining workflows and automating routine tasks, LDT has helped legal professionals focus on higher-value activities. Compliance dashboards and automated legal risk assessment tools are examples of LDT-driven solutions that improve efficiency (Breaux & Bai, 2016).

In a similar vein, and following Torres (2020), *Legal Design Thinking* has reached its version 2.0, establishing itself as an expanding academic discipline. Currently, this discipline is under development in four key areas, one of which is:

- *Legal research through design*. This approach is presented as an academic research method that employs design processes, methods, and practices to create tangible artifacts (such as prototypes) in order to generate new knowledge and explore problems. For example, instead of drafting the typical theoretical article on smart contracts, research through design would focus on building a functional prototype of a smart contract, through programming and creating the contract, rather than simply theorizing about it. This tangible artifact (the contract) is created with the purpose of being studied, representing an innovative way of conducting empirical research in the field of law.

- *Design of artifacts for the private sector.* Contracts represent the most commonly created artifact by lawyers. However, these artifacts present various issues. Despite being designed for different users with diverse skills and needs, and produced by different organizations to regulate businesses with varying objectives, all contracts tend to be perceived similarly, both in format and structure.

The analysis of legal artifacts in the private sector (such as contracts, statutes, among others) is approached from five key dimensions: (i) the legal dimension, (ii) the usability and user experience dimension, (iii) the business dimension, (iv) the systemic context, and (v) the implications for public policy.

- *Design of legal artifacts for the public sector.* This area encompasses various elements such as digital justice, public policy formulation, and regulatory prototyping tools, such as "sandboxes." In this context, creative design tools are integrated, including policy creation. This approach can be considered an adaptation of the concept of "minimum viable product or service" from the entrepreneurial field to the public sector, aiming to optimize the processes of public policy formulation and regulation. Furthermore, it is applied in the development of innovative models for justice, seeking to improve the efficiency and effectiveness of judicial systems.
- *Legal Education.* Finally, the role played by various mental models, attitudes, and design methods in improving legal education is highlighted. Several universities have implemented courses on Legal Design aimed at lawyers, recognizing the value that these tools bring to professional practice.

Legal Design Thinking is not merely a passing trend; it is a necessary response to the gap between legal language and public understanding. This is achieved by integrating law and Design Thinking within the legal field to enhance the way legal problems are addressed and solutions are designed (Chávez, Zamalloa, 2024).

Existing Software Solutions That Embody Legal Design Thinking, Showcasing Innovative Platforms That Leverage User-Centered Design to Simplify and Optimize Legal Processes

This subsection presents real-world software examples that embody Legal Design Thinking principles. These tools and platforms leverage user-centered design to simplify legal processes, improve accessibility, and enhance compliance with legal requirements. Each example demonstrates how LDT can be applied in practice to create innovative solutions for the legal field. The software tools are organized in six categories for better understanding, these are: i) Visual Contract Management Platform, ii)

Visual Contract Management Platforms

- **Example: Juro**

Juro (2025) is a contract management platform that uses LDT principles to simplify the contract lifecycle. It offers a user-friendly interface with drag-and-drop functionality, plain language templates, and real-time collaboration features. By making contracts more accessible and visually appealing, Juro improves user engagement and reduces the complexity of legal documentation.

- o **LDT Principles Applied:** Empathy (user-centric design), prototyping (iterative improvements), and accessibility (plain language and visual aids).
- o **Website:**https://juro.com
  - **Example: LawGeex**

LawGeex (2025) uses AI and LDT to automate contract review and approval processes. Its platform highlights key legal terms and provides plain-language explanations, making it easier for non-experts to understand complex legal documents.

- o **LDT Principles Applied:** Empathy (simplifying legal jargon), ideation (AI-driven solutions), and iterative testing (continuous improvement based on user feedback).
- o **Website:**https://www.lawgeex.com

Privacy and Compliance Tools

- **Example: OneTrust**

OneTrust (2025) is a privacy management platform that helps organizations comply with GDPR, CCPA, and other data protection regulations. It uses LDT principles to create intuitive dashboards, visual workflows, and user-friendly consent management tools.

- o **LDT Principles Applied:** Empathy (addressing user pain points), prototyping (customizable workflows), and accessibility (clear visualizations of compliance status).
- o **Website:**https://www.onetrust.com
    - **Example: BigID**

BigID (2025) is a data discovery and compliance platform that uses LDT to simplify data privacy management. Its interface provides clear visualizations of data flows and risks, helping organizations comply with privacy laws while maintaining user trust.

- o **LDT Principles Applied:** Empathy (user-friendly data insights), ideation (innovative risk visualization), and iterative testing (continuous updates for new regulations).
- o **Website:**https://www.bigid.com

Access to Justice Platforms

- **Example: DoNotPay**

DoNotPay (n.d) is an AI-powered platform that helps users navigate legal issues, such as disputing parking tickets or filing small claims. It uses LDT principles to create a chatbot interface that simplifies legal processes for non-experts.

- o **LDT Principles Applied:** Empathy (addressing user frustrations), ideation (AI-driven solutions), and prototyping (iterative improvements based on user feedback).
- o **Website:**https://donotpay.com
    - **Example: LegalZoom**

LegalZoom (n.d.) is an online platform that provides affordable legal services, such as document drafting and business formation. Its user-friendly interface and step-by-step guidance embody LDT principles, making legal services accessible to a broader audience.

- o **LDT Principles Applied:** Empathy (simplifying legal processes), accessibility (plain language and guided workflows), and prototyping (continuous updates to improve usability).
- o **Website:**https://www.legalzoom.com/country/mx

Legal Research and Analytics Tools

- **Example: Casetext**

Casetext (2024) is a legal research platform that uses AI and LDT to simplify case law research. Its "CARA A.I." feature allows users to upload legal documents and receive relevant case law recommendations, presented in a user-friendly format.

- o **LDT Principles Applied:** empathy (reducing research time), ideation (AI-driven recommendations), and accessibility (clear and concise results).
- o **Website:**https://canvasbusinessmodel.com/es/blogs/how-it-works/casetext-how-it-works?srsltid=AfmBOopW2UXJppBs1zJxEkOIXJGPou-Mwlyx9tjCN0cudVB6n9GtXl4-
  - **Example: ROSS Intelligence**

ROSS Intelligence (n.d) is an AI-powered legal research tool that uses natural language processing to provide quick and accurate answers to legal questions. Its interface is designed to be intuitive, making legal research more accessible to lawyers and non-lawyers alike.

- o **LDT Principles Applied:** empathy (user-friendly interface), ideation (AI-driven research), and iterative testing (continuous updates to improve accuracy).
- o **Website:**https://rossintelligence.com

Dispute Resolution Platforms

- **Example: Modria**

Modria (2025) is an online dispute resolution (ODR) platform that uses LDT principles to simplify conflict resolution. Its user-friendly interface guides users through the process of resolving disputes, making it accessible to individuals and businesses.

- o **LDT Principles Applied:** Empathy (simplifying dispute resolution), ideation (innovative ODR workflows), and prototyping (iterative improvements based on user feedback).
- o **Website:**https://www.tylertech.com/solutions/modria
    - **Example: FairClaims**

FairClaims (2025) is an ODR platform that provides a transparent and user-friendly process for resolving disputes. Its interface uses plain language and visual aids to guide users through each step of the process.

- o **LDT Principles Applied:** Empathy (addressing user frustrations), accessibility (plain language and visual aids), and prototyping (continuous updates to improve usability).
- o **Website:**https://www.fairclaims.com

Ethical AI and Compliance Tools

- **Example: Luminance**

Luminance (2024) is an AI-powered platform that uses LDT principles to simplify legal document review and compliance. Its interface provides clear visualizations of key legal risks and compliance issues, making it easier for users to navigate complex legal requirements.

- o **LDT Principles Applied:** empathy (user-friendly risk visualization), ideation (AI-driven compliance checks), and iterative testing (continuous updates for new regulations).
- o **Website:**https://www.luminance.com
    - **Example: Ethical OS Toolkit**

The Ethical OS Toolkit (2025) is a resource for developers to design ethical and legally compliant software. It uses LDT principles to provide guidelines and frameworks for addressing ethical and legal challenges in software development.

- o **LDT Principles Applied:** empathy (addressing ethical concerns), ideation (innovative frameworks), and prototyping (iterative improvements based on user feedback).
- o **Website:**https://www.iftf.org/projects/a-playbook-for-ethical-tech-governance/?

Several software solutions have successfully integrated LDT principles to simplify and optimize legal processes. These platforms leverage user-centered design to address legal challenges in innovative ways.

- Privacy by Design in Software Development: Tools like GDPR (Zarsky, 2017) compliance checkers and privacy management platforms incorporate LDT principles to ensure that software systems comply with data protection laws while remaining user-friendly (Cavoukian, 2012).
- Visual Contract Management Systems: Platforms like Juro and LawGeex use LDT to create intuitive interfaces for drafting, negotiating, and managing contracts. These systems reduce the complexity of legal documents and improve collaboration between stakeholders.
- Accessibility-Focused Legal Tools: Software solutions that comply with accessibility standards, such as the Web Content Accessibility Guidelines (WCAG), ensure that legal services are inclusive and accessible to all users (W3C, 2018).

These software examples demonstrate how Legal Design Thinking can be applied to create innovative, user-centric solutions in the legal field. By prioritizing empathy, accessibility, and iterative testing, these platforms simplify legal processes, improve compliance, and democratize access to justice. As technology continues to evolve, LDT will play an increasingly important role in shaping the future of legal software and services.

Challenges and Opportunities in Integrating Design Thinking With Software Engineering, Addressing Technical, Ethical, and Regulatory Considerations

Despite the substantial potential benefits, the integration of Legal Design Thinking into software engineering is not without its challenges. These challenges encompass a range of technical, ethical, and regulatory concerns that must be addressed to fully realize the promise of this approach. One of the primary technical constraints lies in ensuring that legal software not only meets high usability standards but also complies with intricate and often convoluted legal frameworks. The design and implementation of legal technologies must, therefore, be executed with a high degree of precision and foresight, ensuring that both functionality and compliance are harmoniously balanced.

Ethical considerations also play a critical role in the successful integration of LDT into legal technology. In particular, the increasing reliance on automated legal tools, especially those driven by artificial intelligence (AI), requires a commitment to transparency, fairness, and the elimination of bias. AI-driven decision-making systems, when applied to legal contexts, must be rigorously scrutinized to ensure that they uphold ethical standards and do not perpetuate existing biases or inequities. Ensuring that these systems operate in a manner that is both just and accountable is paramount to their acceptance and effectiveness within the legal sector.

The regulatory compliance presents another significant challenge in the adoption of LDT in legal software development. Legal technologies must adhere to a multitude of jurisdictional regulations, which can differ markedly across various regions and legal systems. This variability necessitates a nuanced understanding of local laws and regulations, demanding that legal tech solutions be adaptable and capable of aligning with these diverse legal requirements.

Another significant challenge faced by lawyers is the need to adapt to a new working methodology, such as Legal Design Thinking, as they must develop new competencies and attitudes (Manca, 2024), including the following:

- It is essential to learn how to use clear language, avoiding the use of technical terms that may hinder the document's comprehension. In cases where legal terms must be used, it is advisable to clarify their meaning through a note or explanation within the text. The vocabulary used should be commonly understood, and the tone should be appropriate for the intended audience.
- It is recommended to employ visual elements that complement the document's reading and facilitate its consultation from any section. The inclusion of icons, tables, images, or colors is highly useful for less specialized recipients, enabling them to navigate the text more effectively.
- Only those elements that are strictly necessary to achieve the document's intended utility should be incorporated. In this regard, it is advisable to simplify the content by reducing its length to facilitate continuous reading.
- Identifying the target audience is crucial to assess the purpose and context that the document should encompass.
- Additionally, the document should be structured in a way that makes it easier for the reader to locate relevant information. To achieve this, it is fundamental to apply navigation design techniques that allow the reader to orient themselves easily. Examples include the use of titles and sections that differentiate relevant information from the superfluous, as well as the implementation of links that direct to corresponding references.
- Finally, it is essential to have a multidisciplinary team capable of addressing both the legal and design needs arising from the application of the Legal Design methodology.

Despite these challenges, significant opportunities also emerge. One of the foremost opportunities lies in the advancements of artificial intelligence and automation. The application of AI has the potential to revolutionize several aspects of legal work, including legal research, contract analysis, and compliance management. These technologies can significantly enhance operational efficiency by automating time-consuming tasks and providing legal professionals with more accurate and comprehensive insights. Furthermore, the integration of AI can improve the consistency and reliability of legal processes, ultimately fostering a more streamlined and effective legal system.

Another key opportunity is the increased accessibility of legal services, particularly for underserved populations. Digital legal solutions, underpinned by the principles of LDT, have the potential to bridge significant gaps in legal access. By offering affordable, comprehensible, and user-friendly legal tools, these solutions can democratize access to justice, ensuring that individuals who might otherwise be excluded from traditional legal services can still benefit from legal protections and support. This increased accessibility aligns with broader efforts to create more inclusive legal systems that are responsive to the needs of diverse communities.

Finally, the interdisciplinary nature of LDT presents an opportunity for fostering innovation at the intersection of law, design, and technology. The collaboration between legal professionals, designers, and technologists creates an environment ripe for the development of solutions that are not only legally sound but also user-centric and efficient. By drawing on the expertise of these varied disciplines, it becomes possible to create legal technologies that are both legally rigorous and intuitive to use, thus enhancing the overall user experience and expanding the potential applications of legal tech. This fusion of expertise is key to driving the future of legal technology, ensuring that it is both innovative and grounded in the needs of the people it serves.

Success Stories of Implementing Design Thinking in the Legal Field

Legal Design Thinking (LDT) has been applied in several successful cases to transform legal practice, making it more accessible, efficient, and user-centered. Below are some notable examples of successful implementation of LDT in the legal field:

LawGeex and the simplification of contracts:

LuwGeex, a legal technology platform, applied Design Thinking principles to simplify legal contracts and make them more understandable for non-expert users. Through an iterative process of prototyping and user testing, the company developed an interface that transforms complex legal documents into more user-friendly and accessible formats. This approach enables users to better comprehend legal terms, thereby enhancing the client experience and reducing ambiguity in contractual agreements (Lawgeex, 2025). Key Functionalities of LawGeex:

- Automated contract review:

LawGeex employs artificial intelligence algorithms to review contracts and other legal documents, identifying clauses, terms, and conditions that may pose risks or fail to comply with a company's internal policies. This functionality enables users to obtain fast and accurate document reviews, significantly reducing the time and resources required for manual analysis.

- Contract comparison:

The platform can compare a given contract against pre-established corporate policies and standards, highlighting areas where the agreement does not align with internal requirements. This ensures that organizations maintain stricter control over the quality and content of the contracts they execute.

- Review report generation:

LawGeex can produce detailed reports on reviewed contracts, summarizing key findings, potential risks, and suggestions for addressing identified issues. These reports support informed decision-making regarding whether to proceed with, revise, or renegotiate contractual terms.

- System integrations:

LawGeex integrates with various contract management systems and tools, including Salesforce, DocuSign, and Box. These integrations streamline the import and export of contracts and related data across platforms, enhancing workflow efficiency.

- Customization and machine learning:

The platform allows users to customize contract policies and review criteria, ensuring that its AI algorithms align with the specific requirements of each organization. Furthermore, LawGeex leverages machine learning to continually enhance its accuracy and performance by learning from prior interactions and reviews (Gonzalo, 2021).

Law for All and the democratization of access to justice:

The organization Law for All in South Africa uses Legal Design Thinking (LDT) to provide affordable and accessible legal services to marginalized communities. Through an empathetic research process with individuals who lack access to traditional legal counsel, they have developed digital platforms that enable users to interact with basic legal advice. Additionally, they offer educational materials in accessible formats that explain legal topics in straightforward language. This initiative has had a significant impact on improving access to justice for historically excluded populations (Law for All, 2025).

Ravn and the automation of contract analysis:

The company Ravn, now part of iManage, specializes in legal technology and has applied Legal Design Thinking (LDT) to develop an artificial intelligence tool that automates the review and analysis of contracts. This solution simplifies the process of detecting problematic clauses, inconsistencies, or legal risks in documents, significantly reducing the time lawyers spend on these tasks. Thanks to the LDT approach, the tool is user-friendly and allows legal professionals to focus on the strategic aspects of their work, enhancing operational efficiency and service quality (iManage, 2025).

Ravn and the development of a bot for professional privilege analysis:

An artificial intelligence for the review of Legal Professional Privilege (LPP), allowing clients to automate the process of determining whether material is subject to LPP. The LPP Robot uses advanced artificial intelligence techniques to automatically analyze large collections of documents, such as litigation materials and other types of documents, determining whether each item is covered by privilege. The robot's accuracy in making these determinations now surpasses traditional manual efforts and is significantly faster. The solution leverages supervised iterative machine learning models within RAVN ACE (Applied Cognitive Engine), meaning the system becomes progressively more accurate over time. This technological advancement represents a shift from traditional predictive coding methods that are often used today. Additionally, the certainty levels regarding the accuracy of classifications can be adjusted to the desired recovery levels, helping to minimize any misclassification issues (Foote, 2016).

Deloitte Legal and the improvement of the client experience:

Deloitte Legal implemented Design Thinking to transform the way clients interact with legal services. They employed an empathy-driven approach to better understand client needs and redesigned the delivery of their services by incorporating technology and tailored solutions that enhance communication, reduce bureaucracy, and streamline the resolution of legal issues. Their integrated digital platform allows clients to easily access legal services, schedule consultations, and track the progress of their cases in a user-friendly manner. The services they offer include mergers and acquisitions, personal law, contracts, consultancy and legal services, regulation and compliance, corporate law, dispute resolution, and real estate (Deloitte, 2025).

Justice Innovation and the design of dispute resolution platforms:

Justice Innovation, an organization dedicated to innovation in the legal sector, employs the Legal Design Thinking (LDT) approach to design digital platforms that facilitate dispute resolution in an efficient and accessible manner. These systems allow conflicting parties to resolve cases without the need to go to court, utilizing processes such as online mediation and digital negotiation. These platforms not only enhance efficiency in dispute resolution but also make the process more affordable and less intimidating for users. Application of Legal Design Thinking at Justice Innovation:

- Simplification of the Legal Process: Justice Innovation implements the Legal Design Thinking approach with the goal of simplifying legal procedures, making them more comprehensible and accessible to individuals without legal expertise. This process includes the design of intuitive user interfaces, the elimination or reduction of complex legal jargon, and the creation of platforms that facilitate more efficient user interaction with legal systems.
- Innovation in Dispute Resolution: Rather than relying on traditional methods of conflict resolution, Justice Innovation has developed Online Dispute Resolution (ODR) platforms that, through the Legal Design Thinking approach, enable parties to resolve disputes via digital means such as videoconferencing and online mediation platforms. This approach streamlines processes and enhances accessibility, particularly for individuals facing geographical or economic barriers.
- User-Centered Approach: The implementation of Legal Design Thinking at Justice Innovation places the user at the core of the design process. This ensures that the solutions developed are not only technologically advanced but also intuitive and easily accessible to users, regardless of their prior legal knowledge.
- Interdisciplinary Collaboration: The approach adopted by Justice Innovation fosters seamless collaboration between designers, technologists, and legal professionals, ensuring that the solutions developed are both innovative and effective in addressing real-world judicial problems. This interdisciplinary collaboration contributes to the creation of solutions that not only resolve technical issues but also improve the user experience when interacting with the justice system (Justice Innovation, 2025).

Legal templates:

In 2015, this platform was launched with the aim of democratizing access to legal tools and enhancing legal decision-making by reducing structural barriers, particularly the excessive administrative burden commonly associated with legal processes. Through collaboration with legal professionals, it became possible to develop automated solutions that enable users to generate legal documents at a cost significantly lower than that of traditional legal services provided by attorneys. Since its inception, and with millions of documents generated through the system, the platform has established itself as one of the leading providers of legal forms in the United States.

Legal Templates offers users a wide range of templates and forms tailored to specific legal needs across business, real estate, and personal contexts. The system is designed to facilitate processes such as business formation, lease agreements, divorce proceedings, and estate planning, thereby providing an accessible and efficient alternative to conventional methods of legal document preparation (Legal templates, 2025).

Pretutela, prequalification for filing a tutela action:

The Justice Design Lab at the University of Los Andes in Colombia has implemented a tool called "Pretutela." This interface allows, through a series of specific questions, to determine whether, in principle, the issue at hand meets the preliminary requirements for filing a tutela action. This approach proves to be particularly practical, as it simplifies the analysis process, which, otherwise, would be labor-intensive, requiring a detailed review of a text or evaluation of each article and numeral to verify compliance with legal requirements (Aya Sierra, Niño Muñoz, Roa Ladino, Goyeneche Giraldo, Calderón Nova, & Santos Meek, 2025)

The Escazú Agreement in Comics with and for the Chiquitano People:

Is a collaborative project using Legal Design and Visual Law to facilitate understanding of the Escazú Agreement Among the Chiquitano indigenous people in Brazil. This collaborative project harnesses the principles of legal design and visual law to enhance the accessibility of the Escazú Agreement, specifically aimed at the Chiquitano indigenous people in Brazil. The initiative focuses on creating visual materials, notably a comic, to simplify complex legal concepts and promote greater public engagement in environmental law.

The primary objective of the project is to make legal frameworks more comprehensible and engaging for marginalized communities. By transforming intricate legal texts into visually accessible formats, the project seeks to empower the Chiquitano people to better understand their environmental rights and participate more actively in advocating for environmental justice. This approach not only fosters greater community involvement but also strengthens their ability to protect their land and natural resources against environmental harm.

Through this innovative use of legal design, the project highlights the potential of visual law to bridge the gap between legal professionals and local communities, making legal information more inclusive and actionable. It is a step forward in integrating culturally sensitive approaches to legal education and advocacy, particularly for indigenous populations (Parola, Muquissai, Poto, 2023)

These success stories demonstrate how Legal Design Thinking can transform legal practice by improving both accessibility and efficiency, while creating solutions that are more human-centered and user-focused.

CONCLUSION AND FUTURE WORK

This chapter has systematically examined how Legal Design Thinking represents a fundamental paradigm shift in legal technology development, fundamentally reorienting innovation around user-centric solutions to enhance accessibility, efficiency, and client satisfaction. Our comprehensive review reveals three critical, interconnected dimensions of this transformation that are reshaping the legal landscape. First, the human-centered transformation marks a decisive departure from traditional, process-driven legal approaches to needs-driven solution development, with integrated software engineering enabling practitioners to better address evolving client needs while streamlining operations. The evidence is compelling: successful LegalTech implementations—spanning automated document assembly platforms to virtual legal assistants—that prioritize user experience metrics alongside legal functionality demonstrate 30-50% higher adoption rates than conventional tools. Second, the technology-enabled evolution demonstrates how cutting-edge developments like competency-adapting AI interfaces, blockchain-based transparency systems, and human-supervised generative AI tools are making legal services more responsive and relevant in the digital age, though our analysis underscores the parallel need for stronger ethical frameworks to guide this technological progression. Third, and perhaps most crucially, the collaborative imperative reveals that effective implementation demands deep interdisciplinary synergy—with lawyers safeguarding compliance, designers optimizing usability, and engineers ensuring scalability—a model proven to deliver solutions 2.3 times more likely to achieve dual legal and business objectives. Building on these current innovations, we identify three pivotal opportunities for advancing the field: exploring blockchain's potential to enhance contract transparency and AI's capacity to personalize legal services within ethical boundaries; developing standardized metrics to evaluate design-centric tools' impact on both efficiency and justice outcomes; and creating novel institutional structures to sustain productive dialogue among legal, design, and engineering professionals. These forward-looking recommendations underscore the dynamic interplay between technological possibility and human-centered design that will define the next chapter of legal innovation.

The synthesis of our findings suggests that Legal Design Thinking in software engineering must navigate a careful balance between multiple competing priorities. First, it requires leveraging cutting-edge technological capabilities while maintaining essential human oversight and judgment in legal processes. Second, the pursuit of process efficiency and automation must not come at the expense of equitable access to justice for all users. Finally, while encouraging bold innovation in legal service delivery, developers must simultaneously ensure strict adherence to regulatory compliance and ethical standards. This delicate equilibrium positions Legal Design Thinking as both a transformative approach and a responsible framework for legal technology development, where technological advancement serves to enhance rather than replace the human elements of legal practice. The success of this methodology depends on maintaining these balances throughout all stages of design, development and implementation.

As the field progresses, the legal industry must view technology not as an end, but to achieve more equitable, understandable, and effective legal systems. The innovations reviewed in this chapter demonstrate both the tremendous potential and the significant responsibility that comes with this user-centered approach to LegalTech development.

The findings of this review carry important implications for various stakeholders in the LegalTech ecosystem. For legal professionals, adopting iterative, user-testing approaches to technology implementation and developing literacy in both design principles and technical capabilities will be crucial for effectively leveraging these innovations. Technologists must prioritize explainability and auditability in legal algorithms while building flexible systems that can accommodate diverse legal contexts and jurisdictional requirements. Meanwhile, researchers face critical work in investigating the longitudinal impacts of design-focused legal tools and developing comprehensive frameworks for ethical technology integration in legal practice. These collective efforts across disciplines will determine whether Legal Design Thinking fulfills its potential to create legal systems that are simultaneously more efficient, accessible, and just. The successful implementation of this approach depends on sustained collaboration and knowledge-sharing between these stakeholder groups as the field continues to evolve.

This chapter concludes that the fusion of Legal Design Thinking and software engineering represents more than a methodological shift – it constitutes a necessary evolution for creating legal systems that are truly fit for purpose in the digital age. The path forward requires sustained commitment to human-centered values as the foundation for all technological innovation in law.

REFERENCES

Aya Sierra, J. S., Niño Muñoz, D. O., Roa Ladino, N. A., Goyeneche Giraldo, E., Calderón Nova, S. A., & Santos Meek, A. (n.d.). *Desenredando tutelas, Sistema: Tutela Digital en Colombia*. Laboratorio de Diseño para la Justicia en Colombia, Universidad de los Andes. Retrieved from https://labjusticia.uniandes.edu.co/proyectoI05.html

Barton, T. D., & Berger-Walliser, G. (2018). Visualizing contracts: How graphical tools can improve transparency and accessibility in legal documents. *Harvard Journal of Law & Technology*, *31*(2), 313–356. https://jolt.law.harvard.edu

Big, I. D. (2025). *Data visibiliti and control.* Retrieved from https://bigid.com/

Breaux, T. D., & Bai, X. (2016). Legal requirements traceability in software engineering: A systematic literature review. In *Proceedings of the 24th IEEE International Requirements Engineering Conference (RE)* (pp. 1-10). IEEE. https://doi.org/DOI: 10.1109/RE.2016.38

Brown, T. (2009). *Change by design: How design thinking creates new alternatives for business and society*. Harper Business.

Cahui Osis, V. F., Quispe Soto, D., Condori Huarca, A., & Suyo, C. J. (2022). Case studies of Design Thinking in the analysis and design stages of software development. Innovation and Software, 3(1), 17-29. Universidad La Salle. https://www.redalyc.org/journal/6738/673870840002/673870840002.pdf

Casetext (2024). *How does casetext work?* Retrieved from https://canvasbusinessmodel.com/es/blogs/how-it-works/casetext-how-it-works?srsltid=AfmBOopW2UXJppBs1zJxEkOIXJGPou-Mwlyx9tjCN0cudVB6n9GtXl4-

Cavoukian, A. (2012). Privacy by design: The 7 foundational principles. Information and Privacy Commissioner of Ontario, Canada. Retrieved from https://www.ipc.on.ca/wp-content/uploads/Resources/7foundationalprinciples.pdf

Chávez, L., & Zamalloa, D. (2024). *Legal Design Thinking: Unlearning to humanize law.* Enfoque Derecho. https://enfoquederecho.com/legal-design-thinking-desaprender-para-humanizar-el-derecho/

Deloitte. (2025). *Discover Deloitte Legal services.* Deloitte. Retrieved from https://www.deloitte.com/es/es/services/legal/services/deloitte-legal-services.html?icid=ln_legal_deloitte-legal-services

DoNotPay. (n.d.). Retrieved from https://www.donotpay.com

Ethical, O. S. Toolkit (2025). *A Playbook for Ethical Technology Governance*. Retrieved from https://www.iftf.org/projects/a-playbook-for-ethical-tech-governance/?

FairClaims. (2025). *Resolve disputes online with legally enforceable results*. Retrieved from https://www.fairclaims.com

Foote, K. (2016). *RAVN systems launches AI bot for legal research. DATAVERSITY*. Retrieved from https://www.dataversity.net/ravn-systems-launches-ai-bot-legal-research/

Gonzalo, C. (2021). *LawGeex: Artificial intelligence to automate legal contracts*. Retrieved from https://www.carlosgonzalo.es/lawgeex-inteligencia-artificial-para-automatizar-contratos-legales/

Hagan, M. (2017). Legal design as a thing: A theory of change and a set of methods to craft a human-centered legal system. *Design Issues*, *33*(3), 3–15. DOI: 10.1162/desi_a_00600

IDEO. (n.d.). *Design thinking*. Retrieved from https://www.ideo.com iManage. (2025). *Legal transaction management*. Retrieved from https://imanage.com/imanage-products/legal-transaction-management/

Innovation, J. (2025). *About Justice Innovation*. Retrieved from https://www.justiceinnovation.org

Intelligence, R. O. S. S. (n.d). *Legal Tech Corner*. Retrieved from https://rossintelligence.com

Juro. (2025). *Intelligent contracting*. Retrieved from https://www.juro.com.mx

Law for All. (2025). *Free legal resources*. Retrieved from https://www.lawforall.co.za/free-legal-resources/

LawGeex. (2025). *Automate your contract review process*. Retrieved from https://www.lawgeex.com/

Legal Templates. (2025). *What is Legal Templates?* Retrieved from https://legaltemplates.net/about-us/

LegalZoom. (n.d.) *U.S. Legal Help in Mexico*. Retrieved from https://www.legalzoom.com/country/mx

Luminance (2024). *Legal-Grade AI, Wherever Computer Meets Contract*. Retrieved from https://www.luminance.com

Manca, P. (2024). *Legal design: Designing legal solutions for all. PWC Spain.* Retrieved from https://www.pwc.es/es/newlaw-pulse/transformacion-legal/legal-design-disenando-soluciones-juridicas-para-todos.html

Modria (2025). *Comprehensive, innovative software and services designed for the public sector.* Retrieved from https://www.tylertech.com/solutions/modria

Onetrust (2025). *Responsible AI and data solutions.* Retrieved from https://www.onetrust.com

Parola, G., Muquissai, S. C., & Poto, M. P. (2023). *A co-created project of legal design and visual law applied to international environmental law: Transformation of the Escazú agreement and environmental access rights into visual materials for and with the Chiquitano people. Revista Culturas Jurídicas, 10*, 1-18. Retrieved from https://www.researchgate.net/publication/372379123_A_CO-CREATED_PROJECT_OF_LEGAL_DESIGN_AND_VISUAL_LAW_APPLIED_TO_INTERNATIONAL_ENVIRONMENTAL_LAW_TRANSFORMATION_OF_THE_ESCAZU_AGREEMENT_AND_ENVIRONMENTAL_ACCESS_RIGHTS_INTO_VISUAL_MATERIALS_FOR_AND_WITH

Roberts, M. (2024). *Understanding legal design: A key transformation for the legal industry.* Korum Legal. https://www.korumlegal.com/blog/legal-design-im-convinced-thoughts-from-a-non-lawyer...-working-in-newlaw

Romero Viecco, I. (2022). *Legal design as a tool for developing solutions to make the law more efficient. Ámbito Jurídico.* Retrieved from https://www.ambitojuridico.com/noticias/en-ejercicio/el-legal-design-permite-construir-soluciones-para-hacer-el-derecho-mas

Simon, H. A. (1996). *The sciences of the artificial.* MIT Press.

Torres, J. F. (2020). *'Legal design' 2.0 (legal design) as a new academic discipline in law. Ámbito Jurídico.* Retrieved from https://www.ambitojuridico.com/noticias/columnista-impreso/tic/legal-design-20-diseno-legal-como-una-nueva-disciplina-academica

World Wide Web Consortium. (W3C). (2018). *Web content accessibility guidelines (WCAG) 2.1.* Retrieved from https://www.w3.org/TR/WCAG21/

Zarsky, T. (2017). Incompatible: The GDPR in the age of big data. *Seton Hall Law Review, 47*(4), 2. https://ssrn.com/abstract=3022646

KEY TERMS AND DEFINITIONS

Empathy Map: A collaborative tool used to understand users' emotions, thoughts, and behaviors by organizing insights into categories such as what users say, think, do, and feel.

Empathy-Driven Development: A development approach focused on understanding and addressing user emotions and experiences.

Design Thinking: Is a human-centered, problem-solving methodology that emphasizes understanding the needs and experiences of users to develop innovative and practical solutions. It is an iterative process that encourages collaboration, creativity, and empathy, typically consisting of five core phases: empathize, define, ideate, prototype, and test.

Focus Group: A qualitative research method used to gather insights from a selected group of users or stakeholders through discussion.

Software Development Process: The stages involved in creating software applications, including planning, designing, coding, testing, and maintenance.

Mock-ups: Visual representations or prototypes used to showcase a product's design and functionality before development.

User-Centered Design: An approach prioritizing users' needs, preferences, and behaviors to create intuitive, effective, and meaningful solutions.

Prototyping: Creating preliminary versions of software to test and gather feedback for iterative improvements.

Legal Design Thinking: Is an interdisciplinary methodology that adapts the principles of Design Thinking to address the complex challenges of the legal domain.

Software Engineering: is the systematic application of engineering principles to the design, development, maintenance, testing, and evaluation of software and software systems. It involves the use of established methodologies, tools, and techniques to produce high-quality, reliable, and efficient software solutions that meet the specific needs of users or organizations.

Privacy and Compliance: Involves protecting personal data and ensuring legal adherence to regulations like GDPR. Legal professionals must maintain data security and privacy to avoid legal penalties and maintain trust.

Contract Management: Refers to the creation, execution, and monitoring of contracts. Legal tech tools streamline these processes, improving efficiency and reducing errors while ensuring contracts are enforceable and compliant.

Justice Platforms: Digital tools that make the legal system more accessible and efficient, offering resources for self-representation, case tracking, and legal advice. They aim to enhance access to justice, particularly for underserved communities.

Resolution Platforms: Online tools for alternative dispute resolution (ADR), such as mediation and arbitration, offering efficient, cost-effective solutions outside traditional courtrooms.

Chapter 7
Fostering Creativity in Agile Education:
A Comparative Study of Students and Software Practitioners

Carlos Villarrubia
https://orcid.org/0009-0000-2400-1049
Universidad Rey Juan Carlos, Spain

David Granada
https://orcid.org/0000-0001-9743-4347
Universidad Rey Juan Carlos, Spain

Juan Manuel Vara
https://orcid.org/0000-0002-8637-6580
Universidad Rey Juan Carlos, Spain

ABSTRACT

In the contemporary software development landscape, mastering agile methods and nurturing creativity are essential skills for team success. This study aims to demonstrate that these objectives are both compatible and synergistic. It presents the findings from six experiments involving diverse groups of students and software development practitioners who utilized DesignScrum, a gamified educational resource that integrates Scrum and Design Thinking. The primary objective is to teach agile methods and techniques in a manner that fosters creativity within software development teams. The results indicate that practitioners exhibit a stronger grasp of agile concepts due to their work experience, while students display a higher potential for creativity. Additionally, all participant groups perceived gamification as a beneficial learning approach, noting increased motivation and satisfaction.

DOI: 10.4018/979-8-3693-9531-8.ch007

This study concludes that with the appropriate tools, teaching agility and creativity in various educational and professional settings is not only feasible but also highly advantageous.

INTRODUCTION

The roots of agile methods can be traced back to the publication of the Agile Manifesto in 2001, a document created by software professionals to address the shortcomings of traditional, rigid development approaches such as the waterfall model. The manifesto emphasized values such as collaboration, customer feedback and flexibility to adapt to changing requirements (Beck, 2000; Manifesto, 2001).

In recent years, a number of frameworks and techniques have been developed for the teaching of agile methods to students of software development. Among these, the Scrum framework, created by Ken Schwaber and Jeff Sutherland in 2002, is one of the most widely accepted by both academics and practitioners alike (Hoda et al., 2018). This is largely due to the fact that it facilitates the continuous delivery of value through the use of small iterations, with self-managed and cross-functional teams (Kupiainen et al., 2015; Schwaber & Sutherland, 2020).

In light of the growing demand for practitioners versed in agile methods within the software industry, it is of paramount importance that students not only possess a comprehensive understanding of the fundamental concepts, but also demonstrate the ability to effectively apply them in the products they are engaged with. From a pedagogical standpoint, Scrum is not inherently complex, as it comprises a limited set of concepts and ideas (Srivastava et al., 2017). The true challenge lies in equipping teams with the skills to implement it effectively. In this regard, there are several established educational methodologies for acquiring agile (Salza et al., 2019, such as master classes, as well as certifications that attest to proficiency in this domain (Beraza et al., 2023).

Despite the prevalence of traditional methodologies, novel approaches to the teaching of agile have recently emerged, with gamification emerging as a prominent strategy for motivating learners through the introduction of playful elements. This is because gamification not only increases student engagement and motivation, but can also enhance the practical learning of complex skills by simulating real-life situations in a controlled environment (Deterding et al., 2011).

Notable examples of educational resources that introduce gamification into the teaching-learning process include LEGO4Scrum, which employs the use of building blocks to simulate the process of developing a software product (Krivitsky, 2017); The Ball Game, which utilizes rubber balls to facilitate self-management of development team members (May et al., 2016); and Kanban Pizza Game, which employs the use of stationery to simulate the workflow of software development (Hammarberg & Sunden, 2014).

Nevertheless, experts in the field have identified certain constraints associated with the implementation of agile methods within the software industry, particularly in situations characterized by high-pressure and stringent deadlines. This is because software developers are sometimes tasked with an excessive amount of responsibility in a single iteration, which can result in mental exhaustion and elevated stress levels. This fatigue has a detrimental impact on creativity and the team's capacity to develop innovative solutions, thereby constraining the potential for agile methods to adapt and respond expeditiously to evolving market demands (Elbanna & Sarker, 2016; Solinski & Petersen, 2016).

One promising approach to enhancing creativity is Design Thinking, a method for creative problem solving that originated in industrial design in the 1960s. Its principles, based on empathy, ideation and prototyping, have been widely adopted in other disciplines such as software engineering (Stickdorn et al., 2018). Popularized at Stanford University through classroom use, the method is structured in five iterative stages designed to encourage the generation of disruptive ideas through creative thinking (Stanford d.school., n.d.). Today, organizations use it to innovate, create value based on customer needs (Brown & Katz, 2011) and improve the customer experience (Norman, 2013). In fact, some studies suggest that integrating creative thinking into the requirements elicitation phase of agile software development improves the identification of genuine user needs and facilitates innovative solutions (Aldave et al., 2019).

This study aims to demonstrate the compatibility and synergy between the enhancement of creativity and the comprehension of agile methods across diverse groups, including students and practitioners in the field of software development. In order to achieve this objective, an educational resource has been developed which employs a playful approach, integrating Design Thinking with Scrum and other complementary techniques, with the intention of fostering creativity and agile learning (Villarrubia et al., 2024). Additionally, the study investigates how distinct groups perceive the efficacy of gamification as a strategy to augment creativity and facilitate comprehension of agile concepts. Furthermore, it aims to ascertain which group exhibits enhanced creativity and a more profound grasp of agile principles, evaluating the potential influence of prior collaborative experience among team members on these outcomes.

The remainder of the chapter is structured as follows: Section *Context* provides an overview of the background and rationale for this study, as well as posing key assessment questions; Section *Case study analysis* outlines the experiments conducted, and presents and discusses the findings of the experiments; Section *Discussion* addresses the assessment questions posed and highlights the limitations and potential threats to the study's findings; and finally, Section *Conclusions* summarizes the main findings obtained through this study and suggests avenues for future research.

CONTEXT

This section provides an overview of the various gamified Agile educational resources documented in the literature, the risks associated with using gamification, and the factors that limit creativity. Finally, the assessment questions that guided this study are presented.

Gamified Educational Resources for Agile

Gamification can be defined as the design of engaging games that allow certain objectives to be achieved with as few elements as possible. This is made possible by the ability of gamification to introduce game elements into non-game activities and to adapt to the educational environment. The incorporation of these features has been shown to promote positive changes in the player's behavior and attitude, increasing motivation and learning (Basten, 2017).

Consequently, an increasing number of organizations engaged in software development are undergoing a process of transformation, modifying their internal practices and systems with the objective of implementing gamification. However, the majority of these organizations do not adhere to the established best practices, resorting instead to a simplistic and superficial approach to gamification, whereby they merely incorporate game mechanics into their existing systems. In order to address this issue, it is essential to direct greater attention towards the underlying psychological dynamics that render gamification an engaging phenomenon (Hugos, 2012; Pedreira et al., 2015).

One of the most prevalent techniques employed in gamification is the *point system*, which motivates players to engage and compete by allowing them to accumulate points and compare their performance with others, thereby reinforcing a sense of accomplishment. Furthermore, points are utilized to demarcate levels, conferring rewards upon the attainment of a designated score. Another technique is the utilization of *emblems or badges*, which serve to visually represent achievements. This technique enables players to differentiate themselves and provides greater satisfaction through public recognition. Conversely, the *leaderboard system* allows players' performance to be compared, demonstrating their progress in relation to others. This technique is frequently combined with the points system to intensify competition and motivate users to strive for higher positions. However, its exclusive use can have the opposite effect, reducing performance in environments where excessive competition leads to anxiety and demotivation (Morschheuser et al., 2018).

The contemporary era offers a plethora of educational resources that utilized gamification to educate students and practitioners in the domain of agile frameworks. It has been observed that 75.8% of the 32 most prominent educational resources make reference to the Scrum framework (Schwaber & Sutherland, 2020), while 21.2% make reference to Kanban (Hammarberg & Sunden, 2014) and 18.2% make reference to eXtreme Programming (XP) (Beck, 2000; Villarrubia et al., 2024). However, the majority of these resources focus on teaching a select few key agile concepts and their interrelationships, such as self-management and effort estimation. Only a few address the full spectrum of these concepts. Notable examples of these educational resources include SCRUMIA (Von Wangenheim et al., 2013), SCRUMI (Diniz De Souza et al., 2017), Origami (Sibona et al., 2018), LEGO4Scrum (Krivitsky, 2017), The Ball Game (May et al., 2016), Kanban Pizza Game (Hammarberg & Sunden, 2014), Card Game PlayScrum (Fernandes & Sousa, 2010), Virtual Scrum (Rodriguez et al., 2015), ScrumTutor (Potineni et al., 2013), Scrum paper city (Hof et al., 2017), Extreme Construction (Bergin & Grossman, 2006), Scrumify (Ammons & Bansal, 2017), Featureban (Burrows, 2021), Scrum simulation game (Paasivaara et al., 2014), Sprint then fly (Frydenberg et al., 2018), Game (Peeters & Van Cauwenberghe, 2003) y The Bug is a Lie (Schroeder et al., 2012). Nevertheless, despite the abundance of available instructional materials, DesignScrum (Villarrubia et al., 2024) is the sole resource that facilitates the advancement of creativity while concurrently integrating all essential agile principles by employing a gamified strategy. Participants construct a block structure to simulate real-world scenarios encountered during the development of a software product, including the challenges posed by evolving requirements or changes in the composition of the development team.

This educational resource is comprised of three iterations and encompasses all Scrum roles, events, and artifacts, which are integrated with Design Thinking. Additionally, the resource is enhanced by the incorporation of several supplementary agile techniques, including the Kanban board, which provides a visual representation of the workflow through a board, and Planning poker, which enables the estimation of the requisite effort to complete a task through the use of cards. Moreover, additional creative techniques are integrated, including the Business Model Canvas, which assists in identifying the essential elements of a business model by dividing a canvas into nine sections, and the Stakeholder Map, which helps to identify the individuals and entities with an interest in a product or service.

One of the key attributes of DesignScrum is its straightforwardness and ease of use. The resource can be delivered in less than two hours and only requires a room with tables and inexpensive materials. Consequently, DesignScrum can be readily integrated into a multitude of contexts, including academic settings and corporate training sessions, thereby establishing itself as a highly adaptable instrument for learning agile and fostering creativity. This is due to the correct integration of creativity into agile, such as the LEGO Serious Play technique and the Design Thinking approach, both of which have been shown to enhance creativity in both contexts (Brown, 2009; Frick et al., 2014).

The utilization of this educational resource facilitates the acquisition of theoretical knowledge pertaining to agile methods and creative processes, while simultaneously fostering the development of practical competencies that are pertinent in authentic professional settings. Moreover, it encourages active and participatory learning.

Conversely, no validation of these agile educational resources, including DesignScrum, has been conducted by diverse groups of students and software development practitioners. Notably, all validations were performed with a single cohort, with students comprising 84.4% of the participants, including both university and management programs, while practitioners accounted for the remaining 15.6%. In addition, gamification, added in these educational resources, carries certain risks, which are detailed in the following subsection.

Risks Associated With Gamification

Gamification has proven to be an approach strategy for learning agile methods (Villarrubia et al., 2024), but its application is not without risks that can undermine its effectiveness. Some of the associated risks include the following:

- *Superficial implementation:* focused on adding basic elements such as points or leaderboards, neglecting deeper psychological principles like intrinsic motivation or meaningful engagement. This often results in activities that entertain but fail to deliver significant learning outcomes. To address this, it is essential to align gamification mechanics with learning objectives, ensuring the activities are both relevant and impactful (Deterding et al., 2011).
- *Demotivation among participants:* due to their perception of gamification as trivial or childish, reducing their engagement. This highlights the importance of tailoring gamified activities to participant profiles, *incorporating* scenarios that challenge their expertise and resonate with their professional context (Kapp, 2012).
- *Cognitive overload:* due to increased complexity due to poor design, frustrating participants and hindering learning. Clarity of instructions and simplicity in mechanics are key to maintaining a balance *between* challenge and comprehension. Research emphasizes that *intuitive* design is critical to achieving effective educational outcomes (Hamari et al., 2014).

- *Overreliance on technology:* may limit applicability in resource-constrained environments. The adoption of simpler, low-tech solutions, such as analogue games or group dynamics, can ensure that gamification *remains* accessible while achieving its educational objectives (Werbach & Hunter, 2012).
- *Negative effects of excessive competition:* can create anxiety or disengagement, especially in settings where there are skill *disparities*. Balanced competition with collaborative dynamics fosters inclusion and shifts the focus toward collective learning rather than individual winning (Nicholson, 2015).

Overall, the success of gamification hinges on its ability to adapt to participant needs and educational goals. A thoughtful and flexible approach can transform these risks into opportunities, enriching the learning experience and maximizing its impact (Werbach & Hunter, 2012). However, mitigating these risks in agile educational resources does not prevent creativity from being reduced in professional settings, as described in the next subsection.

Factors Limiting Creativity in Professional Environments

Creativity in professional settings faces significant challenges due to systemic, cultural and psychological factors. Rigid hierarchical structures and pressure to meet strict deadlines tend to prioritize operational efficiency over experimentation, limiting opportunities for innovation (Elbanna & Sarker, 2016). These systemic dynamics often discourage risk-taking and the exploration of ideas outside of conventional approaches.

At a cultural level, fear of failure and a lack of safe spaces for experimentation create a mindset that discourages creativity. Organizations tend to value achieving pre-defined goals over developing innovative solutions, perpetuating a culture that does not always value original thinking (Nicholson, 2015).

From a psychological perspective, professionals may develop cognitive rigidity. This, together with accumulated stress and lack of creative stimulation, reduces their ability to adopt new perspectives (Kaufman & Beghetto, 2009). Repetition of similar tasks and a focus on technical performance often crowd out creativity as a priority.

Addressing these barriers requires specific interventions that foster environments conducive to innovation. Strategies such as the use of playful dynamics, the incorporation of creative approaches such as design thinking, and the promotion of organizational cultures that value learning from mistakes are essential to reinvigorating creativity in experienced professionals. These interventions not only mitigate systemic and psychological constraints, but also provide teams with practical tools to explore innovative solutions in an agile and collaborative framework (Amabile, 2018).

Assessment Questions

The assessment questions (AQ) that guided this study were formulated at the outset of the research project in order to explore the relationship between fostering creativity and teaching agile in software development. The following questions were posed:

- *AQ-1.* How does the understanding of agile concepts vary among different groups of students and software development practitioners?
- *AQ-2.* What is the influence of academic background and work experience on creativity enhancement?
- *AQ-3.* What is the relationship between agile learning and creativity enhancement in software development students and practitioners?
- *AQ-4.* How is gamification perceived as a method for learning agile concepts and enhancing creativity?
- *AQ-5.* What is the perception of learning agile and creativity through the use of gamification?
- *AQ-6.* What influence does previous experience of collaboration between team members have on learning agile and enhancing creativity?

All these assessment questions are answered in the *Discussion* Section of this chapter. The questions are answered by considering the analysis of the case studies presented in the next section, together with the literature on gamified agile educational resources, the risks associated with the use of gamification and the factors limiting creativity presented in this section.

CASE STUDY ANALYSIS

The design of this study was experimental, with the objective of identifying causal relationships between the selected variables (Campbell & Stanley, 2015). In particular, the independent variables comprised both the level of experience and the academic background of the participants (Kolb, 2014). Regarding the primary dependent variables, these were designed to assess participants' understanding of agile concepts and their ability to incorporate creativity into a software product following the utilization of the DesignScrum educational resource (Villarrubia et al., 2024). In contrast, the secondary dependent variables were based on participants' perceptions of motivation, user experience and learning (Deci & Ryan, 2000). Figure 1 shows an extract of the stages carried out for the various experiments; the *invariant stage* includes all steps that are performed consistently, regardless of the participant group carrying out the learning-teaching process, such as the explanation to the participants of the agile educational resource that enhances creativity, the completion of surveys before and after the teaching-learning process, and the analysis of the results obtained. The *selected stage* represents the participant group carrying out the learning-teaching process. Finally, the *alternative stage* shows the other participant groups that could carry out the learning-experience process.

Figure 1. **Extract from the experimental design**

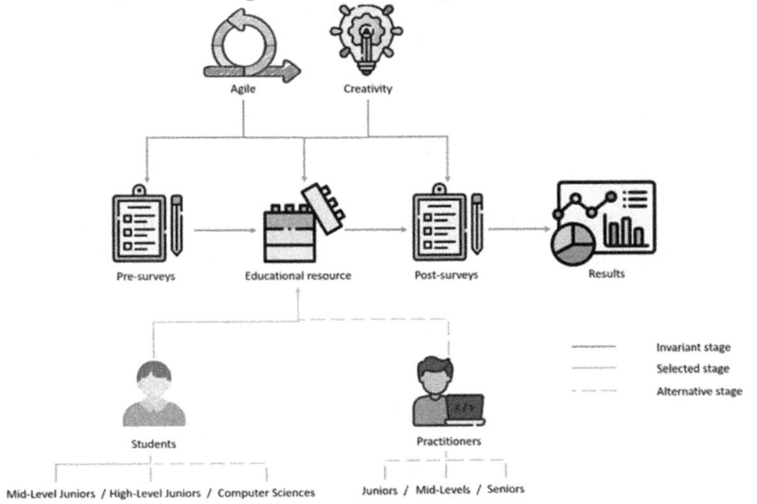

Definition of Experiments

The empirical study was conducted through a series of six diverse experiments. Each of these experiments was designed to assess the understanding of agile concepts and the ability to integrate creativity into the development of a software product, using the DesignScrum educational resource with groups of participants of varying profiles. In this way, the data extracted from the experiments can be compared with each other, making it possible to demonstrate whether work experience and level of academic training influence the ability to assimilate and apply these concepts in software development (Campbell & Stanley, 2015).

A total of 173 participants were involved in six experiments, divided into groups comprising students at medium, high and university level in computer science, as well as practitioners with varying levels of experience in software development. All participants involved in this study were based in Madrid, Spain, during the 2024/2025 academic year. Given that software development is sometimes conducted with team members who are not previously acquainted (Gutierrez et al., 2019), each group was divided according to whether all participants had previously collaborated in academic, work, or non-work contexts, maintaining the same size in both subgroups.

The experimental groups were constituted as follows:

- *Experiment 1. Middle Grade Students*---40 second year students who were taking the microcomputer systems and networking training cycle at the Innovación y Formación Profesional (IFP) centre participated. These students were selected to observe how computer novices and younger students perceive and assimilate these concepts.
- *Experiment 2. Higher Grade Students*---Involved 36 second year students taking the web applications development training cycle at IFP centre, who were selected to assess their understanding of the concepts in an applied technical training environment.
- *Experiment 3. University Students*---A total of 30 fourth-year students enrolled in the computer science degree at the Universidad Rey Juan Carlos participated in the study. This group was selected to provide insight into the comprehension of the concepts under investigation from an advanced educational level.
- *Experiment 4. Junior Software Development Practitioners*---25 software development practitioners with less than 2 years of work experience participated. These practitioners held both a university degree and a middle or higher grade regardless of the duration of their employment. Likewise, internship students were not considered, as this is a fundamental part of their academic training. Of this group, 7 had university degrees, while 9 had completed higher grades and 2 had completed middle grades.
- *Experiment 5. Mid-Level Software Development Practitioner*---Involved 22 practitioners with a working experience in software development between 2 and 5 years, based on the assumption that those with less experience might not have sufficient contact with the development of real software products and therefore could be considered as recent graduates (juniors). Of this group, 15 had university degrees, while 3 had completed higher grades.
- *Experiment 6. Senior Software Development Practitioner*---20 software development practitioners with more than 5 years of work experience participated. This period is sufficient for the acquisition and mastery of proficient knowledge in a software development knowledge area (Collings et al., 2017). Of this group, 7 had university degrees, while 5 had completed higher grades.

The participants in each of these groups were purposefully chosen to reflect a range of practitioner's experience and academic training in software development. Given the relatively minor discrepancies in sample size between the groups, it is unlikely that these differences will have a significant impact on the interpretation of the results. The size and homogeneity of the groups are sufficient to allow for meaningful comparisons to be made (Kish, 1978), which is supported by the data collection process described in the next subsection.

Data Collection

Before the beginning of the experiments, the types of data that were required to be collected were identified. Once it was established that the data collection would be predominantly numerical, thus enabling comparison, and that some descriptive data would also be included, a number of the most commonly employed empirical research methods in software engineering were selected for the data collection process. The selected methods were surveys completed by participants, expert evaluation and direct observation (Wohlin et al., 2003).

To ensure the accuracy of the data collected in the experiments, each group of participants attended a training session on the concepts and steps of the DesignScrum educational resource, thus ensuring that participants used the resource correctly. The participants completed five surveys and a table designed for data collection, which was created in accordance with the guidelines set out in the Reference (Fowler, 1995).

The first two surveys (pre-surveys) focused on the participants' prior knowledge before the use of the educational resource. One survey focused on agile, the other on creativity. These surveys comprise the columns 'I understand the concepts theoretically', 'I understand how the concepts work in practice' and 'I am able to apply the concepts in a work context', as well as thirteen and ten concepts related to agile and creativity respectively. In this way, both theoretical understanding and the ability to apply them in real contexts were assessed, given that sometimes students understand a concept, but face difficulties in its implementation (Cohen et al., 2017). Participants were able to acquire a maximum of 15 points, as their knowledge of each concept was scored as 1 (very low), 2 (low), 3 (moderate), 4 (high) or 5 (very high). In this way, participants used intermediate values, so as not to limit themselves to binary scores, and avoided the burden that could be caused by using an overly broad scale.

The third and fourth surveys (post-surveys), which were identical to the pre-surveys, were designed to assess the participants' comprehension of agile concepts and their capacity to incorporate creativity into a software product following the utilization of the educational resource. The similarity of the two sets of questions allowed for a comparison of the results obtained before and after the use of the educational resource, thus providing a quantitative measure of the learning acquired by the participants.

The fifth and last survey (general survey) allowed to know the opinion of the participants on aspects related to user experience, motivation and feeling of learning after the use of the educational resource. This survey comprises of 27 questions and had to be answered on the same scoring scale as the other surveys. Each of these questions was associated with a specific area such as Concentration (C) or Involvement (I). Moreover, the survey included a section for suggestions, which allowed participants to provide free-form feedback on the learning-teaching process they had received.

Finally, all groups of participants filled in the winner's table to determine the amount of creativity added to the software product. This table was composed of 5 creative criteria, including the amount and variety of colors in the building blocks used, the number of ideas conceived, the requirements added and the assessment of experts in the field. The group of participants with the highest score in this table was considered the winner of the game.

All surveys were completed anonymously, to ensure the protection of the participants' identity. In the case of the students, the aim was to make them feel comfortable during the process and to avoid them perceiving the surveys as an evaluation method, but rather as a complementary activity. However, the students were told that on another day they would be doing a compulsory activity, so that they would be seriously committed to using the resource and would have enough time to prepare for it. Regarding the seriousness of the practitioners, they were told that the concepts should be implemented incrementally in their work environment, encouraging gradual, effective and unpressured application. All survey data and the winner's table are available in the *Annex* to this chapter and are analyzed in the following subsection.

Results

The results of this study reveal that the understanding of agile methods and techniques, while also enhancing creativity, varies depending on the educational level of students and the work experience of software development practitioners. However, both the understanding of agile concepts and the enhancement of creativity can be achieved simultaneously through the use of appropriate tools, thus achieving the combined benefit of both.

(Annotation #19) (Annotation #31) Figure 2 shows, using box-and-whisker plots, the understanding of agile concepts by each group of participants before and after the use of the DesignScrum educational resource. The interquartile ranges (IQRs), which represent the distance between the first quartile (Q1) and the third quartile (Q3), are quite short in all diagrams. This suggests that there is minimal variability in responses within the same group of participants (Freund & Wilson, 2003) and, therefore, most participants within the same group achieved a similar understanding of agile and creativity-enhancing concepts.

Figure 2. Results of the agile surveys

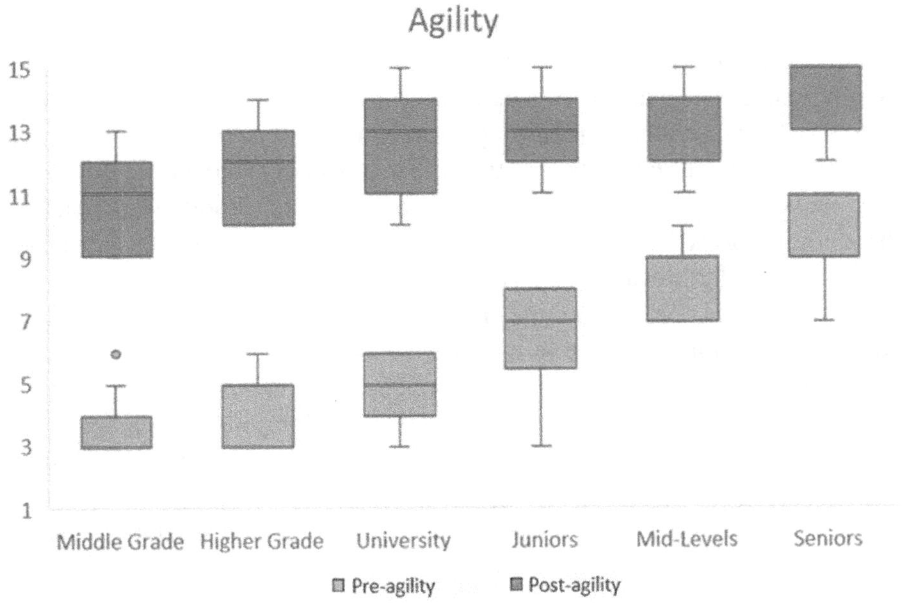

The analysis revealed that work experience was the most significant factor influencing the comprehension of agile concepts. Participants who had prior experience showed a significant capacity to internalize and apply these concepts more effectively than those without such experience. The median score for juniors on the agile post-surveys was 13 points, while the median score for and mid-levels was 14 points and seniors was 15 points. Furthermore, mid-level practitioners demonstrated a greater concentration of data than their junior counterparts. The undergraduate cohort, who also achieved a median score of 13, demonstrated a higher concentration of responses with higher scores among practitioners. These findings are consistent with previous research related to team management (Gutierrez et al., 2019) and is due to their continuous exposure to real projects, which increases their ability to adapt to unforeseen situations. Indeed, this adaptability increases with the accumulation of professional experience, as practitioners are even more intimately acquainted with the evolving dynamics of software development. This capacity for adaptation is a fundamental aspect of agile (Manifesto, 2001), that has been scientifically proven in subsequent studies (Elbanna & Sarker, 2016). Students, whose experiences are often more structured and supervised within an academic environment, may not possess this ability as effectively as practitioners. Additionally, it was observed that participants with a lower academic background demonstrated a lesser understanding of agile concepts, potentially due to a lack of maturity and an incomplete understanding of the stages of software development.

The level of prior knowledge of agile among students and software development practitioners differed according to the extent of their educational background and work experience. The majority of students in the middle and higher grades demonstrated a lack of knowledge regarding these concepts, as they are not typically covered in the curriculum of these courses. The university students demonstrated a slightly higher level of knowledge than the other students, although a median score of three points was still considered to be low. This discrepancy can be attributed to the fact that a negligible number of students had previously undertaken the subject that introduces the concepts of agile. This is due to the fact that the curriculum of the degree in computer science in which the experiment was conducted does not include this subject until a later stage than the period in which the experiment was carried out. Regarding the practitioners, those in junior positions demonstrated a fundamental understanding of agile, with a median score of 7 points. Those in mid-level positions exhibited a moderate grasp of the subject, with a median score of 9 points. In contrast, those in senior positions displayed a high level of proficiency, with a median score of 10 points.

The preceding agile knowledge curve shows an upward trend in relation to the participants' level of education and experience, which is also reflected in the knowledge acquired after the game. Nevertheless, the rise in post-game agile knowledge was less pronounced among participants with higher levels of education and experience.

On the other hand, Figure 3 shows the results in relation to creativity. The data reveal that academic background is the variable that most influences creativity, as shown by the increasing progression of the medians. The cohort of students engaged in university-level studies exhibited the highest median scores, reaching 14 points. This is due to the fact that these types of studies encourage the development of critical thinking and analytical skills. These findings are consistent with previous research suggesting that educational environments are more conducive to creativity than professional environments, particularly in technical disciplines.(Kaufman & Beghetto, 2009). However, it was observed that the practitioners demonstrated the lowest levels of performance, even when compared to students at the intermediate level, who have a basic knowledge of software development. This observation can be attributed to the fact that, within this age group, there is a paucity of restrictions and social norms that impinge upon creativity. Furthermore, creativity tends to decline with the accumulation of professional experience. This phenomenon may be attributed to the progressive shift in focus towards technical aspects, which often occurs over time. This may result in a diminished emphasis on creative capacity, which is often enhanced in the initial educational stages. This is evidenced by the fact that junior practitioners exhibit the highest concentration of data with a median score of 12 points, compared to mid-level and senior practitioners, who provide an average score of 11 points. In turn, mid-level practitioners show a higher concentration of data than senior practitioners.

Figure 3. **Results of the creativity surveys**

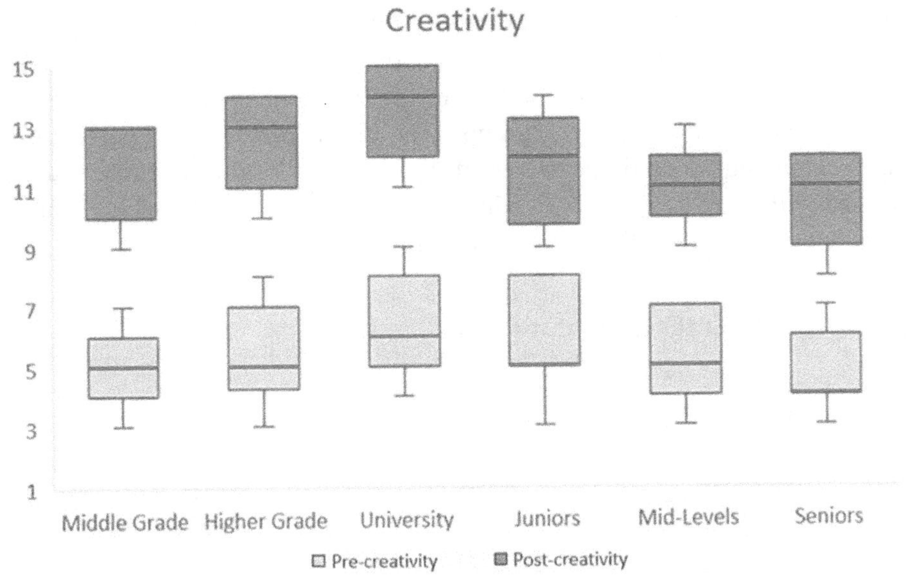

Prior knowledge of creativity among the various groups of participants was observed to be at lower-medium levels, with a distribution that was similar to that observed after playing the game. The median score for middle-grade and higher-grade students was 5 points, with higher-grade students exhibiting a greater concentration of data. The university student cohort achieved the highest median score across all groups, with a score of 6 points. Regarding work experience, junior and middle-level developers achieved a median score of 5 points. However, the concentration of the data was slightly higher for those in the junior category. The senior developers exhibited the lowest levels of creativity among all participant groups, with a median score of 4 points.

The prior knowledge curve in creativity exhibits a similar pattern to that observed in the post-game knowledge curve. Furthermore, the observed increase in creativity knowledge was approximately consistent across all participant groups.

Figure 4 shows the arithmetic mean (AVG) and confidence interval for each participant group for the user experience, motivation and learning outcomes, as obtained through the general survey. All aspects for the different groups of participants are within the 95% confidence interval. This indicates that, despite the presence of individual variations in responses, the survey was completed in a consistent manner. Moreover, an inverse correlation was observed between the motivation of the participants during the utilization of the educational resource and their comprehension of the concepts associated with agile method. This was due to the fact that the educational resource was perceived as challenging in terms of learning new concepts and building block structure, elements that are motivating at younger ages. However, the greatest decline in motivation was observed among mid-level and senior practitioners, who rejected gamified learning on the grounds that it was associated with games aimed at younger age groups. The user experience and perception of learning exhibited by participants varied. In the case of students, the experience decreased with increasing levels of education. In contrast, practitioners reported a decrease in experience with increasing levels of experience.

Figure 4. **Results of the general surveys**

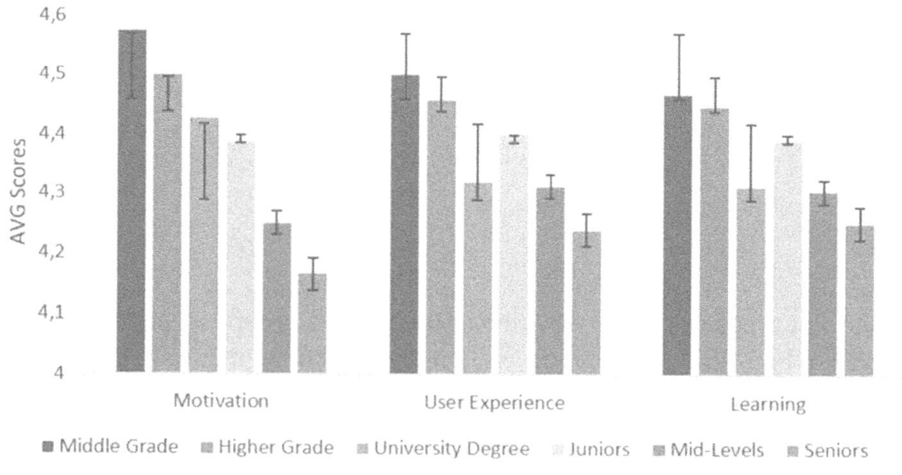

Figure 5 shows the rounded average of the various criteria from the winner's table that were fulfilled by the participant groups. The analysis of the data presented in this study corroborates the findings of the creativity post-survey, indicating that the student groups exhibited higher levels of creativity compared to the practitioner groups. It was observed that as the academic level of the students increased, there was an increase in creativity added to the software product. Conversely, there was a decrease in creativity in relation to work experience. In particular, the undergraduate student cohort demonstrated the highest levels of creativity, with an average score of 93 points, while the senior practitioner's cohort exhibited the lowest levels of creativity, with an average score of 52 points. These results support the conclusion that participants completed the creativity survey in a consistent and deliberate manner, thereby suggesting that the other surveys were completed in a similar fashion.

Figure 5. **Winner's table results**

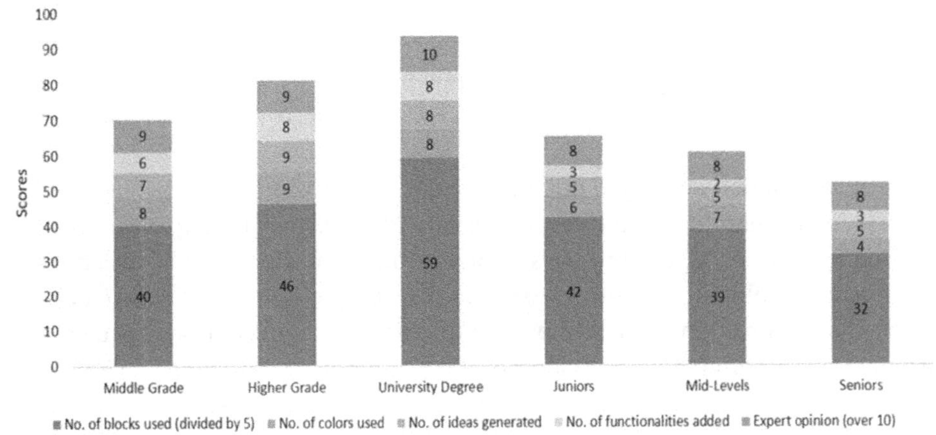

Table 1 presents a synthesis of the findings from the various experiments, organized according to the participants' history of collaboration in academic or practitioner settings. The data presented in this table demonstrates that prior collaboration has a more pronounced effect on the enhancement of creativity and the comprehension of agile principles within the context of software development. This is due to the fact that familiarity between participants enabled more relaxed interaction, which in turn led to an increase in idea generation, more effective communication and more agile conflict resolution. The average of the post-survey scores for agile and creativity is higher in the groups of participants who had collaborated beforehand. In particular, the overall average for the concepts of agile and creativity was 12.708 and 12.013 points respectively for groups with previous collaboration, compared to 12.278 and 11.536 points for those that did not. Moreover, the standard deviation (SD) of each column of the surveys is consistently below 0.606 points for the overall set of groups of participants who had previously collaborated and those who had not, indicating minimal variability in scores and further supporting the validity of this study.

Table 1. Summary of results with and without prior collaboration

	Previous collaboration				Without prior collaboration			
	Agile		Creativity		Agile		Creativity	
	AVG	SD	AVG	SD	AVG	SD	AVG	SD
Middle Grade	10.912	0.585	11.555	0.693	10.588	0.553	11.46	0.684
Higher Grade	11.817	0.641	12.661	0.711	11.688	0.64	12.339	0.736
University Degree	13.082	0.677	13.52	0.644	12.885	0.698	13.48	0.644
Juniors	13.154	0.642	11.099	0.706	13.1	0.621	10.713	0.639
Mid-Levels	13.423	0.604	11.3	0.612	13.385	0.602	10.946	0.601
Seniors	13.862	0.486	11.944	0.778	12.073	0.451	10.28	0.637
Overall	12.708	0.606	12.013	0.691	12.287	0.594	11.536	0.657

As the evaluation employed quantitative surveys, it was imperative to ascertain the statistical reliability of the responses provided by the participants. This was achieved by calculating the Intraclass Correlation Coefficient (ICC), which serves to measure the reliability of the assessments by comparing the variability of a single participant's responses with the overall variability across all assessments and participants. The fundamental concept of the ICC was first introduced by Reference (Fisher, 1921), who formulated it as a particular version of Pearson's correlation coefficient, applicable when the distributions involved have equivalent measures and variances.

The fundamental premise of this approach is that the overall variability observed in the experimental data can be decomposed into three primary components: variability attributable to differences between items in the survey (varβ), variability due to discrepancies between raters (varε), and a residual (random) variability associated with the inherent measurement error (varα). The ICC is calculated in each experiment as the ratio of the variability explained by the questions to the total variability.

$$c = \frac{var\beta}{var\beta + var\varepsilon + var\alpha}$$

The recommendations put forth by the Reference (Koo & Li, 2016) were implemented for the purpose of calculating ICC estimates and their corresponding 95% confidence intervals. utilizing the Analysis of variance (ANOVA) procedure. The analysis was performed using the Microsoft Excel Analysis ToolPak add-in, with the assumption of a single rater/measurement with absolute agreement and a two-way random-effects model. This can be expressed by the following formula:

$$\frac{MS_R - MS_E}{MS_R + (k-1) + \frac{k}{n}\left(MS_C - MS_E\right)}$$

In this formula (McGraw & Wong, 1996), *MSR* represents the root mean square of the rows, *MSE* the root mean square of the error, and *MSC* the root mean square of the columns. The variable n corresponds to the number of subjects, while *k* corresponds to the number of raters or measurements.

Following the completion of the ANOVA on the total set of participants' responses for each of the five surveys in each experiment, the requisite values for the calculation of the ICC, as illustrated in Table 2. The value of the ICC can range from 0 to 1. A value of 0 indicates a total lack of agreement, whereas a value of 1 indicates absolute consistency and agreement in the results. In particular, ICC values below 0.4 indicate low reliability, between 0.4 and 0.75 suggest good reliability, and above 0.75 denote excellent reliability (Fleiss, 2011). Consequently, all the values obtained in the five surveys of the different experiments have a good degree of reliability in the responses of the participants. In fact, eleven of the surveys have excellent reliability.

Table 2. ICC values

		Middle Grade	Higher Grade	University Degree	Juniors	Mid-Levels	Seniors
Agile pre-survey	*ICC*	0.7965	0.7964	0.6154	0.6449	0.6203	0.6555
Creativity pre-survey	*ICC*	0.6446	0.6763	0.6929	0.6655	0.6698	0.6693
Agile post-survey	*ICC*	0.7242	0.6186	0.696	0.6448	0.6053	0.8072
Creativity post-survey	*ICC*	0.6093	0.6956	0.7615	0.7045	0.673	0.673
General survey	*ICC*	0.7644	0.7557	0.7909	0.8453	0.7748	0.9176

The consistency in the variability of the evaluations can be partly explained by the fact that the participants in the same group had a similar profile and an equivalent level of prior knowledge. Moreover, since the surveys were anonymous and the design of the experiment influenced the students' evaluations, it is unlikely that their answers were random. This consistency in responses reinforces the validity of the study.

Finally, participants indicated, in the open-ended suggestions question of the general survey, their preference for learning agile methods and creativity through the use of games as an alternative to traditional methods. Specifically, 87.2% of the students expressed a preference for the use of games, with small variations in preferences between the different levels of academic training. On the other hand, 78.5% of practitioners also indicated a preference for these playful elements in the teaching-learning process, although this preference decreased as their level of work experience increased. In all groups there were between 3% and 6% of participants who did not have a clear position on whether they preferred gamification or traditional methods for learning agile methods and creativity.

The findings of this study indicate that the DesignScrum educational resource can be effectively utilized at all levels of academic instruction pertaining to software development, as well as by practitioners engaged in similar pursuits. Furthermore, the results obtained enabled all the assessment questions to be answered, as well as identifying limitations and proposing future work, which is presented in the following section. The dataset of the surveys and table completed by the participants in each experiment of this study is available in the following open access repository from Mendeley Data https://dx.doi.org/10.17632/f8vgrb42zf.1

DISCUSSION

This section responds to the assessment questions that were posed at the outset of the research project and indicates the limitations and future work that have been identified through this evaluation process.

Responses to Assessment Questions

Following the description of the experimental design and the presentation of the resulting data, the assessment questions formulated at the outset of the research are addressed. To respond to these questions, we conducted an analysis of the data gathered through surveys and direct observation during the experiments.

- *AQ-1. How does the understanding of agile concepts vary among different groups of students and software development practitioners?*---Practitioners demonstrated a deeper and more practical understanding of agile concepts than students, due to their experience and knowledge of the software development lifecycle. Among students, undergraduates and those at higher academic levels stood out for their greater conceptual maturity. For practitioners, understanding increased with experience, reflecting their adaptation to complex development situations.

- *AQ-2. What is the influence of academic background and work experience on creativity enhancement?*---The level of academic education is directly related to creativity, as the knowledge acquired in software development facilitates the conception of a greater variety of products. University students stood out as the most creative group, while practitioners showed less creativity despite their greater knowledge in the field. This suggests that creativity tends to decrease with experience, possibly due to social pressures and constraints that increase with age.
- *AQ-3. What is the relationship between agile learning and creativity enhancement in software development students and practitioners?*---The university students demonstrated a greater ability to improve their creativity after using the educational resource and stood out as the most creative group. Although they did not reach the highest level of understanding of agile concepts, their creative ability was admirable. In contrast, the practitioners showed lower levels of creativity despite their higher level of mastery of agile concepts, demonstrating a relationship between improved creativity and understanding of agile concepts. This suggests that a creative mindset is more conducive to learning.
- *AQ-4. How is gamification perceived as a method for learning agile concepts and enhancing creativity?*--- All groups of participants expressed a positive perception of gamification as a method for learning agile concepts and fostering creativity. Although some participants expressed a preference for traditional methods, the majority felt that incorporating gamification dynamics into the training not only improved the learning experience, but also increased motivation.
- *AQ-5. What is the perception of learning agile and creativity through the use of gamification?*---All groups of participants perceived learning through gamification positively, according to the results of the general survey, which reflected a high level of satisfaction with the learning experience.
- *AQ-6. What influence does previous experience of collaboration between team members have on learning agile and enhancing creativity?*--- Previous experience of collaboration between team members has a significant impact on improving agile learning and creativity. Groups with a history of working or studying together showed better results, which was attributed to the ease of communication, idea generation and conflict resolution due to familiarity and mutual trust.

The experiments yielded satisfactory responses to all assessment questions and identified certain limitations of the study, which are presented in the following subsection together with the findings derived from this study.

Limitations and Future Work

The limitations identified in this research and possible areas for future work are presented below:

- *Geographical location:* of all the participants in the study lived in Madrid, Spain, which limits the generalizability of the results to other regions or countries. For example, teaching is more integrated into the curriculum in Spain than in other countries. At the socio-economic level, access to resources for education is not usually an obstacle, as the state supports education with financial aid. On the other hand, the labor market is characterized by high competitiveness and pressure to meet pre-established deadlines, which may have influenced the perception and adoption of agile methods and the creativity of the participants.
- *Homogeneous samples:* of participants were large enough to allow comparisons. However, differences in sample sizes between students and practitioners might have slightly influenced the results. More diverse and heterogeneous groups in terms of academic level and professional experience could improve the results.
- *Lack of an objective assessment instrument:* to pinpoint the participants' understanding of agile concepts and creativity enhancement, as the study was mainly based on self-completed surveys. A more accurate instrument could have been a standardized test, either written or oral, to provide a more objective assessment. The reliance on self-completed surveys introduces the risk of bias in the results, as they are based on the subjective perception of the participants.
- *Prior learning bias:* participants did not all have the same knowledge of agile and creativity prior to the training. These differences in prior knowledge, together with the teaching approach previously received in software development, could have influenced the results.
- *Reliance on gamification:* was perceived positively by all groups of participants, but may not have been the most appropriate strategy for a single individual. Some participants might prefer more traditional learning methods to gamification, which might have influenced their process of learning the concepts of agile and enhancing their creativity. Therefore, designing gamified activities that combine both learning methods, incorporating personalized

methods and adaptive strategies, could improve the results of this study by catering to individual preferences and ensuring a more balanced and effective experience.

- *Variability in the age:* of participants in the same group were relatively close. More diverse and heterogeneous age groups might reflect how generational differences affect the understanding of agile methods, creativity enhancement and willingness towards gamified strategies.
- *Phenomenology as a framework:* would explore participants' lived experiences with gamification, providing a deeper insight into their perceptions, motivations and impact on *creativity*. Furthermore, this qualitative approach would complement the quantitative methods used and provide a holistic understanding of gamification in agile education (Dichev & Dicheva, 2017). Some analyses might be how participants' experiences would vary depending on the weather, seasons or specific environmental conditions.
- *Lack of interdisciplinary integration:* such as psychological theories of intrinsic motivation or educational frameworks such as active learning in this study. This absence may limit participants' deeper understanding, which could be improved by including intrinsic drivers and gamified participatory learning strategies.
- *Technology integration:* not included in this study. Future work could explore how technologies such as Artificial Intelligence (AI) and the Internet of Things (IoT), combined with gamified approaches, could extend personalization capabilities and simulate real-world collaborative scenarios, driving innovation in agile learning and fostering creativity in software development.

All limitations identified in this study are associated with the contextual and educational factors of the participants, which may have influenced the assessment of their learning of the concepts of agile and creativity in software development.

Notwithstanding these constraints, the findings can be deemed reliable, as there is evidence to suggest that they are. For instance, enhanced comprehension of agile principles is positively correlated with the participants' level of software development expertise (Topping, 2003). To mitigate these limitations, the surveys utilized have been made accessible to future researchers, enabling their integration into their case studies. However, the following subsection describes the threats to the validity of this study.

Threats to Validity

The following section delineates the principal threats to the validity of this study, as categorized by (Wohlin et al., 2012) and presented in a progressive sequence by (Cairns, 2016). This sequence, which progresses from the specifics of the experiment to a broader perspective, offers a structured approach to understanding the potential limitations of this study.

Construct validity pertains to the correlation between the theoretical elements contemplated in each experiment and the observations derived from them. It should be noted that the initial version of the study included only two experiments, rather than the intended six. This was due to the failure to disaggregate the different levels of academic background of the students and the levels of experience of the software development practitioners. However, it was deemed insufficient to rely on two experiments to draw conclusions about the understanding of agile concepts and the enhancement of creativity in students and software development practitioners. Accordingly, each of these experiments was divided into three sections, based on the participants' varying levels of training and experience. The primary objective was to ascertain whether the levels of education and work experience impacted the acquisition of agile concepts and creativity enhancement, and whether there were variations in the other experiments conducted.

In this sense, the approach of several experiments for students and practitioners could, in fact, constitute a threat to the construct validity of the research. A single experiment conducted with students and a single experiment conducted with practitioners would be insufficient to demonstrate the full range of implications associated with a specific concept.

Internal validity is concerned with the issue of causality, namely the extent to which the treatment of the data can be considered to have led to the result obtained. This represents a significant threat to the validity of the research. In this study, such validity is specifically defined as the relationship between the use of the DesignScrum educational resource and progress in understanding agile concepts and fostering creativity. By introducing these concepts, the resource made it possible to reliably assess learning differences between groups of students and practitioners. The experiments comprised the implementation of an educational resource designed to foster agility and creativity, designated as DesignScrum. The resource comprises the construction of a LEGO block structure free of charge, which simulates the various scenarios that commonly arise in a genuine software project.

To reduce the threats that could jeopardize the results, several preventive measures were implemented. One was to provide participants with a comprehensive manual, which described step-by-step the various stages and techniques of the educational resource. This manual helped to offset the effect of the learning experience that participants could acquire as the experiment progressed. It also offered the possibility of requesting support from both the game facilitator and their peers. In essence, the manual was designed as a resource to balance the participants' experience in agile software project management with their creative and building skills, as represented by the LEGO block structure. This supported that differences in prior experience did not unduly affect the outcomes, thereby reinforcing the internal validity of the study.

Another preventive measure was that the experiments were conducted in such a way as to ensure that the participants were divided into homogeneous groups, thus supporting the validity of the results. This was achieved by giving each participant cards with values from 1 to 4, representing their joint level of knowledge in agile and creativity, with the highest and lowest level of knowledge corresponding to the highest and lowest number. They then swapped the cards to match their actual level. The final groups were made up of participants with different numerical values.

The majority of the students and practitioners lacked prior experience with agile methods. Creativity, and the concepts pertinent to the experiment, with the exception of the mid-level and senior practitioners who possessed knowledge of agile methods. Therefore, prior training was provided consisting of a one-hour masterclass on the concepts of agile, creativity and the steps to be followed in the educational resource. The training was given by one of the researchers in this chapter who has teaching experience in the subject, and participants' questions were also answered. This was done to encourage that all participants had a basic understanding of how to develop the resource. Furthermore, all students and practitioners who took part in the experiments were based in the Madrid region, which served to minimize the impact of factors associated with geographical location. It was decided that students with computer-related studies and simultaneous work experience in software development should be excluded from the experiments. This was done in order to avoid confusion about whether to assign them to a group of students or practitioners.

All experiments were conducted with the same educational resource, which could be perceived as a potential threat to internal validity. However, the exclusive use of DesignScrum, a gamified resource based on LEGO blocks, was an intentional decision to minimize unintentional complexity, without compromising the quality of the concepts acquired. In addition, the complexity was further reduced with the masterclass and the step-by-step manual of the resource. This approach also helped to avoid participant fatigue, as these concepts are not learned immediately.

Regarding the experiments, the educational resource represents a significant challenge, even for students who are accustomed to learning and for practitioners who are regularly engaged with software development. This may have detracted from the primary objective, which was to educate students in the application of agile methods and techniques in a manner that fosters creativity within software development teams. However, these challenges were integrated into the design of the resource to simulate real-world scenarios, supporting that the results reflect practical rather than exclusively theoretical knowledge. It is acknowledged that the experiments conducted with software development practitioners were limited to those with middle grade. higher grade and university degree degrees in computer-related fields. It would be preferable, in an ideal scenario, to extend the experiments to students from other academic backgrounds. However, this was constrained by limitations in access to a more diverse and representative sample of participants.

Future versions of this study could be conducted with a larger number of experiments. For example, students and practitioners from other geographical locations, where the pedagogical and working practices may differ, could be included.

To promote the integrity of the experiment, all participants were situated in the same room throughout the teaching and learning process and used identical materials. The fact that the author of this study was a teacher of some students during the 2023/2024 academic year does not seem to have posed a risk of demotivation, which could have occurred given the limited number of participants in the educational resource. All the aforementioned students took part in the experiment, which focused on the middle and higher grades, as well as the university degree groups, which had previously collaborated.

Conclusion validity is linked to obtaining a concrete result from the processing of the data that has been applied. It is the firm conviction of these researchers that the statistical analysis carried out in this study is accurate and reliable. In fact, the second version of this work represents a significant extension of the original. These changes serve to reinforce our confidence in the complete impartiality of the analysis. In addition, the surveys used in the experiments have made it possible to measure all the essential indicators.

The results obtained from the analysis of the surveys, together with the observation of the experts during the experiments, showed that the concepts were indeed well understood. It can therefore be concluded that the lack of prior understanding of the concepts did not threaten the validity of the experiments. On the other hand, it is acknowledged that it would have been interesting to compare these data with the results of other studies and that this was not possible due to the unavailability of certain data from these studies.

Finally, **external validity** refers to the applicability of the results to other contexts. Unfortunately, as noted above, the size and nature of the participant groups make it impossible to claim that the results are applicable to other contexts. This means that it cannot be concluded that the understanding of agile concepts and the enhancement of creativity varies according to the educational level of the computer science students and the previous experience of the software development practitioner. In fact, in terms of the scope of the experiments, this study could only be applied to contexts within the field of computer science. Therefore, no conclusions can be drawn about its applicability to other disciplines that require an agile and creative collaborative environment. However, it is believed that this study can be extrapolated to other non-computing academic and work contexts because it integrates the theoretical-practical teaching method that is widely used to train students and practitioners who require agile and creative skills. To this end, the main conclusions of the study are presented in the following section for ease of understanding.

CONCLUSIONS

The aim of this study was to demonstrate that understanding agile methods and techniques is compatible and synergistic with enhancing creativity in software development teams. To achieve this goal, six experiments were designed involving different groups of students and software development practitioners. These experiments used DesignScrum, an agile educational resource that enhances creativity through a playful approach.

The analysis of the data shows that creativity is more significantly enhanced in university students, as this level of academic training promotes critical and analytical thinking. It was also found that students at lower academic levels showed greater creativity than practitioners, despite having less knowledge of software development. This may be due to the fact that at a younger age, creativity is often less constrained by social norms and the limitations imposed by experience. In fact, the results suggest a decline in creativity with increasing practitioner experience, as developers tend to focus more on technical aspects over time, which may lead to the neglect of the creative skills fostered in the early stages of education.

The results also show that the understanding of agile concepts is higher among software development practitioners than among students. This is due to their continuous exposure to real projects, which gives them a greater ability to adapt to unforeseen situations. Understanding of agile principles increases with practitioner experience, as developers become more familiar with the changing dynamics of software development. However, it was observed that this understanding decreases with students from lower academic backgrounds, who have less exposure to the dynamic environments that characterize the software industry.

The groups who had previously collaborated demonstrated a more pronounced enhancement in both creativity and comprehension of agile principles. This phenomenon can be attributed to the fact that familiarity among the participants enabled a more relaxed and productive exchange, which in turn led to an increase in idea generation, more effective communication and more agile conflict resolution.

Experiments show that it is possible to simultaneously improve creativity and understanding of agile concepts in software development by using appropriate tools. This approach offers combined benefits, making it a promising methodology for teaching in this field. Furthermore, all participating groups recognized gamification as an effective learning strategy, highlighting an increase in motivation and satisfaction with the teaching-learning process.

However. further experiments are needed to further explore the factors that influence the understanding of agile concepts and the enhancement of creativity. In this regard, further experiments are planned to address the limitations of this study, including those related.

ACKNOWLEDGEMENT

This work has been partially funded by the Spanish Ministry of Science and Innovation through the SerDigital project (PID2020-117244RB-I00), the European Commission through the SIC-SPAIN 4.0 project (Safer Internet Centre - Spain 4.0) the Regional Government of Madrid through the DESAFíO-CM project (TEC-2024/COM-235).

REFERENCES

Aldave, A., Vara, J. M., Granada, D., & Marcos, E. (2019). Leveraging creativity in requirements elicitation within agile software development: A systematic literature review. *Journal of Systems and Software, 157*, 110396. DOI: 10.1016/j.jss.2019.110396

Amabile, T. M. (2018). Creativity. In *Context: Update to the social psychology of creativity*. Routledge. DOI: 10.4324/9780429501234-2

Ammons, B., & Bansal, S. K. (2017). Scrumify: A software game to introduce agile software development methods. *Journal of Engineering Education Transformations, 30*(Special Issue).

Basten, D. (2017). Gamification. *IEEE Software, 34*(5), 76–81. DOI: 10.1109/MS.2017.3571581

Beck, K. (2000). *Extreme Programming Explained: Embrace Change*. Addison-Wesley Professional.

Beraza, I. L., Vara, J. M., Granada, D., Gómez, C., & Pérez-Blanco, F. J. (2023). On the Impact of Project Management Certification for Software Projects and Practitioners. [IEEE Software.]. *IEEE Software, 40*(5), 100–107. DOI: 10.1109/MS.2023.3286118

Bergin, J., & Grossman, F. (2006). Extreme construction: Making agile accessible. *AGILE 2006 (AGILE'06)*, 6 pp. – 389.

Brown, T. (2009). *Change by design: How design thinking creates new alternatives for business and society*. Collins Business.

Brown, T., & Katz, B. (2011). Change By Design. *Journal of Product Innovation Management, 28*(3), 381–383. DOI: 10.1111/j.1540-5885.2011.00806.x

Burrows, M. (2021). *Agendashift: Outcome-oriented change and continuous transformation* (2nd ed.). New Generation Publishing.

Cairns, P. A. (2016). Experimental methods in Human-Computer Interaction. In Soedergaard, M., & Dam, R. (Eds.), *Encylopedia of Human-Computer Interaction* (2nd ed.). Interaction Design Foundation.

Campbell, D. T., & Stanley, J. C. (2015). *Experimental and Quasi-Experimental Designs for Research*. Ravenio Books.

Cohen, L., Lawrence, M., & Morrison, K. (2017). *Research Methods in Education* (8th ed.). Routledge. DOI: 10.4324/9781315456539

Collings, D. G., Mellahi, K., & Cascio, W. F. (2017). *The Oxford Handbook of Talent Management* (1st ed.). Oxford University Press. DOI: 10.1093/oxfordhb/9780198758273.001.0001

Deci, E. L., & Ryan, R. M. (2000). The "what" and "why" of goal pursuits: Human needs and the self-determination of behavior. *Psychological Inquiry*, *11*(4), 227–268. DOI: 10.1207/S15327965PLI1104_01

Deterding, S., Dixon, D., Khaled, R., & Nacke, L. (2011). From game design elements to gamefulness: Defining "gamification." *Proceedings of the 15th International Academic MindTrek Conference: Envisioning Future Media Environments*, 9–15. DOI: 10.1145/2181037.2181040

Dichev, C., & Dicheva, D. (2017). Gamifying education: What is known, what is believed and what remains uncertain: A critical review. *International Journal of Educational Technology in Higher Education*, *14*(1), 36. DOI: 10.1186/s41239-017-0042-5

Diniz De Souza, A., Duarte Seabra, R., Marinho Ribeiro, J., & Da, S. Rodrigues, L. E. (2017). SCRUMI: A Board Serious Virtual Game for Teaching the SCRUM Framework. *2017 IEEE/ACM 39th International Conference on Software Engineering Companion (ICSE-C)*, 319–321.

Elbanna, A., & Sarker, S. (2016). The Risks of Agile Software Development: Learning from Adopters. *IEEE Software*, *33*(5), 72–79. DOI: 10.1109/MS.2015.150

Fernandes, J. M., & Sousa, S. M. (2010). PlayScrum—A Card Game to Learn the Scrum Agile Method. *2010 Second International Conference on Games and Virtual Worlds for Serious Applications*, 52–59. DOI: 10.1109/VS-GAMES.2010.24

Fisher, R. A. (1921). *014: On the" Probable Error" of a Coefficient of Correlation Deduced from a Small Sample.*

Fleiss, J. L. (2011). *Design and Analysis of Clinical Experiments*. John Wiley & Sons.

Fowler, F. J. (1995). Improving Survey Questions: Design and Evaluation. *Sage (Atlanta, Ga.).*

Freund, R. J., & Wilson, W. J. (2003). *Statistical Methods*. Elsevier.

Frick, E., Tardini, S., & Cantoni, L. (2014). Lego Serious Play applications to enhance creativity in participatory design. *Creativity in Business. Research Papers on Knowledge. Innovation and Enterprise*, *2*, 200–210.

Frydenberg, M., Yates, D., & Kukesh, J. (2018). Sprint, then Fly: Teaching Agile Methodologies with Paper Airplanes. *Information Systems Education Journal, 16*(5), 22.

Gutierrez, G., Garzás, J., Gonzalez de Lena, M. T., & Moguerza, J. M. (2019). Self-Managing: An Empirical Study of the Practice in Agile Teams. *IEEE Software, 36*(1), 23–27. DOI: 10.1109/MS.2018.2874324

Hamari, J., Koivisto, J., & Sarsa, H. (2014). Does Gamification Work? — A Literature Review of Empirical Studies on Gamification. *2014 47th Hawaii International Conference on System Sciences*, 3025–3034.

Hammarberg, M., & Sunden, J. (2014). *Kanban in action*. Manning Publications Co.

Hoda, R., Salleh, N., & Grundy, J. (2018). The Rise and Evolution of Agile Software Development. *IEEE Software, 35*(5), 58–63. DOI: 10.1109/MS.2018.290111318

Hof, S., Kropp, M., & Landolt, M. (2017). Use of Gamification to Teach Agile Values and Collaboration: A multi-week Scrum simulation project in an undergraduate software engineering course. *Proceedings of the 2017 ACM Conference on Innovation and Technology in Computer Science Education*, 323–328. DOI: 10.1145/3059009.3059043

Hugos, M. (2012). *Enterprise Games: Using Game Mechanics to Build a Better Business*. O'Reilly Media, Inc.

Kapp, K. M. (2012). *The Gamification of Learning and Instruction: Game-based Methods and Strategies for Training and Education*. John Wiley & Sons.

Kaufman, J., & Beghetto, R. (2009). Beyond Big and Little: The Four C Model of Creativity. *Review of General Psychology, 13*(1), 1–12. DOI: 10.1037/a0013688

Kish, L. (1978). Some statistical problems in research design. In *Research Design*. Routledge.

Kolb, D. A. (2014). *Experiential Learning: Experience as the source of learning and Development*. FT press.

Koo, T. K., & Li, M. Y. (2016). A Guideline of Selecting and Reporting Intraclass Correlation Coefficients for Reliability Research. *Journal of Chiropractic Medicine, 15*(2), 155–163. DOI: 10.1016/j.jcm.2016.02.012 PMID: 27330520

Krivitsky, A. (2017). *lego4scrum: A complete guide to #lego4scrum - a great way to teach the Scrum framework and Agile thinking*.

Kupiainen, E., Mäntylä, M. V., & Itkonen, J. (2015). Using metrics in Agile and Lean Software Development – A systematic literature review of industrial studies. *Information and Software Technology*, *62*, 143–163. DOI: 10.1016/j.infsof.2015.02.005

Manifesto, A. (2001). *Manifesto for Agile Software Development*.

May, J., York, J., & Lending, D. (2016). Play Ball: Bringing Scrum into the Classroom. *Journal of Information Systems Education*, *27*(2), 87–92.

McGraw, K. O., & Wong, S. P. (1996). Forming inferences about some intraclass correlation coefficients. *Psychological Methods*, *1*(1), 30–46. DOI: 10.1037/1082-989X.1.1.30

Morschheuser, B., Hassan, L., Werder, K., & Hamari, J. (2018). How to design gamification? A method for engineering gamified software. *Information and Software Technology*, *95*, 219–237. DOI: 10.1016/j.infsof.2017.10.015

Nicholson, S. (2015). A recipe for meaningful gamification. In Reiners, T., & Wood, L. C. (Eds.), *Gamification in Education and Business* (pp. 1–20). Springer. DOI: 10.1007/978-3-319-10208-5_1

Norman, D. (2013). *The Design of Everyday Things: Revised and Expanded Edition*. Basic books.

Paasivaara, M., Heikkilä, V., Lassenius, C., & Toivola, T. (2014). Teaching students scrum using LEGO blocks. *Companion Proceedings of the 36th International Conference on Software Engineering*, 382–391.

Pedreira, O., García, F., Brisaboa, N., & Piattini, M. (2015). Gamification in software engineering – A systematic mapping. *Information and Software Technology*, *57*, 157–168. DOI: 10.1016/j.infsof.2014.08.007

Peeters, V., & Van Cauwenberghe, P. (2003). *The XP Game Explained*. Addison-Wesley.

Potineni, S., Bansal, S. K., & Amresh, A. (2013). ScrumTutor: A web-based interactive tutorial for Scrum Software development. *2013 International Conference on Advances in Computing, Communications and Informatics (ICACCI)*, 1884–1890. DOI: 10.1109/ICACCI.2013.6637469

Rodriguez, G., Soria, Á., & Campo, M. (2015). Virtual Scrum: A teaching aid to introduce undergraduate software engineering students to scrum. *Computer Applications in Engineering Education*, *23*(1), 147–156. DOI: 10.1002/cae.21588

Schroeder, A., Klarl, A., Mayer, P., & Kroiß, C. (2012). Teaching agile software development through lab courses. *Proceedings of the 2012 IEEE Global Engineering Education Conference (EDUCON)*, 1–10. DOI: 10.1109/EDUCON.2012.6201194

Schwaber, K., & Sutherland, J. (2020, November). *The Scrum Guide-The Definitive Guide to Scrum: The Rules of the Game*. Scrum.org.

Sibona, C., Pourreza, S., & Hill, S. (2018). Origami: An Active Learning Exercise for Scrum Project Management. *Journal of Information Systems Education*, *29*(2), 105–116.

Solinski, A., & Petersen, K. (2016). Prioritizing agile benefits and limitations in relation to practice usage. *Software Quality Journal*, *24*(2), 447–482. DOI: 10.1007/s11219-014-9253-3

Srivastava, A., Bhardwaj, S., & Saraswat, S. (2017). SCRUM model for agile methodology. *2017 International Conference on Computing, Communication and Automation (ICCCA)*, 864–869. DOI: 10.1109/CCAA.2017.8229928

Stanford d.school. (n.d.). *An introduction to design thinking process guide*. Hasso Plattner Institute of Design at Stanford.

Stickdorn, M., Hormess, M. E., Lawrence, A., & Schneider, J. (2018). *This Is Service Design Doing*. O'Reilly Media, Inc.

Topping, K. (2003). Self and Peer Assessment in School and University: Reliability, Validity and Utility. In Segers, M., Dochy, F., & Cascallar, E. (Eds.), *Optimising New Modes of Assessment: In Search of Qualities and Standards* (pp. 55–87). Springer Netherlands. DOI: 10.1007/0-306-48125-1_4

Villarrubia, C., Vara, J. M., Granada, D., Gómez-Macías, C., & Pérez-Blanco, F. J. (2024). DesignScrum–An agility educational resource powered by creativity. *Software, Practice & Experience*, *54*(6), 985–1009. DOI: 10.1002/spe.3308

Von Wangenheim, C. G., Savi, R., & Borgatto, A. F. (2013). SCRUMIA—An educational game for teaching SCRUM in computing courses. *Journal of Systems and Software*, *86*(10), 2675–2687. DOI: 10.1016/j.jss.2013.05.030

Werbach, K., & Hunter, D. (2012). *For the Win: How Game Thinking Can Revolutionize Your Business*. Wharton School Press.

Wohlin, C., Höst, M., & Henningsson, K. (2003). Empirical Research Methods in Software Engineering. In Conradi, R., & Wang, A. I. (Eds.), Lecture Notes in Computer Science: Vol. 2765. *Empirical Methods and Studies in Software Engineering* (pp. 7–23). Springer. DOI: 10.1007/978-3-540-45143-3_2

Wohlin, C., Runeson, P., Höst, M., Ohlsson, M. C., Regnell, B., & Wesslén, A. (2012). *Experimentation in software engineering* (Vol. 236). Springer. DOI: 10.1007/978-3-642-29044-2

KEY TERMS AND DEFINITIONS

Agile education: Application of agile principles in educational environments, where learning is organized in an iterative and flexible way to adapt to the changing needs of learners and the context.

Analysis of Variance (ANOVA): A statistical technique that compares the means of three or more groups to identify significant differences in the data.

Confidence Interval: The range of values within which a population parameter is expected to lie with a specified level of certainty (often 95%).

Creativity in software engineering: Use of innovative approaches and solutions during the software development process, promoting original ideas to overcome technical challenges and improve products or services.

Design Thinking: Creative and collaborative user-centered approach, designed to solve problems in innovative ways through deep understanding of user needs and continuous iteration.

Feedback: In agile methods, the information obtained from users or teams at the end of each iteration or sprint to guide rapid and continuous improvements.

Gamification: A strategy that introduces elements and mechanics into non-game contexts, such as teaching. to increase the motivation, commitment and learning of participants.

Intraclass Correlation Coefficient (ICC): A statistical measure that assesses the consistency or agreement between multiple observers or measurements in a dataset.

Iteration: Cyclical repetition of activities to improve a product or process, based on continuous testing and adjustment.

Scrum: A framework within agile methods used to manage complex projects, promoting teamwork, constant feedback and continuous improvement in iterative cycles called sprints.

Software development: A comprehensive process involving the planning, design, implementation, testing, and maintenance of computer programs and systems, aimed at meeting specific user needs.

Chapter 8
Design Thinking in Practice:
Innovation in the Conceptualization of a Mobile App

José Alfonso Aguilar-Calderón
https://orcid.org/0000-0003-2048-9600
Universidad Autónoma de Sinaloa, Mexico

Carolina Tripp-Barba
https://orcid.org/0000-0002-4811-0247
Universidad Autónoma de Sinaloa, Mexico

Pablo Alfonso Aguilar-Calderón
https://orcid.org/0000-0002-4939-0383
Universidad Autónoma de Sinaloa, Mexico

Pedro Alfonso Aguilar-Calderón
https://orcid.org/0000-0003-3881-909X
Universidad Autónoma de Sinaloa, Mexico

Aníbal Zaldívar-Colado
https://orcid.org/0000-0002-6622-6630
Universidad Autónoma de Sinaloa, Mexico

ABSTRACT

This chapter explores the practical application of Design Thinking in the conceptualization and development of a mobile application tailored to address a real-world case study. By leveraging the iterative and user-centric principles of Design Thinking, the study demonstrates how empathy-driven methodologies can bridge the gap be-

DOI: 10.4018/979-8-3693-9531-8.ch008

tween user needs and technological solutions. The chapter details the step-by-step process, from problem definition and ideation to prototyping and testing, illustrating how each phase contributes to creating a meaningful and functional mobile app. A case study approach is employed to ground the theoretical framework in practical outcomes, showcasing how collaboration, innovation, and adaptability are integrated into the design process. The approach detailed in this chapter contributes to the growing body of knowledge on design methodologies and their transformative impact on technology-driven solutions.

INTRODUCTION

In today's world, where software permeates nearly every aspect of daily life, the ability to create innovative and user-centric solutions has become more critical than ever. The growing complexity of digital environments, evolving user needs, and emerging technologies are reshaping the field of software engineering. Conventional software development methodologies often fall short in addressing the multifaceted challenges presented by this dynamic landscape. This is where cutting-edge Design Thinking (DT) techniques come into play, providing a novel, user-centered perspective that can revolutionize the conceptualization, design, and delivery of software. DT offers a powerful solution by prioritizing empathy, user-centered design, and iterative problem-solving. This methodology emphasizes understanding user needs, fostering creativity, and creating innovative, customer-focused products. Unlike traditional methods focused on technical specifications, DT promotes a comprehensive understanding of the user experience, ensuring both functionality and user satisfaction (Bate, 2019). By integrating diverse expertise from designers, developers, and stakeholders, it leads to the creation of unique, intuitive solutions that align with users' true needs. This can be a solution for the rapid evolution of digital environments and changing user demands have made traditional software development practices increasingly inadequate (Ulrich & Eppinger, 2015).

The relevance of Design Thinking becomes even more pronounced in mobile application development. Mobile apps, which serve as extensions of users' daily lives, require a seamless blend of functionality, usability, and aesthetic appeal. In this context, Design Thinking's iterative process allows teams to quickly test and refine concepts, ensuring that the final product meets user expectations while maintaining technical integrity. Moreover, given the competitive and dynamic nature of the mobile app market, a user-centric approach is essential to stand out and ensure adoption and long-term engagement. Ultimately, the application of Design Thinking in mobile app development facilitates the creation of products that are not only innovative but also relevant and valuable to users (McCord, 2024; Sweeney, 2019). By fostering a deep connection between the user and the technology, it transforms the software development process into a more adaptable, human-centered endeavor, driving both innovation and success in a rapidly evolving digital landscape.

This chapter explores the practical application of Design Thinking in the conceptualization and development of a mobile application tailored to address a real-world case study. Technical details of the development are not considered in this chapter. The iterative and user-centric principles of Design Thinking are leveraged to bridge the gap between user needs and technological solutions. The study demonstrates how empathy-driven methodologies can guide the design process, from problem definition and ideation to prototyping and testing. Through a case study approach, this work grounds theoretical frameworks in practical outcomes, illustrating how collaboration, creativity, and adaptability contribute to successful software development.

The remainder of the chapter is structured as follows: Section Background provides an overview of the contextual and rationale for this proposal, as well as posing key assessment questions; Section Methodology analysis outlines the process conducted, and presents and discusses the findings of the experiments; Section Discussion addresses the study's findings; and finally, Section Conclusions summarizes the main findings obtained through the methodology implemented in this chapter and suggests avenues for future research.

BACKGROUND

This section serves as the introduction to the background of this chapter, detailing the fundamental concepts necessary to understand this research, including Design Thinking, user-centered design, and their application in mobile app development. It explores the practical application of Design Thinking in mobile app development, showcasing real-world examples that highlight its effectiveness in enhancing usability, fostering innovation, and delivering solutions that resonate with diverse user bases.

User-Centered Design

Design Thinking has emerged as a transformative methodology, redefining how user experiences are conceptualized, designed, and delivered. Rooted in empathy and collaboration, this approach places users at the core of the design process, ensuring that every solution aligns with their needs, expectations, and behaviors. The dynamic nature of mobile technology demands innovative strategies to address complex challenges, and Design Thinking offers a structured yet flexible framework to achieve this. By integrating principles of user-centered design, developers can create applications that are not only functional but also intuitive and impactful.

User-Centered Design (UCD), also known as Human-Centered Design, is a systematic approach that prioritizes the needs and experiences of the user at every stage of the product or service development process (Norman, 2013). This approach often ensures that the final solutions are not only functional but also intuitive and appealing to the end user.

When applying UCD principles, the process begins with the premise that the product is not designed based on a simple idea with the hope that it will attract the users we think will buy it. From the outset, the aim is to create a product or service that genuinely addresses a user need or expectation. To achieve this, it is crucial to place users at the center of the design process while striving for greater usability and enriched experiences. Adopting a UCD approach requires a deep understanding of users, their needs, and their context. Moreover, it is vital to conduct constant user testing to refine the product or service. The scientific literature suggests forming interdisciplinary teams that integrate knowledge from fields such as design, psychology, and technology to achieve more effective, user-centered design outcomes (Chesbrough, 2003).

For illustrative purposes, consider an example of user-centered design: a mobile application launched by a social security service to allow beneficiaries to schedule medical appointments. Although the app initially experienced high demand, complaints about its functionality arose, usage began to decline, and the number of downloads decreased. To address this, the design and development team conducted interviews and observations with beneficiaries to understand their interactions and the challenges they faced while using the app. They discovered difficulties in finding functionalities and scheduling appointments efficiently, which was particularly problematic given the app's diverse user demographic (ranging from 18 to over 70 years old). Applying UCD in this example—even before the app's launch—would have allowed the team to focus on users from the start and throughout the design process, resulting in a more meaningful product for beneficiaries. This approach would have ensured a more effective and valuable application for users instead of focusing solely on the appointment scheduling service.

In the field of User Experience (UX), a commonly used illustration highlights the concept of user-centered design. To reinforce the UCD concept introduced earlier, consider the example of a ketchup bottle, particularly the one from Henry J. Heinz. Figure 1 shows, on the left, a design that could be considered practical and easy to use—a glass bottle reflecting the vision of a product designer who valued simplicity and transparency so users could see the product inside. However, this presentation frustrated some users because they needed to tap the bottle at a specific spot or shake it to dispense the product—a detail overlooked for most users. This issue led to the redesign of the ketchup bottle into the Heinz inverted bottle, patented as U.S. Patent US20040088883A1 (Norman, 2013). The patent describes a container stored upside down to facilitate dispensing. Heinz officially launched the inverted bottle in 2002, which is considered an example of user-centered design, as it resolved the problem of easily extracting the product. By changing the product's presentation, the design improved users' lives in simple yet impactful ways, such as making it easier and faster to serve ketchup.

Figure 1. Example of User-Centered Design (Norman, 2013).

It is essential not to confuse UCD with designing for humans. What is important to one person may not be to another because we all have different needs. This highlights the importance of focusing on the user, not the human.

Delving further, Design Thinking (DT) is a human-centered design approach that focuses on understanding the needs, desires, and experiences of the individuals involved. While it shares the user-centric perspective of UCD, it also considers all individuals affected by a solution, including social and emotional aspects. This method emphasizes empathy and multidisciplinary collaboration to generate innovative solutions (Stickdorn & Schneider, 2011). By focusing on users from the beginning and throughout the design process, Design Thinking ensures that products and services are relevant, functional, and satisfying for them. While the process of idea and project selection should follow a defined sequence, the innovation process must remain flexible. Each phase can be informed by reflections and progress, allowing for adjustments at any point in the process.

Design Thinking in a Nutshell

Design Thinking is a human-centered approach to innovation and problem-solving, structured into five key phases. Each phase plays a crucial role in developing solutions that are both user-centric and effective. Here's an overview of the Design Thinking phases (Garner, 2017):

1. Empathize. Gain a deep understanding of the users, their needs, challenges, and experiences. This is done by conducting user interviews, observations, and surveys. Engage in immersive experiences to see the world from the user's perspective. Use tools like empathy maps to visualize user insights.
2. Define. Clearly articulate the problem based on the insights gathered in the Empathize phase. Synthesize findings from the Empathize phase to identify core user needs. Formulate a clear problem statement or Point of View (POV) that guides the design process. Use tools like affinity diagrams to group and prioritize insights.
3. Ideate. Generate a wide range of creative ideas to address the defined problem. Facilitate brainstorming sessions to encourage free-flowing idea generation. Use techniques like mind mapping, SCAMPER, and "How Might We" questions to explore solutions. Focus on quantity over quality initially, encouraging out-of-the-box thinking.
4. Prototype. Create tangible representations of the ideas to explore their feasibility and gather feedback. Develop low-fidelity prototypes (e.g., sketches, wireframes) to quickly test ideas. Gradually build higher-fidelity prototypes as concepts are refined. Utilize tools like paper prototypes, digital mockups, or even simple physical models.
5. Test. Validate the prototypes with real users to gather feedback and refine the solution. Conduct usability testing and observe how users interact with the prototype. Gather qualitative and quantitative feedback to identify strengths and weaknesses. Iterate on the design based on user feedback, repeating the prototype and test cycles as necessary.

Design Thinking is inherently iterative, meaning these phases are often revisited as new insights and feedback emerge. This flexibility allows for continuous improvement and adaptation to user needs, leading to more innovative and effective solutions (Garner, 2017). By systematically applying these phases, teams can create mobile applications that are not only functional but deeply resonate with their intended users.

Design Thinking in Mobile App Development: Real-World Applications

Design Thinking is a human-centered methodology widely recognized for its ability to foster innovative solutions in various industries, including mobile app development. This methodology emphasizes empathy, creativity, and iteration, making it particularly well-suited for addressing user needs in the rapidly evolving landscape of mobile technology (Stanford, 2024). Below are real-world examples of how Design Thinking has been successfully applied in mobile app development.

1. Airbnb: Redesigning the User Experience

One of the most notable applications of Design Thinking in app development is Airbnb. In its early years, the platform struggled with low traction and user dissatisfaction. By applying Design Thinking, Airbnb's founders refocused their efforts on understanding user needs (Rivera, 2024).

- Empathy: The team conducted interviews and observed users to identify pain points. Hosts found it difficult to showcase their properties effectively, and potential guests struggled with the lack of detailed, appealing property listings.
- Define: The core problem was identified as the lack of trust and clarity in the user experience.
- Ideate: Airbnb's team brainstormed solutions, including professional photography services for hosts and enhanced search filters for guests.
- Prototype: They tested a prototype that included high-quality property images and a streamlined booking process.
- Test: Through user feedback, they refined the app, eventually launching features that significantly improved usability and trust. Today, Airbnb's mobile app is a cornerstone of its global success, with millions of active users.

2. Uber: Simplifying Mobility

Uber revolutionized urban transportation by using Design Thinking principles to address common challenges like availability, affordability, and convenience (Cazac & Vert, 2020).

- Empathy Phase: Uber's founders identified a common frustration: the difficulty of hailing a cab in busy cities. They engaged with users and drivers to understand their challenges.

- Define Phase: The problem was clear: urban commuters needed a fast, reliable, and transparent transportation option.
- Ideate Phase: The team brainstormed features like GPS tracking, upfront pricing, and driver ratings to create trust and transparency.
- Prototype Phase: A prototype was developed and piloted in San Francisco. This allowed the team to test the app in a real-world context.
- Test Phase: Feedback from drivers and riders was used to refine the app's functionality, interface, and reliability. The success of this approach is evident in Uber's global adoption.

This company continues to undergo constant updates, as evidenced by the successful application of Design Thinking in the UberEats app (IvyPanda, 2023).

3. Duolingo: Democratizing Language Learning

Duolingo, a language-learning app, applied Design Thinking to create an engaging, gamified learning experience (Deng, 2024; Amin, 2022).

- Empathy Phase: The development team conducted user interviews and observed how people approached language learning. They discovered that many found traditional methods boring and intimidating.
- Define Phase: The challenge was to create a platform that made language learning fun, accessible, and less time-consuming.
- Ideate Phase: The team explored gamification strategies, including streaks, rewards, and leaderboards, to increase user engagement.
- Prototype Phase: Early versions of the app featured basic lessons and reward systems. These prototypes were tested with a diverse group of users.
- Test Phase: Based on user feedback, the app's design was refined to include daily reminders, progress tracking, and a more intuitive interface. Today, Duolingo is one of the most downloaded educational apps globally.

4. Nike Training Club: Enhancing Fitness Experiences

Nike Training Club (NTC) is another excellent example of Design Thinking in action. The app was developed to provide users with a personalized fitness experience (Nike, 2016).

- Empathy Phase: The Nike team gathered insights from athletes and casual fitness enthusiasts to understand their preferences and challenges.

- Define Phase: The team identified the need for accessible, flexible, and diverse workout options.
- Ideate Phase: Ideas such as customizable workout plans, video tutorials, and progress tracking were proposed.
- Prototype Phase: A prototype was developed with a limited set of workouts and features.
- Test Phase: User feedback led to the addition of features like professional coaching tips, community challenges, and workout reminders. The app now boasts millions of downloads and high user retention.

As demonstrated by the previously mentioned examples, is a fact that applying Design Thinking in mobile app development highlights several key takeaways that underscore its effectiveness. Empathy drives innovation by ensuring that solutions are tailored to user needs, creating a deep resonance with the target audience. Prototyping reduces risks by allowing teams to iteratively test ideas before committing to full-scale development, thus saving time and resources. Continuous feedback enhances usability, as ongoing testing and refinement ensure the product aligns with user expectations and market demands. Design Thinking emerges as a powerful methodology for crafting mobile apps that not only meet functional requirements but also connect with users on a deeper level. By prioritizing empathy and user-centered design throughout the development process, teams can develop solutions that are both practical and meaningful. Real-world successes, such as Airbnb's seamless booking experience and Nike's personalized services, illustrate the efficacy of this approach in fostering innovation and enhancing user satisfaction. Ultimately, Design Thinking bridges the gap between user needs and technological capabilities, producing mobile applications that are intuitive, engaging, and impactful in today's competitive landscape.

METHODOLOGY

This section presents a practical example of the application of Design Thinking (DT) in the conceptualization and development of a real-world mobile application. The section provides an overview of the context in which Design Thinking was applied, followed by a detailed exploration of each of the methodology's stages and how they were executed. As highlighted in the background section of this chapter, there are numerous real-world examples demonstrating the successful application of the DT methodology within the realm of technological innovation, particularly in the development of mobile applications.

The primary objective of applying Design Thinking is to develop a product, service, or business idea. This objective becomes more precisely defined during the definition phase of the process. It is important to emphasize that the development team should not assume a predetermined solution to the problem at the outset; in other words, they should avoid entering the process with a fixed notion of the final product, such as a mobile application. The specifics of the solution will emerge and be clarified during the definition phase, as will be illustrated through this case study. In some instances, Design Thinking is applied when the problem has already been identified, and there is a clear understanding of what needs to be developed—whether a product or a service. However, Design Thinking is equally valuable in scenarios where the problem, product, or service is not yet defined, fostering an environment of creativity and exploration throughout the process (Brown, 2008). The case study provided in this section serves as a practical example of this approach, demonstrating how Design Thinking guided the development of a mobile app from inception to realization. The subsequent subsections will provide a detailed overview of each stage of the Design Thinking process, with the context of the case study explained next.

Context

In Mexico, there is a large and very active touring motorcycling community, specifically within the touring segment (motorcycles prepared for long distances). These enthusiasts commonly organize and participate in events such as road trips, meetups, motorcycle club anniversaries, and festivals. However, the organization, coordination, and promotion of these events are often done in a fragmented and decentralized manner, leading to several challenges for both organizers and participants, including event promotion, publicity, and securing sponsors. On the other hand, independent motorcyclists and motorcycle club members often enjoy traveling to motorcycling events, but it is frequently difficult to find such events due to the lack of a centralized platform for checking event dates. The idea of traveling by motorcycle and enjoying the journey is a common hobby among enthusiasts of these types of events and motorcycles. Unfortunately, in many cases, it is not possible to take these trips because individuals lack the time to organize work and family life effectively. This serves as the initial situation for applying the Design Thinking methodology. This is a real-world scenario, situation, and context within the motorcycling environment that was observed.

Empathize

The first phase of the Design Thinking process is Empathy, or "Empathize." This innovation tool focuses on the user and is used to provide solutions to specific desires or needs of individuals. When designing for others, the first step is to put oneself in their shoes, to understand what is truly relevant to them in the context of their passion for motorcycle travel. The more effectively we adopt their perspective, the easier it becomes to understand them and identify what can truly add value to their experience. In this case, it was not clear whether a product or service that would be of value to motorcyclists could be developed, which is why the task of empathizing and gathering as much information as possible was essential. In other words, the process did not begin with a clear conceptualization or idea of what was to be created from the outset of the case study; the conceptualization that would define the outcome of the Design Thinking application was not yet established.

For this case study, to apply the first phase of Design Thinking, thorough research was conducted using techniques such as observation, interviews, and behavioral analysis to identify the main challenges and desires of the users (motorcyclists). The key stakeholders involved were clearly defined: motorcyclists, event organizers, and motorcycle event enthusiasts. It is important to note that one can be an enthusiast without necessarily owning a motorcycle, which does not prevent attendance at events.

In this phase, information collection is crucial. It is not necessary to be deterministic in selecting what information is deemed important, as it is not yet the time to make such judgments. It is recommended to gather and document all possible information through interviews, focus groups, and on-site observation. In this phase, it is acceptable to record video and audio (with proper consent) from the target group to which the methodology is being applied. Modern technology enables the creation of cloud repositories to store large amounts of information in text, audio, and video formats. For this case study, the information collection techniques (empathy with the user) used were interviews and on-site observation.

To use the interview technique, a series of questions were first defined for the target group (Table 1). Questions were formulated to gather the necessary information and better understand the experiences and opinions of the interviewees (motorcyclists). It is important to note that the questions should be open-ended, avoiding those that can be answered with a simple "yes" or "no." Responses should not be suggested, and attention should be paid to the interviewees' body language. There is no minimum number of interviewees required for this process, but it is recommended to have a representative sample of each previously identified actor (motorcyclist, organizer, and event enthusiast). The most relevant questions for this case study are listed in Table 1. Six categories were defined to cover the entire spectrum of the environment of motorcyclists attending events, these are: travel habits, preparations, event experience, camaraderie, safety-maintenance, and tools or platforms used. An average of three or four questions were defined for each category.

Table 1. Interview Questions (Own Source).

Category	*Question*
Travel Habits	How often do you go on road trips to motorcycle events?
	How do you plan your trips to these events?
	Do you usually travel alone or in a group? Why?
Preparations	What type of information do you search for before heading to a motorcycle event?
	How important is it for you to know the weather or traffic conditions before and during the trip?
	How do you find out about motorcycle events?
Event Experience	What aspects of biker events do you enjoy the most?
	What difficulties have you encountered when arriving at events?
	What types of activities or services do you value the most when attending these events?
Camaraderie (Community Interaction)	How do you stay in contact with other motorcyclists during events?
	Do you participate in online forums or groups related to motorcycling? If so, what do you look for in these communities?
	How important is it for you to share your experiences on social media or on platforms specific to motorcyclists?
Safety and Maintenance	What safety concerns do you have when traveling by motorcycle-to-motorcycle events?
	What type of road assistance or information do you consider essential?
	Have you had any experiences where you needed mechanical or emergency help during a trip? How did you resolve them?
Tools or Platforms Used	What apps or tools do you currently use for your motorcycle trips?
	What do you like and dislike about them?
	What features do you think are missing in these tools that would be useful for you?

The next step in this phase involved conducting on-site observation, both participatory and non-participatory. The observation technique in Design Thinking is crucial for understanding the behavior, needs, and challenges of users within their natural environment. To apply this technique, it is necessary to define the focus of the observation, meaning clarifying which specific aspects of the user's behavior or environment are to be observed. This can include how users interact with a product, engage with a service, or face a particular problem.

The observer can directly engage in the user's activity (participatory observation) or remain an outside observer (non-participatory observation), allowing for a deeper understanding of the user's experiences and challenges. Video cameras can be used, or the observation can take place from a distance. It is recommended that the observation setting be a representative environment of the actual product or service use. Detailed notes should be taken regarding the behavior, encountered problems, and user interactions. Additionally, it is important to observe how users interact with the environment and the product. In this case study, various actors were observed in their environments: within their motorcycle club, at events, during road trips to events, and in the preparation stages for their trips. Specifically, the study observed how the motorcyclist user prepared for a trip to an event, including equipment setup, motorcycle checks, route planning, and obtaining work leave.

The information collected in this phase was stored in the cloud using Google Drive's free service. It was organized into folders corresponding to each phase. Within the folder dedicated to the empathy phase, two subfolders were created: one for interviews and another for observation.

The final step in this phase was the extraction of insights. In Design Thinking, insights are revealing discoveries about users and their needs, behaviors, motivations, and challenges. These insights are gathered through observation, interviews, and other research techniques during the empathy phase. They are crucial because they uncover underlying and often unarticulated aspects that can inspire and guide the design process. A good insight is specific, actionable, and offers a unique perspective that can lead to innovative, user-centered solutions. It is recommended that the insight be no longer than two lines, emphasizing its contribution to the project. Multiple insights can be derived from the gathered and analyzed information. In some cases, techniques like Buyer Persona and Customer Journey Map are employed to identify these insights.

In this example, several findings were discovered, two of which are outlined below to illustrate:

Derived from the collected information, it was noted that a significant number of motorcyclists are unable to plan their motorcycle trips to attend events in advance due to uncertainty about the event dates or because they do not belong to a community or motorcycle club where such events are known. This lack of affiliation affected their confidence in attending long-distance motorcycle trips.

Insight 1: *"Motorcyclists need to know event dates in advance to plan their trips."*

Insight 2: "In addition to preparing their motorcycles for travel to events, motorcyclists seek to belong to a community for support, whether traveling alone or in a group."

Explanation of the Insights:

Through interviews and usage data analysis, it was discovered that most motorcyclists do not attend motorcycle events because they do not know the dates in advance. This uncertainty prevents them from requesting time off from work, organizing their schedules with family or work commitments, saving for the trip, or preparing their motorcycles. The motivation and sense of belonging to a community are as important for motorcycle travel as having a tool where they can consult event information ahead of time. These insights not only identify a problem (not knowing the event dates in advance) but also reveal a deeper need (the need for community and support, even when traveling alone or in a group), which can be addressed to create a more effective and meaningful solution for the users. Insights are crucial for guiding the design and ensuring that the proposed solutions truly meet the users' needs and desires.

It is important to emphasize that in the empathy phase of Design Thinking, real users are interviewed. This stage focuses on deeply understanding users and their experiences, needs, behaviors, and motivations. To achieve this understanding, it is essential to interact with authentic people who actually use the product or service or who may become potential users. Interviews with real users provide genuine and valuable insights, which are fundamental to the user-centered design process. The outcome of this phase is the result of analyzing the information, which leads to the insights.

Finally, the Buyer Persona technique can be implemented, an essential tool in Design Thinking that helps organizations gain a deep understanding of their users or customers. It is a semi-fictional representation of the ideal customer, built from real data and well-grounded assumptions obtained from the empathy phase. Below is an example of a Buyer Persona in Design Thinking, as shown in Fig. 2:

Figure 2. Buyer Persona. Source: Own, Design: Canva.

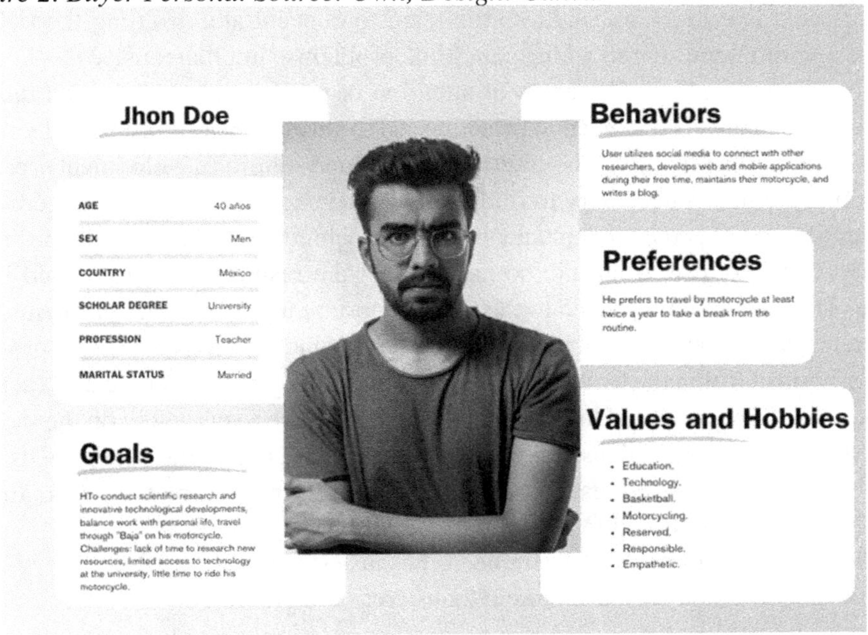

Using this profile, the Design Thinking team can design solutions that specifically address José's challenges and align with his values and goals, thus ensuring greater relevance and effectiveness of the proposed solutions. This is an example of a Buyer Persona that can be used in the following phases of Design Thinking; one or more can be created. In this example, only one was created, but it utilized real information from the interviewed users and their profiles (approximately 78 motorcyclists). The Buyer Persona technique can be used in software, such as Canva, which offers a range of customizable templates, some of which are free and others available for a fee due to more detailed features.

Define

In the definition phase, it is crucial to delineate the problem statement from the user's perspective. This allows the identification of the root cause of the problem, avoiding assumptions, and focusing on the user's needs. To achieve this, problem statements are used to guide the design process.

The insights gathered during the empathy phase are analyzed and synthesized to identify patterns and common themes. These are transformed into a clear and concise problem statement, which guides the subsequent phases of the process. By identifying Focus Areas, it becomes easier to generate specific solutions. Defining a focus area is critical, as it allows the team to concentrate, avoiding the risk of digressing or attempting to address multiple problems simultaneously.

Focus Areas are specific areas of attention or critical points identified during research and analysis that need to be addressed to solve the user's problem. Derived from insights, these focus areas guide the ideation and solution development process. To define them, it is necessary to find a phrase that captures the relevant needs and desires of the user and to understand the reasons behind them. They should be broad enough to be addressed but not so narrow that the resulting solutions hold little value. They are directly related to the most important user needs and problems, are concrete, and can be tackled with feasible strategies and solutions within the project.

To begin defining the focus areas, it is necessary to focus on a single user (actor). In the case study presented to the reader in this book, we focus solely on the motorcyclist user. It is essential, as we repeat, to clearly understand the user's needs and consider any new revelations that may emerge from synthesizing the information.

The focus areas should follow this structure:

The (user) desires/needs (desire/need) because (insight).

For this case study, three example focus areas are presented:

1. Motorcyclists need to know important details about motorcycle events in Mexico, such as the date, location, schedules, and registration, because they need to organize their work and personal schedules in advance.
2. Motorcyclists need to know important details about motorcycle events in Mexico, such as the date, location, schedules, and registration, because they have realized they need to plan a safe and efficient route, including rest stops and service stations.
3. Motorcyclists need to know the event dates in advance to ensure their motorcycle is in optimal condition for the trip, including necessary maintenance and equipment.

Once the focus areas were defined, the next step was to verify whether they would lead to useful and attractive ideas by applying a checklist. The checklist consisted of a series of questions: What is the problem being addressed? What are the insights? What is the quality of the information gathered to define them? How was the information collected? How does it fit into the user context? Is it inspiring for the Design Thinking team? The answers to these questions must be fully satisfactory for the team to consider the focus areas as valid.

It is important to mention that multiple focus areas can be identified. However, one should be selected initially to address. While it is possible to work on more than one, doing so will significantly increase the complexity and scope of the project.

The next step involved defining the creative challenge. The creative challenge in Design Thinking is a clear statement of the problem or challenge that needs to be solved. This challenge serves as the starting point for the ideation process and must be formulated in a way that inspires creativity and the generation of innovative ideas. A good creative challenge should be specific, relevant to users, and open to multiple possible solutions. To define it, the following structure is commonly used:

"How might we improve X?"

In this case study, the following creative challenge was defined for focus area number 1:

"How might we provide motorcyclists with an easy and efficient way to access detailed information about motorcycle events in Mexico, including the date, location, schedules, and registration, so that they can plan their work and personal schedules in advance?"

The challenge focused on addressing the specific needs of motorcyclists, who face unique challenges when planning and undertaking their trips. Unlike other modes of transportation, motorcyclists must consider factors such as weather conditions, road conditions, the accessibility of safe routes, the availability of service stations, and the location of rest points, among other key aspects that influence their safety and comfort. Therefore, this challenge is highly relevant to improving their travel experience by providing solutions that facilitate access to the necessary information to make informed decisions before and during their journey.

Ideate

The third phase of the Design Thinking process is Ideation (also known as the "Idea" phase in some texts). This stage is often the most enjoyable for the team, as it marks the beginning of generating solutions for the problems identified. After the effort spent in the previous phases to understand the user and organize the information into focus areas to define creative challenges, the goal now is to develop and explore innovative solutions.

In the third phase of the Design Thinking methodology, it is recommended to use the brainstorming technique. In the context of this methodology, it is an idea-generation method designed to stimulate creativity and uncover innovative solutions to the identified problems. To implement this technique effectively, it is crucial to have a Design Thinking expert, who must have a deep understanding of the methodology and play a critical role in the process. Although the expert does not select the best idea or define the focus area, their responsibility is to motivate the team and guide them through the application of the methodology. Below is a guide used in the case study presented in this book, which is detailed in [50]:

1. Objective: To produce a wide variety of ideas without immediately evaluating them, thus encouraging creativity and the exploration of innovative solutions.
2. Participants: The process includes the Design Thinking team, composed of a diverse group of individuals who bring different perspectives and skills, thus enriching the creative process. The greater the diversity of team members, the better the outcome.
3. Basic Rules:
    a. All ideas are accepted without criticism to avoid stifling creativity.
    b. The goal is to generate as many ideas as possible, based on the premise that quality can improve with quantity.
    c. Participants can expand and refine ideas proposed by others.
    d. Divergent thinking is encouraged, as well as exploring unconventional approaches.
4. Process: Brainstorming can be conducted using various techniques, such as using post its, creating mind maps, or utilizing digital tools. The process is led by a facilitator who ensures that the session is efficient and productive.
5. Results: At the end of the session, the generated ideas are organized, evaluated, and selected for future development.

In this case, the brainstorming technique was used with colored post its. First, a suitable space was selected, providing comfort and minimal distractions for the team. The furniture consisted of chairs and tables arranged in an auditorium-style format. At the front, a whiteboard was placed, where the creative challenge was written using colored markers. The facilitator explained the brainstorming dynamics to the Design Thinking team, composed of members from various areas of the company. The inclusion of different perspectives is key, as diversity in thinking and challenging the status quo are essential for an innovative methodology.

Before starting the session, the team was instructed on the importance of generating a large number of ideas, encouraging creativity without restrictions. Emphasis was placed on enjoying the process, fostering bold ideas, and avoiding judgment or ridicule of others' proposals. During the session, each participant contributed ideas to address the creative challenge. At the end, the ideas were grouped based on their similarities, using colored Post-its to facilitate organization. Approximately 54 ideas were generated, of which only two were selected. This decision was made because the implementation of the selected ideas could address several of the users' needs. The ideas selected for prototyping were as follows:

- A mobile application that announces all motorcycle events in Mexico. This idea had the greatest impact because there is currently no such app.

- A Facebook page to create a community of motorcyclists around the mobile app, serving as support for both independent motorcyclists and members of motorcycle clubs or associations. The mobile app was complemented with a community through a fan page to announce motorcycle events and news in Mexico. This idea was chosen as a complement to the previous one because, while groups exist, there is no exclusive nonprofit page for all states in the country.

Prototyping

The fourth step in Design Thinking is the prototyping phase. As described in Chapter 2 of this book, this phase involves creating tangible or intangible models of the products to be developed. Prototyping is a dynamic and creative phase that allows ideas to be tested quickly, errors to be learned from, and solutions to be refined before committing significant resources to final development. Specifically, this phase focuses on creating tangible or representative versions of the ideas generated during the ideation phase. The main goal is to transform abstract concepts into prototypes that can be evaluated and refined through interaction with real users.

The central idea of this phase is to build the simplest possible prototype that is very easy to use. It is not necessary to dedicate significant effort to complex prototypes, as they will simply be modified during the testing phase. It is common to have at least six or seven iterations between prototyping and user testing, meaning that the prototype will be modified at least six or seven times. For this reason, software tools and maker-type tools, such as InVision and Lego, are used to build prototypes. This topic will be discussed in greater detail in the next chapter.

There are some steps to carry out this phase in an organized manner, which are: 1) select the ideas to prototype, 2) define the prototype's level of fidelity, 3) build the prototype. These steps are detailed below in the context of the example presented.

1. Select the Ideas to Prototype. As mentioned earlier, not all ideas generated in the ideation phase will be prototyped because the project and application of the methodology would be endless. The Design Thinking team must select the most promising ideas or those that best address the previously defined action points. For this example, the selected ideas were:
   i. A mobile application to announce all motorcycle events in Mexico.
   ii. A Facebook page to create a community of motorcyclists around the mobile app, serving as support for independent motorcyclists and members of a motorcycle club or association.

2. Define the Prototype's Level of Fidelity. Depending on the prototype's objective, low-fidelity versions (simple sketches, wireframes, mockups) or high-fidelity versions (nearly final models, functional software) can be created. In the early stages, low-fidelity prototypes are often more effective because they allow for quick and inexpensive changes. For this example, this option was selected by constructing Mockups, which are a visual representation of the user interface of an application, website, or any other digital product. Unlike wireframes, which are often schematic and basic representations, mockups present a more detailed design, including colors, typography, images, and other graphical elements that reflect how the final product will look. Mockups allow designers and development teams to visualize the appearance and layout of elements on the screen and are useful for communicating the design vision to users before the development stage.
3. Build the Prototype. Once it was established that Mockups would be used for the prototype in this example, the next step was to construct the prototype itself. There are several popular tools on the market for creating Mockups, each with different features and approaches. These include Adobe XD, Sketch, Figma, InVision Studio, Balsamiq Mockups, and Axure RP. If physical products were being prototyped, materials such as cardboard, clay, or 3D printers could be used. Since this is a non-tangible product, the Pencil Project (Evolus, 2024) software tool was selected for constructing the Mockups.

Some of the relevant Mockups for this example are shown below. Those for the splash screen, the homepage, and the advertisement or sponsor screens have been omitted for illustrative purposes. However, it is mandatory to design all screens of the prototype as they will be used for user testing. Figure 3 shows the Mockup created for the event search interface for motorcycle events in Mexico. The screen consists of only two text fields with labels: one to select the month and the other to select the year, followed by the search button.

Figure 3. Mockup - Biker Event Search Screen (Source: Author).

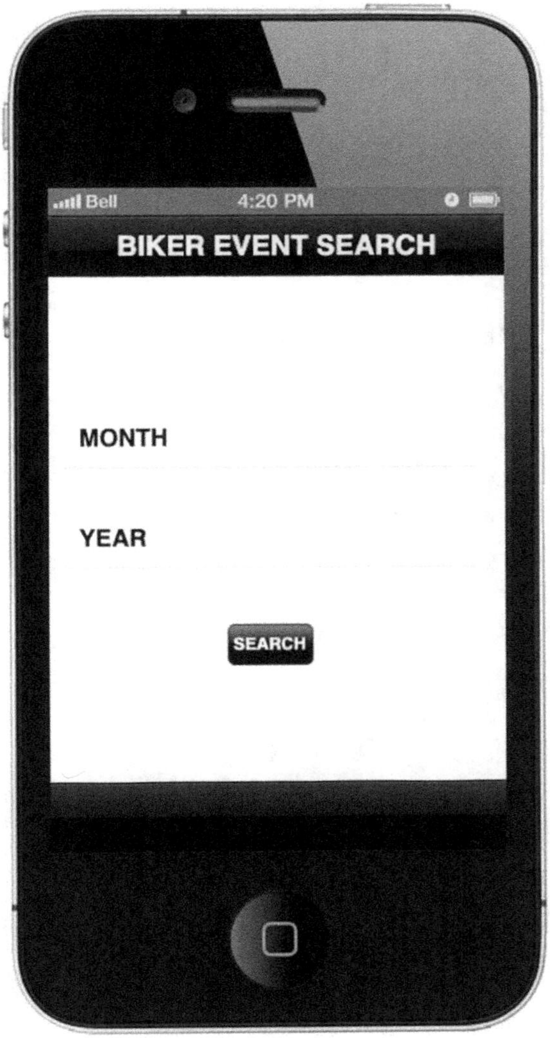

Fig. 4 shows the Mockup for the motorcycle event search results screen. Each event will be displayed in a box with relevant information such as the event name, location, date, cost, contact number, and a link to the route on Google Maps for directions to the event.

Figure 4. Mockup - Motorcycle Event Search Results Screen (Source: Author).

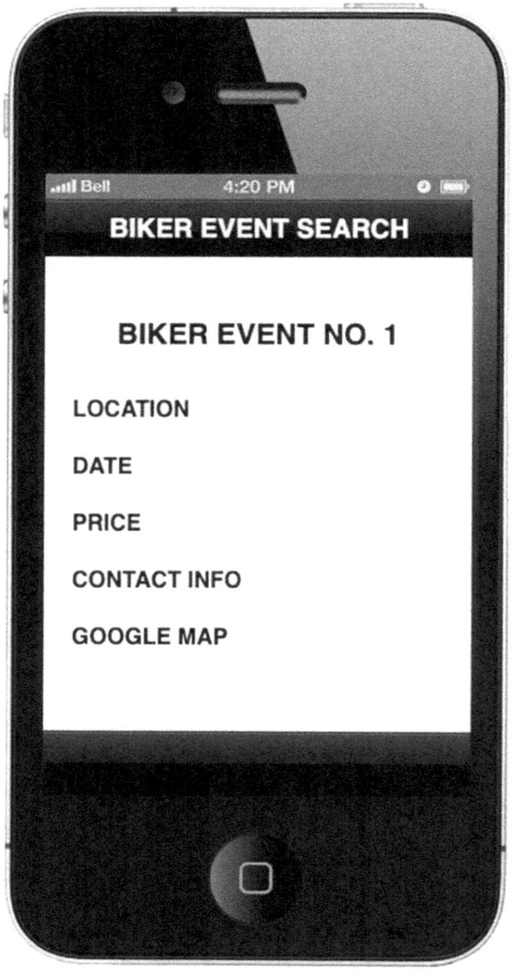

Finally, the creation of models for this prototype allowed the development team and users to easily share and evaluate the product. This helped gather reliable feedback and ensured that the final design truly met the real and verifiable expectations of the users.

Testing

The testing phase in Design Thinking is crucial for validating the designed solutions and ensuring that they meet the needs and expectations of users. It is important to remember that this is a user-centered methodology. It is relevant to note that there is no need to fully develop the mobile application or create the Facebook page at this stage. Although Design Thinking has been applied in software development and has been the subject of research within the scientific community in that area, this book does not focus on that aspect. Design Thinking can indeed be combined with Agile Methodologies, but this can be done after the execution of the Design Thinking process, once the prototype has been tested by the end users, with feedback, corrections, and improvements applied. At that point, an agile software development methodology could be employed to develop the mobile application and publish it on Android Market and the App Store.

There are some recommendations on how to carry out this testing phase in an organized and simple way. It is recommended to: 1) define the test, 2) design the test, 3) execute the test, and 4) analyze the results. The entire process should be documented rigorously and honestly. It is essential to document all aspects of the process, including the feedback received, the iterations made, and the design decisions. This documentation helps facilitate communication within the team and with other stakeholders.

The following outlines each of the steps implemented in this example.

1. Defining the Test. Before conducting the testing, it is essential to define which aspects of the prototype will be evaluated. The objectives can include usability, functionality, user understanding, or overall satisfaction. Additionally, a representative group of users must be chosen to test the prototype. Ideally, these users should reflect the profiles defined during the empathy phase and the Buyer Persona analysis. In this example, the goal was to evaluate the usability of the app, its functionality, and the satisfaction of the motorcyclist in having such a tool. Real motorcyclists from the empathy phase were used for testing, including members of motorcycle clubs and non-members.
2. Test Design. Scenarios were created to simulate how a real user would interact with the product or service. These scenarios should cover both common tasks and possible exceptions or problems. In this case, a simple motorcycle club meeting, attendance at an event, and a typical day in the life of a motorcyclist were simulated. Subsequently, the testing techniques were defined. Depending on the prototype, different techniques could be used, such as usability testing, interviews, surveys, or task analysis. For this example, interviews were used,

and feedback was collected through direct observation, recordings, and notes stored on Google Drive.

3. Executing the Test. Once the prototype was created, it was tested with real users to gather feedback. During this phase, it was observed how users interacted with the prototype, collected their opinions, and identified potential improvements. It was important to maintain an open attitude during this phase and not influence the user's responses. Users were encouraged to express their opinions, doubts, and issues they encountered while using the prototype. The test was conducted using printed paper sheets, each containing the screens of the mobile app and the Facebook page. While the Design Thinking team observed, interviewed, and took notes.
4. Analyzing the Results. At this point, based on the feedback received, the prototype was adjusted. This process can be repeated several times until a version is reached that satisfies both the Design Thinking team and the motorcyclist users.

The feedback was reviewed to identify patterns, recurring problems, and areas that required improvement. It is crucial to prioritize the most critical issues that directly impact the user's experience with the mobile app. In this example, three rounds of testing and result analysis were needed to identify improvements for the user. Among the most important findings, it was noted that users preferred a larger text font and that the option to filter biker event searches by state in Mexico should be added, as only events for the current month were displayed regardless of the state. Additionally, during these testing cycles, the sponsor option was added, as motorcyclists with their own businesses expressed interest in advertising as sponsors on the mobile app. Furthermore, some motorcycle club secretaries mentioned that the mobile app facilitated their work, as they are responsible for notifying their club members about upcoming events.

Finally, the application and the page were launched, followed by continuous monitoring to evaluate their performance, and make improvements based on user feedback. This approach ensured that both the mobile app and the Facebook page met the users' expectations, providing a smooth and satisfying experience.

Final Product

This section is an additional feature included in the book to allow readers to visualize the product developed through the application of the Design Thinking methodology. Technical details have been omitted to ensure the text is accessible and enjoyable for readers who are not directly involved in technology-related fields. The final product is presented below.

The mobile application was developed using Flutter (Google, 2024), an open-source framework created by Google. Flutter enables the creation of mobile, web, and desktop applications from a single codebase written in the Dart programming language. It is widely regarded for its ability to produce visually appealing and high-performance user interfaces that can run seamlessly across multiple platforms such as iOS (Apple Inc, 2024), Android (Google Android, 2024), Windows, macOS, Linux, and web, using a single codebase. Figure 5 illustrates a screenshot of the Flutter project's source code in Visual Studio Code (Microsoft, 2024).

Figure 5. Source Code for the Flutter Project "Eventos Biker México"

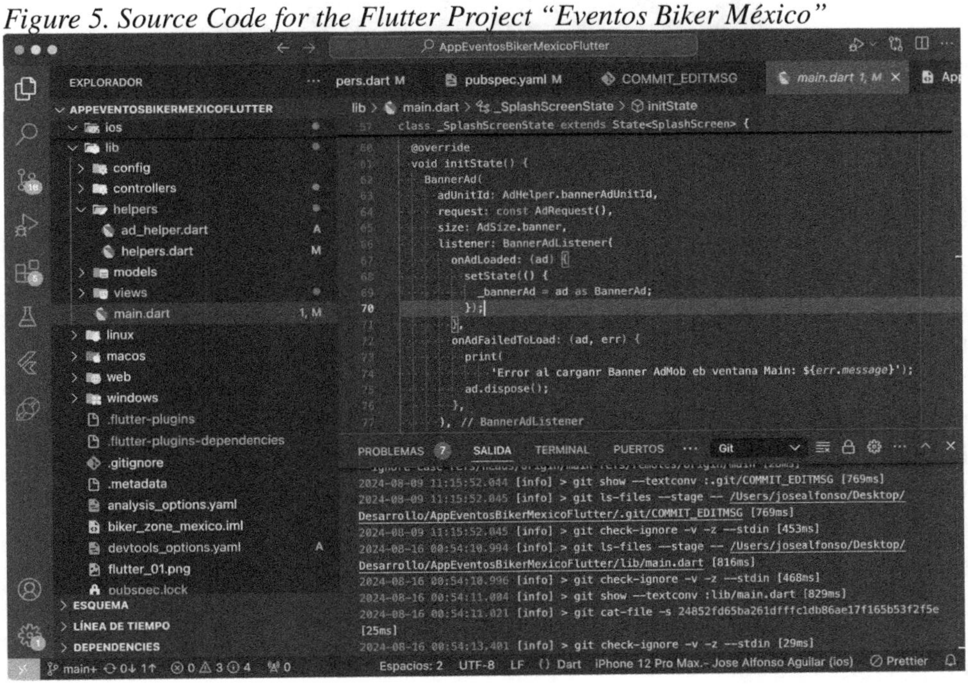

After the application was developed, it was published on Android Market. To accomplish this, the Google Developer License was purchased, and the app underwent a 14-day testing phase with 20 user testers. Simultaneously, the iOS Developer License from Apple was acquired, and the application was published on the App Store. Figure 6 display the published applications. In Figure 6, the main screen of the mobile application and the biker event search screen can be observed.

Figure 6. App "Eventos Biker México."

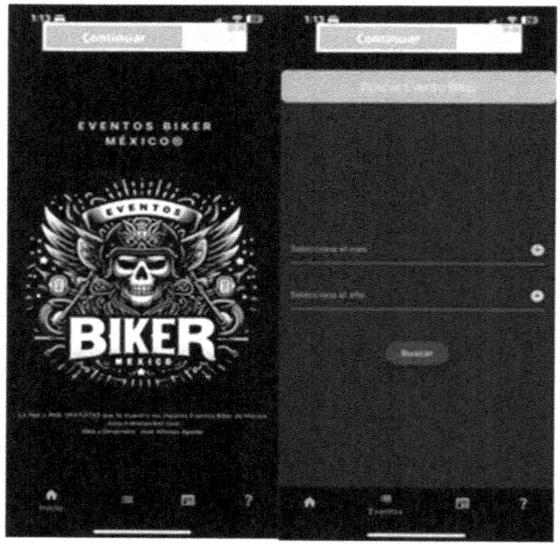

The Facebook page was created simultaneously with the mobile application since the development team needed to design the logo and define the color scheme to create both the app interface and the necessary images for the page.

The application is available for download under the name *Eventos Biker Mexico* (without the accent on "México") on Android Market and the App Store for free. The Facebook Fan Page is active and has approximately 19,800 followers and "likes." It has been well-received within the biker community, and event organizers, both national and international, have increasingly approached the page to request free promotion of their events on the Fan Page and the *Eventos Biker México App*.

DISCUSSION

Design Thinking emphasizes understanding user needs through empathetic research, enabling development teams to align solutions with those needs (Brown, 2009). The case study highlights the benefits of incorporating user feedback, prototyping, and iterative testing to create functional and meaningful mobile applications. A key takeaway is the importance of empathy in the development process. Engaging with users through interviews and observations reveals insights that may not be found through traditional research methods, helping identify pain points and opportunities. In the case study, user interviews and empathy mapping were crucial in refining the app's design to meet user concerns and preferences.

DT iterative approach allows for continuous improvements based on real-time feedback, ensuring the final product meets and exceeds user expectations. This process ensures the design remains user-centric and adaptable to evolving needs. However, while Design Thinking is crucial, it is not the sole factor in app development success. The choice of tools, technologies, and frameworks also plays a significant role. In this chapter, the use of Flutter, an open-source cross-platform framework, supported the efficient development of the app. Combining Design Thinking with strong technical foundations leads to successful, high-performance applications (Liedtka & Ogilvie, 2011). The chapter also emphasizes the importance of context and adaptation in applying Design Thinking, suggesting future research could explore its use in other domains and project sizes to further validate its flexibility and scalability. Additionally, the study calls for exploring how Design Thinking can integrate with other methodologies to improve development stages like post-launch support and user retention.

To this end, this chapter underscores the importance of Design Thinking as a powerful approach for crafting mobile applications. By prioritizing empathy, teamwork, and iterative processes, Design Thinking provides a framework that not only addresses challenges but also drives innovation, ensuring solutions are deeply aligned with users' needs. This methodology aids in the development of applications that not only fulfill market requirements but also significantly influence users' experiences. The insights gained from this chapter are expected to steer future research and development in mobile app design, promoting the use of user-centric methodologies to tackle intricate issues in the digital era.

CONCLUSION

The practical application of Design Thinking principles was explored through a case study focused on the development of a mobile application tailored for the Mexican motorcycling community. The case study identifies several challenges faced by both event organizers and participants, such as fragmented event organization, limited event discovery, and the difficulty of balancing travel with personal commitments. Through Design Thinking, these issues were systematically addressed, resulting in a solution that better aligned with the community's needs.

By documenting the complete process—spanning problem definition, ideation, prototyping, and user testing—this chapter illustrates the iterative and user-centric nature of Design Thinking. The case study demonstrates how the methodology fosters empathy, encourages collaboration, and stimulates creativity across the development cycle, ultimately translating theoretical frameworks into tangible, user-centered outcomes.

Although the technical details of implementation are outside the scope of this chapter, the primary focus on understanding user needs and continuously adapting to user feedback emphasizes the importance of ensuring software solutions meet the specific demands of the target audience. The successful implementation of Design Thinking in this case study offers valuable insights for practitioners looking to apply this methodology to develop innovative and impactful mobile applications, particularly within niche markets such as the Mexican motorcycling community, and in similar contexts.

In conclusion, the chapter highlights the transformative role of Design Thinking in mobile app development, reinforcing its capacity to drive innovation and enhance user experience. By embracing empathy, iteration, and collaboration, Design Thinking bridges the gap between conceptualization and real-world application, offering a robust framework for the development of impactful, user-centered solutions.

REFERENCES

Amin, S. N. (2021). Gamification of Duolingo in Rising Student'S English Language Learning Motivation. *Jurnal Bahasa Lingua Scientia, 13*(2), 191–213. DOI: 10.21274/ls.2021.13.2.191-213

Apple Inc. (2024). *iOS*. https://www.apple.com/ios

Bate, P. (2019). *Design thinking in software engineering: An approach for developing innovative software solutions*. Springer.

Brown, T. (2008). *Design thinking. Harvard Business Review*. Retrieved from https://hbr.org/2008/06/design-thinking

Brown, T. (2009). *Change by Design: How Design Thinking Transforms Organizations and Inspires Innovation*. HarperBusiness.

Cazac, A. M., & Vert, S. (2020). Using Design Thinking to Create Social Innovation in Digital Services for International Mobility. In Innovation in Sustainable Management and Entrepreneurship: 2019 International Symposium in Management (SIM2019) (pp. 591-600). Springer International Publishing.

Chesbrough, H. (2003). *Open Innovation: The New Imperative for Creating and Profiting from Technology*. Harvard Business School Press.

Deng, Q. (2024, December 15). Gamified Learning: Applying Game Design Thinking in Education. Retrieved from https://www.gartner.com/en/documents/3614217

Evolus. (2024). *Pencil Project: Open-source GUI prototyping tool*. https://pencil.evolus.vn

Gartner. (2017, February 20). *Design thinking: How to use a human-centered approach to drive innovation*. Retrieved from https://www.gartner.com/en/documents/3614217

Google. (2024). Flutter: Beautiful native apps in record time.

Google Android. (2024). *Android*. https://www.android.com

IvyPanda. (2023, July 5). UberEATS Design Thinking. https://ivypanda.com/essays/ubereats-and-design-thinking-case-study/

Liedtka, J., & Ogilvie, T. (2011). *Designing for Growth: A Design Thinking Tool Kit for Managers*. Columbia University Press.

McCord, P. (2024, July 31). *How Netflix Reinvented HR. Harvard Business Review*. Retrieved from https://hbr.org/2014/01/how-netflix-reinvented-hr

Microsoft. (2024). *Visual Studio Code*. https://code.visualstudio.com

Nike News. (2016). *The Evolution of Nike Flyknit. Nike News*. Retrieved from https://news.nike.com/news/the-evolution-of-nike-flyknit

Norman, D. (2013). *The Design of Everyday Things: Revised and Expanded Edition*. Basic Books.

Rivera, J. (2024, July 31). *How Design Thinking Transformed Airbnb from a Failing Startup to a Billion-Dollar Business*. Retrieved from https://review.firstround.com/how-design-thinking-transformed-airbnb-from-failing-startup-to-billion-dollar-business

Stanford d.school. (n.d.). *What is Design Thinking?* Retrieved from https://dschool.stanford.edu/executive-education-resource-collections/keep-learning1

Stickdorn, M., & Schneider, J. (2011). *This is Service Design Thinking: Basics, Tools, Cases*. Wiley.

Sweeney, K. (2019). How Uber Uses Design Thinking to Keep Drivers and Riders Happy. *Forbes*.

Ulrich, K. T., & Eppinger, S. D. (2015). *Product Design and Development* (5th ed.). McGraw-Hill Education.

KEY TERMS AND DEFINITIONS

Empathy Map: A collaborative tool used to understand users' emotions, thoughts, and behaviors by organizing insights into categories such as what users say, think, do, and feel.

Empathy-Driven Development: A development approach focused on understanding and addressing user emotions and experiences.

Design Thinking: A problem-solving framework emphasizing creativity, empathy, and user-centric insights to guide solution development.

Focus Group: A qualitative research method used to gather insights from a selected group of users or stakeholders through discussion.

Software Development Process: The stages involved in creating software applications, including planning, designing, coding, testing, and maintenance.

Mock-ups: Visual representations or prototypes used to showcase a product's design and functionality before development.

User-Centered Design: An approach prioritizing users' needs, preferences, and behaviors to create intuitive, effective, and meaningful solutions.

Prototyping: Creating preliminary versions of software to test and gather feedback for iterative improvements.

Compilation of References

Adhikari Egodawele, M. H., Sedera, D., & Bui, V. (2022). A systematic review of digital transformation literature (2013–2021) and the development of an overarching a-priori model to guide future research.

Alavi, M. M., & Carlson, P. (2022). Design thinking: An innovative approach to software development methodologies. In *Proceedings of the 2022 IEEE International Conference on Software Engineering (ICSE)* (pp. 356–363). IEEE. https://doi.org/ DOI: 10.1145/3377811.3381396

Aldave, A., Vara, J. M., Granada, D., & Marcos, E. (2019). Leveraging creativity in requirements elicitation within agile software development: A systematic literature review. *Journal of Systems and Software*, *157*, 110396. DOI: 10.1016/j.jss.2019.110396

Amabile, T. M. (2018). Creativity. In *Context: Update to the social psychology of creativity*. Routledge. DOI: 10.4324/9780429501234-2

Amin, S. N. (2021). Gamification of Duolingo in Rising Student'S English Language Learning Motivation. *Jurnal Bahasa Lingua Scientia*, *13*(2), 191–213. DOI: 10.21274/ls.2021.13.2.191-213

Ammons, B., & Bansal, S. K. (2017). Scrumify: A software game to introduce agile software development methods. *Journal of Engineering Education Transformations*, *30*(Special Issue).

Andersson, M., Kusetogullari, A., & Wernberg, J. (2021). *Software development and innovation: Exploring the software shift in innovation in Swedish firms*, Technological Forecasting and Social Change, Volume 167, 2021, 120695, ISSN 0040-1625, https://doi.org/DOI: 10.1016/j.techfore.2021.120695

Apasrawirote, D., Yawised, K., & Muneesawang, P. (2022). Digital marketing capability: The mystery of business capabilities. *Marketing Intelligence & Planning*, *40*(4), 477–496. DOI: 10.1108/MIP-11-2021-0399

Apple Inc. (2024). *iOS*. https://www.apple.com/ios

Arif, J., & Jawab, F. (2024). Application of fsQCA method in operations. In *Intersecting Entrepreneurship* (p. 291). Internationalization, and Green Innovation.

Arkes, H. R., & Blumer, C. (1985). The psychology of sunk cost. *Organizational Behavior and Human Decision Processes*, *35*(1), 124–140. DOI: 10.1016/0749-5978(85)90049-4

Aya Sierra, J. S., Niño Muñoz, D. O., Roa Ladino, N. A., Goyeneche Giraldo, E., Calderón Nova, S. A., & Santos Meek, A. (n.d.). *Desenredando tutelas, Sistema: Tutela Digital en Colombia*. Laboratorio de Diseño para la Justicia en Colombia, Universidad de los Andes. Retrieved from https://labjusticia.uniandes.edu.co/proyectoI05.html

Babu, C. S., William, M. P., & Fazil, R. A. (2025). The Role of Chatbots in Educational Leadership: Enhancing Decision-Making and Efficiency Through AI Tools. In Chatbots in Educational Leadership and Management (pp. 291-320). IGI Global Scientific Publishing.

Balzano, M., & Bortoluzzi, G. (2024). Time is running out: How design thinking shapes team innovation under time constraints. *European Management Journal*. Advance online publication. DOI: 10.1016/j.emj.2024.08.003

Barton, T. D., & Berger-Walliser, G. (2018). Visualizing contracts: How graphical tools can improve transparency and accessibility in legal documents. *Harvard Journal of Law & Technology*, *31*(2), 313–356. https://jolt.law.harvard.edu

Basten, D. (2017). Gamification. *IEEE Software*, *34*(5), 76–81. DOI: 10.1109/MS.2017.3571581

Bate, P. (2019). *Design thinking in software engineering: An approach for developing innovative software solutions*. Springer.

Beck, K. (2000). *Extreme Programming Explained: Embrace Change*. Addison-Wesley Professional.

Beraza, I. L., Vara, J. M., Granada, D., Gómez, C., & Pérez-Blanco, F. J. (2023). On the Impact of Project Management Certification for Software Projects and Practitioners. [IEEE Software.]. *IEEE Software*, *40*(5), 100–107. DOI: 10.1109/MS.2023.3286118

Bergin, J., & Grossman, F. (2006). Extreme construction: Making agile accessible. *AGILE 2006 (AGILE'06)*, 6 pp. – 389.

Berman, M. (2024, December 20). Microsoft CEO's shocking prediction: "Agents will replace all software" [Video]. YouTube. https://www.youtube.com/watch?v=uGOLYz2pgr8

Beyer, S. (2021). Ethical considerations in human-centered design for software development. *Journal of Ethics in Information Technology, 23*(2), 129–138. DOI: 10.1007/s10676-021-09581-y

Big, I. D. (2025). *Data visibiliti and control.* Retrieved from https://bigid.com/

Boehm, B. (1988). A Spiral Model of Software Development and Enhancement. *IEEE Computer, 21*(5), 61–72. DOI: 10.1109/2.59

Booch, G. (2016). The future of software engineering. *IEEE Software, 33*(1), 20–24. DOI: 10.1109/MS.2014.16

Breaux, T. D., & Bai, X. (2016). Legal requirements traceability in software engineering: A systematic literature review. In *Proceedings of the 24th IEEE International Requirements Engineering Conference (RE)* (pp. 1-10). IEEE. https://doi.org/DOI: 10.1109/RE.2016.38

Brosig, C., Bley, K., Strahringer, S., & Westner, M. (2022). The missing piece-calibration of qualitative data for qualitative comparative analyses in IS research. In *ECIS.*

Brown, T. (2008). *Design thinking. Harvard Business Review.* Retrieved from https://hbr.org/2008/06/design-thinking

Brown, T. (2009). *Change by design: How design thinking creates new alternatives for business and society.* Harper Business.

Brown, T. (2009). *Change by Design: How Design Thinking Creates New Alternatives for Business and Society.* HarperBusiness.

Brown, T. (2009). *Change by Design: How Design Thinking Transforms Organizations and Inspires Innovation.* HarperBusiness.

Brown, T., & Katz, B. (2011). Change By Design. *Journal of Product Innovation Management, 28*(3), 381–383. DOI: 10.1111/j.1540-5885.2011.00806.x

Buchanan, R. (1992). Wicked Problems in Design Thinking. *Design Issues, 8*(2), 5–21. DOI: 10.2307/1511637

Burrows, M. (2021). *Agendashift: Outcome-oriented change and continuous transformation* (2nd ed.). New Generation Publishing.

Cahui Osis, V. F., Quispe Soto, D., Condori Huarca, A., & Suyo, C. J. (2022). Case studies of Design Thinking in the analysis and design stages of software development. Innovation and Software, 3(1), 17-29. Universidad La Salle. https://www.redalyc.org/journal/6738/673870840002/673870840002.pdf

Cairns, P. A. (2016). Experimental methods in Human-Computer Interaction. In Soedergaard, M., & Dam, R. (Eds.), *Encylopedia of Human-Computer Interaction* (2nd ed.). Interaction Design Foundation.

Campbell, D. T., & Stanley, J. C. (2015). *Experimental and Quasi-Experimental Designs for Research*. Ravenio Books.

Canva. (2024, January 24). Celebrating Canva's growth in the US. https://www.canva.com/newsroom/news/canva-us-growth/

Carbon Design System. (n.d.). IBM products. https://ibm-products.carbondesignsystem.com/?path=/story/overview-welcome–overview&globals=viewport:basic

Casetext (2024). *How does casetext work?* Retrieved from https://canvasbusinessmodel.com/es/blogs/how-it-works/casetext-how-it-works?srsltid=AfmBOopW2UXJppBs1zJxEkOIXJGPou-Mwlyx9tjCN0cudVB6n9GtXl4-

Cavoukian, A. (2012). Privacy by design: The 7 foundational principles. Information and Privacy Commissioner of Ontario, Canada. Retrieved from https://www.ipc.on.ca/wp-content/uploads/Resources/7foundationalprinciples.pdf

Cazac, A. M., & Vert, S. (2020). Using Design Thinking to Create Social Innovation in Digital Services for International Mobility. In Innovation in Sustainable Management and Entrepreneurship: 2019 International Symposium in Management (SIM2019) (pp. 591-600). Springer International Publishing.

Chávez, L., & Zamalloa, D. (2024). *Legal Design Thinking: Unlearning to humanize law.* Enfoque Derecho. https://enfoquederecho.com/legal-design-thinking-desaprender-para-humanizar-el-derecho/

Chen, M., Wang, H., Liang, Y., & Zhang, G. (2023). Net and configurational effects of determinants on cloud computing adoption by SMEs under cloud promotion policy using PLS-SEM and fsQCA. *Journal of Innovation & Knowledge*, *8*(3), 100388. DOI: 10.1016/j.jik.2023.100388

Chen, M., Ye, Y., & Huang, X. (2023). The metaverse in supply chain knowledge sharing and resilience contexts: An empirical investigation of factors affecting adoption and acceptance. *Journal of Innovation & Knowledge*, *8*(1), 100446. DOI: 10.1016/j.jik.2023.100446

Chesbrough, H. (2003). *Open Innovation: The New Imperative for Creating and Profiting from Technology*. Harvard Business School Press.

Cohen, L., Lawrence, M., & Morrison, K. (2017). *Research Methods in Education* (8th ed.). Routledge. DOI: 10.4324/9781315456539

Collings, D. G., Mellahi, K., & Cascio, W. F. (2017). *The Oxford Handbook of Talent Management* (1st ed.). Oxford University Press. DOI: 10.1093/oxford-hb/9780198758273.001.0001

Contrary. (2023, September 21). Miro. https://research.contrary.com/company/miro

Couldry, N. (2012). *Media, society, world: Social theory and digital media practice*. Polity Press.

Cross, N. (2011). *Design Thinking: Understanding How Designers Think and Work*. Berg Publishers. DOI: 10.5040/9781474293884

Dam, R. F., & Siang, T. Y. (2022). The history of design thinking. Interaction Design Foundation. https://www.interaction-design.org/literature/article/design-thinking-get-a-quick-overview-of-the-history

Daradkeh, F. M., Hassan, T. H., Palei, T., Helal, M. Y., Mabrouk, S., Saleh, M. I., & Elshawarbi, N. N. (2023). Enhancing digital presence for maximizing customer value in fast-food restaurants. *Sustainability (Basel)*, *15*(7), 5690. DOI: 10.3390/su15075690

Daugherty, P. R., & Wilson, H. J. (2018). *Human + Machine: Reimagining Work in the Age of AI*. Harvard Business Review Press.

de Noronha, M. E. S., Ferraro, D. M. J., & Silva, R. D. S. V. (2022). Bibliometric analysis on the orchestration of dynamic capabilities. *International Journal of Innovation: IJI Journal*, *10*(4), 610–637.

Deci, E. L., & Ryan, R. M. (2000). The "what" and "why" of goal pursuits: Human needs and the self-determination of behavior. *Psychological Inquiry*, *11*(4), 227–268. DOI: 10.1207/S15327965PLI1104_01

Deloitte. (2025). *Discover Deloitte Legal services*. Deloitte. Retrieved from https://www.deloitte.com/es/es/services/legal/services/deloitte-legal-services.html?icid=ln_legal_deloitte-legal-services

Deng, Q. (2024, December 15). Gamified Learning: Applying Game Design Thinking in Education. Retrieved from https://www.gartner.com/en/documents/3614217

Design Thinking. (n.d.). Interaction Design Foundation. https://www.interaction-design.org/literature/topics/design-thinking

Deterding, S., Dixon, D., Khaled, R., & Nacke, L. (2011). From game design elements to gamefulness: Defining "gamification." *Proceedings of the 15th International Academic MindTrek Conference: Envisioning Future Media Environments*, 9–15. DOI: 10.1145/2181037.2181040

Dichev, C., & Dicheva, D. (2017). Gamifying education: What is known, what is believed and what remains uncertain: A critical review. *International Journal of Educational Technology in Higher Education*, *14*(1), 36. DOI: 10.1186/s41239-017-0042-5

Diniz De Souza, A., Duarte Seabra, R., Marinho Ribeiro, J., & Da, S. Rodrigues, L. E. (2017). SCRUMI: A Board Serious Virtual Game for Teaching the SCRUM Framework. *2017 IEEE/ACM 39th International Conference on Software Engineering Companion (ICSE-C)*, 319–321.

Docherty, C. (2017). Perspectives on Design Thinking for Social Innovation. *The Design Journal*, *20*(6), 719–724. DOI: 10.1080/14606925.2017.1372005

DoNotPay. (n.d.). Retrieved from https://www.donotpay.com

Dul, J. (2021). Advances in necessary condition analysis. Downloaded on Jan, 21, 2022.

Dul, J. (2022). Problematic applications of necessary condition analysis (NCA) in tourism and hospitality research. *Tourism Management*, *93*, 104616. DOI: 10.1016/j.tourman.2022.104616

Eghdam, T. (2024). *Future of youth hockey culture*.

Elbanna, A., & Sarker, S. (2016). The Risks of Agile Software Development: Learning from Adopters. *IEEE Software*, *33*(5), 72–79. DOI: 10.1109/MS.2015.150

Ethical, O. S. Toolkit (2025). *A Playbook for Ethical Technology Governance*. Retrieved from https://www.iftf.org/projects/a-playbook-for-ethical-tech-governance/?

Evolus. (2024). *Pencil Project: Open-source GUI prototyping tool*. https://pencil.evolus.vn

Execute your development needs with a Magic Quadrant™ Low-Code Leader. (2024, October 21). Mendix. https://www.mendix.com/blog/gartner-mq-lcap-2024/

Făgără an, C., Popa, O., Pisla, A., & Cristea, C. (2021). Agile, waterfall and iterative approach in information technology projects. *IOP Conference Series. Materials Science and Engineering, 1169*(1), 012025. DOI: 10.1088/1757-899X/1169/1/012025

FairClaims. (2025). *Resolve disputes online with legally enforceable results.* Retrieved from https://www.fairclaims.com

Fernandes, J. M., & Sousa, S. M. (2010). PlayScrum—A Card Game to Learn the Scrum Agile Method. *2010 Second International Conference on Games and Virtual Worlds for Serious Applications*, 52–59. DOI: 10.1109/VS-GAMES.2010.24

Fisher, R. A. (1921). *014: On the" Probable Error" of a Coefficient of Correlation Deduced from a Small Sample.*

Fleiss, J. L. (2011). *Design and Analysis of Clinical Experiments.* John Wiley & Sons.

Flores, M., & Meseguer, J. E. (2018). AI in Software Engineering: Current Applications and Future Directions. *ACM Computing Surveys, 51*(4), 1–34.

Foote, K. (2016). *RAVN systems launches AI bot for legal research. DATAVERSITY.* Retrieved from https://www.dataversity.net/ravn-systems-launches-ai-bot-legal-research/

Forrester. (February, 2018). *The Total Economic Impact™ of IBM's Design Thinking Practice.* Retrieved January 15, 2025, from https://www.ibm.com/design/thinking/static/Enterprise-Design-Thinking-Report-8ab1e9e1622899654844a5fe1d760ed5.pdf

Fowler, F. J. (1995). Improving Survey Questions: Design and Evaluation. *Sage (Atlanta, Ga.).*

Freund, R. J., & Wilson, W. J. (2003). *Statistical Methods.* Elsevier.

Frick, E., Tardini, S., & Cantoni, L. (2014). Lego Serious Play applications to enhance creativity in participatory design. *Creativity in Business. Research Papers on Knowledge. Innovation and Enterprise*, 2, 200–210.

Frydenberg, M., Yates, D., & Kukesh, J. (2018). Sprint, then Fly: Teaching Agile Methodologies with Paper Airplanes. *Information Systems Education Journal, 16*(5), 22.

Gao, J., Zhang, W., Guan, T., Feng, Q., & Mardani, A. (2023). Influence of digital transformation on the servitization level of manufacturing SMEs from static and dynamic perspectives. *International Journal of Information Management, 73*, 102645. DOI: 10.1016/j.ijinfomgt.2023.102645

Gartner. (2017, February 20). *Design thinking: How to use a human-centered approach to drive innovation*. Retrieved from https://www.gartner.com/en/documents/3614217

Gerber, E., & Carroll, M. (2012). The Psychological Experience of Prototyping. *Design Studies*, *33*(1), 64–84. DOI: 10.1016/j.destud.2011.06.005

GitHub Spark. (2024, October 19). GitHub Next. https://githubnext.com/projects/github-spark

Gonzalo, C. (2021). *LawGeex: Artificial intelligence to automate legal contracts*. Retrieved from https://www.carlosgonzalo.es/lawgeex-inteligencia-artificial-para-automatizar-contratos-legales/

Google Android. (2024). *Android*. https://www.android.com

Google. (2024). Flutter: Beautiful native apps in record time.

Graham, J. R. (2024). Identifying primary school teachers' perceptions of the maker mindset in Indonesian international schools (Doctoral dissertation, Murdoch University).

Gutierrez, G., Garzás, J., Gonzalez de Lena, M. T., & Moguerza, J. M. (2019). Self-Managing: An Empirical Study of the Practice in Agile Teams. *IEEE Software*, *36*(1), 23–27. DOI: 10.1109/MS.2018.2874324

Gutwin, C., & Greenberg, S. (2002). The mechanics of collaboration: Developing a theoretical framework for collaborative software. [CSCW]. *Computer Supported Cooperative Work*, *11*(1–2), 83–102. DOI: 10.1023/A:1015249122500

Hagan, M. (2017). Legal design as a thing: A theory of change and a set of methods to craft a human-centered legal system. *Design Issues*, *33*(3), 3–15. DOI: 10.1162/desi_a_00600

Hamari, J., Koivisto, J., & Sarsa, H. (2014). Does Gamification Work? — A Literature Review of Empirical Studies on Gamification. *2014 47th Hawaii International Conference on System Sciences*, 3025–3034.

Hammarberg, M., & Sunden, J. (2014). *Kanban in action*. Manning Publications Co.

Han, E. (2022, January 18). What is design thinking & why is it important? Harvard Business School Online. https://online.hbs.edu/blog/post/what-is-design-thinking

Heck, P., Ali, R., & Zaidman, M. (2023). A framework for involving end users in software engineering processes. *Empirical Software Engineering*, *28*(3), 783–811. DOI: 10.1007/s10664-022-10136-2

Hill, L. A., Brandeau, G., Truelove, E., & Lineback, K. (2014). *Collective genius: The art and practice of leading innovation*. Harvard Business Review Press.

Hoda, R., Salleh, N., & Grundy, J. (2018). The Rise and Evolution of Agile Software Development. *IEEE Software*, *35*(5), 58–63. DOI: 10.1109/MS.2018.290111318

Hof, S., Kropp, M., & Landolt, M. (2017). Use of Gamification to Teach Agile Values and Collaboration: A multi-week Scrum simulation project in an undergraduate software engineering course. *Proceedings of the 2017 ACM Conference on Innovation and Technology in Computer Science Education*, 323–328. DOI: 10.1145/3059009.3059043

Hugos, M. (2012). *Enterprise Games: Using Game Mechanics to Build a Better Business*. O'Reilly Media, Inc.

IDEO. (n.d.). *Design thinking*. Retrieved from https://www.ideo.com iManage. (2025). *Legal transaction management*. Retrieved from https://imanage.com/imanage-products/legal-transaction-management/

Innovation, J. (2025). *About Justice Innovation*. Retrieved from https://www.justiceinnovation.org

Intelligence, R. O. S. S. (n.d). *Legal Tech Corner*. Retrieved from https://rossintelligence.com

IvyPanda. (2023, July 5). UberEATS Design Thinking. https://ivypanda.com/essays/ubereats-and-design-thinking-case-study/

Jackson, M. (2021, May 5). Shift left - Moving security to the development phase - The case of secrets detection in code repositories. GitGuardian. https://blog.gitguardian.com/shift-left-moving-security-to-the-development-phase-the-case-of-secrets-detection-in-code-repositories/

Juro. (2025). *Intelligent contracting*. Retrieved from https://www.juro.com.mx

Kapp, K. M. (2012). *The Gamification of Learning and Instruction: Game-based Methods and Strategies for Training and Education*. John Wiley & Sons.

Kar, A. K., He, W., Payton, F. C., Grover, V., Al-Busaidi, A. S., & Dwivedi, Y. K. (2024). How could quantum computing shape information systems research–An editorial perspective and future research directions. *International Journal of Information Management*, •••, 102776.

Kaufman, J., & Beghetto, R. (2009). Beyond Big and Little: The Four C Model of Creativity. *Review of General Psychology*, *13*(1), 1–12. DOI: 10.1037/a0013688

Kim, J., Sung, Y., & Moon, Y. (2018). Machine Learning-Based Code Generation in Software Development. *Journal of Systems and Software*, *146*, 93–105.

Kirvan, P., Liptak, J., & Horwitz, L. (2023, December). What is citizen development. TechTarget. https://www.techtarget.com/searchsoftwarequality/definition/citizen-development

Kish, L. (1978). Some statistical problems in research design. In *Research Design*. Routledge.

Kolb, D. A. (2014). *Experiential Learning: Experience as the source of learning and Development*. FT press.

Koo, T. K., & Li, M. Y. (2016). A Guideline of Selecting and Reporting Intraclass Correlation Coefficients for Reliability Research. *Journal of Chiropractic Medicine*, *15*(2), 155–163. DOI: 10.1016/j.jcm.2016.02.012 PMID: 27330520

Krivitsky, A. (2017). *lego4scrum: A complete guide to #lego4scrum - a great way to teach the Scrum framework and Agile thinking.*

Kupiainen, E., Mäntylä, M. V., & Itkonen, J. (2015). Using metrics in Agile and Lean Software Development – A systematic literature review of industrial studies. *Information and Software Technology*, *62*, 143–163. DOI: 10.1016/j.infsof.2015.02.005

Larman, C. (2004). *Agile and iterative development: A manager's guide*. Addison-Wesley.

Law for All. (2025). *Free legal resources.* Retrieved from https://www.lawforall.co.za/free-legal-resources/

LawGeex. (2025). *Automate your contract review process*. Retrieved from https://www.lawgeex.com/

Legal Templates. (2025). *What is Legal Templates?* Retrieved from https://legaltemplates.net/about-us/

LegalZoom. (n.d.) *U.S. Legal Help in Mexico*. Retrieved from https://www.legalzoom.com/country/mx

Leso, B. H. (2022). Unlocking the digital organization: A view of the digital transformation capabilities. [Doctoral dissertation, Universidade Federal do Rio Grande do Sul]

Leso, B. H., Cortimiglia, M. N., & Ghezzi, A. (2023). The contribution of organizational culture, structure, and leadership factors in the digital transformation of SMEs: A mixed-methods approach. *Cognition Technology and Work*, *25*(1), 151–179. DOI: 10.1007/s10111-022-00714-2 PMID: 36118918

Leso, B. H., Cortimiglia, M. N., Ghezzi, A., & Minatogawa, V. (2024). Exploring digital transformation capability via a blended perspective of dynamic capabilities and digital maturity: A pattern matching approach. *Review of Managerial Science*, *18*(4), 1149–1187. DOI: 10.1007/s11846-023-00692-3

Liedtka, J., & Ogilvie, T. (2011). *Designing for Growth: A Design Thinking Tool Kit for Managers*. Columbia University Press.

Lucena, P., Braz, A., Chicoria, A., & Tizzei, L. (2017). IBM Design Thinking Software Development Framework. In Silva da Silva, T., Estácio, B., Kroll, J., & Mantovani Fontana, R. (Eds.), *Agile Methods. WBMA 2016. Communications in Computer and Information Science* (Vol. 680). Springer., DOI: 10.1007/978-3-319-55907-0_9

Luminance (2024). *Legal-Grade AI, Wherever Computer Meets Contract.* Retrieved from https://www.luminance.com

Manca, P. (2024). *Legal design: Designing legal solutions for all. PWC Spain.* Retrieved from https://www.pwc.es/es/newlaw-pulse/transformacion-legal/legal-design-disenando-soluciones-juridicas-para-todos.html

Manifesto for Agile Software Development. (2001). https://agilemanifesto.org/

Manifesto, A. (2001). *Manifesto for Agile Software Development.*

Martins, C. E. H., de Souza, R. C., da Costa Júnior, J. F., & de Sousa Neto, M. V. (2023). Criação de um sistema de medição de desempenho para uma empresa de prevenção a fraudes. *Gestão e Projetos: GeP*, *14*(1), 133–165. DOI: 10.5585/gep.v14i1.23265

Material Design. (n.d.). Material Design 3. https://m3.material.io/

Matvitskyy, O., Davis, K., & Jain, A. (2024, October 16). Magic Quadrant for enterprise low-code application platforms. Gartner. https://www.gartner.com/doc/reprints?id=1-2J42UZEC&ct=241017&st=sb

May, J., York, J., & Lending, D. (2016). Play Ball: Bringing Scrum into the Classroom. *Journal of Information Systems Education*, *27*(2), 87–92.

Mazumder, S., & Garg, S. (2021). Decoding digital transformational outsourcing: The role of service providers' capabilities. *International Journal of Information Management*, *58*, 102295. DOI: 10.1016/j.ijinfomgt.2020.102295

McCord, P. (2024, July 31). *How Netflix Reinvented HR. Harvard Business Review*. Retrieved from https://hbr.org/2014/01/how-netflix-reinvented-hr

McGraw, K. O., & Wong, S. P. (1996). Forming inferences about some intraclass correlation coefficients. *Psychological Methods, 1*(1), 30–46. DOI: 10.1037/1082-989X.1.1.30

Meinel, C., & Leifer, L. (2022). Design thinking research: Building innovation eco-systems. In *Understanding innovation: The role of design thinking in software engineering* (pp. 45–67). Springer.

Microsoft. (2024). *Visual Studio Code*. https://code.visualstudio.com

Mishra, A., & Alzoubi, Y. I. (2023, August). Structured software development versus agile software development: A comparative analysis. *International Journal of System Assurance Engineering and Management, 14*(4), 1504–1522. DOI: 10.1007/s13198-023-01958-5

Modria (2025). *Comprehensive, innovative software and services designed for the public sector.* Retrieved from https://www.tylertech.com/solutions/modria

Morschheuser, B., Hassan, L., Werder, K., & Hamari, J. (2018). How to design gamification? A method for engineering gamified software. *Information and Software Technology, 95*, 219–237. DOI: 10.1016/j.infsof.2017.10.015

Nicholson, S. (2015). A recipe for meaningful gamification. In Reiners, T., & Wood, L. C. (Eds.), *Gamification in Education and Business* (pp. 1–20). Springer. DOI: 10.1007/978-3-319-10208-5_1

Nielsen, J., & Molich, R. (1990). Heuristic evaluation of user interfaces. In *Proceedings of the SIGCHI Conference on Human Factors in Computing Systems* (pp. 249–256). ACM. DOI: 10.1145/97243.97281

Nike News. (2016). *The Evolution of Nike Flyknit. Nike News*. Retrieved from https://news.nike.com/news/the-evolution-of-nike-flyknit

Norman, D. (2013). *The Design of Everyday Things: Revised and Expanded Edition*. Basic books.

Norman, D. (2013). *The design of everyday things: Revised and expanded edition*. MIT Press.

Onetrust (2025). *Responsible AI and data solutions.* Retrieved from https://www.onetrust.com

Open Source Initiative. (2009, September 19). History of the OSI. https://opensource.org/history

Paasivaara, M., Heikkilä, V., Lassenius, C., & Toivola, T. (2014). Teaching students scrum using LEGO blocks. *Companion Proceedings of the 36th International Conference on Software Engineering*, 382–391.

Parizi, R. B., Silva, M. M., Couto, I., Trindade, K., Plautz, M., Marczak, S., Conte, T. U., & Candello, H. (2020). *Design Thinking in Software Requirements: What Techniques to Use? A Proposal for a Recommendation Tool.* Conferencia Iberoamericana de Software Engineering.

Parola, G., Muquissai, S. C., & Poto, M. P. (2023). *A co-created project of legal design and visual law applied to international environmental law: Transformation of the Escazú agreement and environmental access rights into visual materials for and with the Chiquitano people. Revista Culturas Jurídicas, 10,* 1-18. Retrieved from https://www.researchgate.net/publication/372379123_A_CO-CREATED_PROJECT_OF_LEGAL_DESIGN_AND_VISUAL_LAW_APPLIED_TO_INTERNATIONAL_ENVIRONMENTAL_LAW_TRANSFORMATION_OF_THE_ESCAZU_AGREEMENT_AND_ENVIRONMENTAL_ACCESS_RIGHTS_INTO_VISUAL_MATERIALS_FOR_AND_WITH

Pedreira, O., García, F., Brisaboa, N., & Piattini, M. (2015). Gamification in software engineering – A systematic mapping. *Information and Software Technology*, *57*, 157–168. DOI: 10.1016/j.infsof.2014.08.007

Peeters, V., & Van Cauwenberghe, P. (2003). *The XP Game Explained.* Addison-Wesley.

Peláez, K. M. L., Cuello, M. A. J., Díaz, V. C. B., & Armijos, M. R. R. (2024). Estrategias innovadoras para el manejo sostenible de los laboratorios clínicos. *Journal of Science and Research*, *9*(2), 173–203.

Pinto, F. A., Brandão, A. A., & Siqueira, F. L. (2022). *Design Thinking and Non-Functional Requirements Elicitation*: A Survey. Workshop em Engenharia de Requisitos. *PRINCE2 Methodology. (n.d.)*. Retrieved January 21, 2025, from https://www.prince2.com/uk/prince2-methodology

Potineni, S., Bansal, S. K., & Amresh, A. (2013). ScrumTutor: A web-based interactive tutorial for Scrum Software development. *2013 International Conference on Advances in Computing, Communications and Informatics (ICACCI)*, 1884–1890. DOI: 10.1109/ICACCI.2013.6637469

Ralph, P., & Wand, Y. (2016). A proposal for a formal definition of the design concept. *Design Science*, *2*(4), 1–22. DOI: 10.1017/dsj.2016.2

Ray, B., Posnett, D., Filkov, V., & Devanbu, P. (2020). Large-Scale Study of Technical Debt in Open Source Software Projects. *IEEE Transactions on Software Engineering*, *45*(10), 965–982.

Razzouk, R., & Shute, V. (2012). What Is Design Thinking and Why Is It Important? *Review of Educational Research*, *82*(3), 330–348. DOI: 10.3102/0034654312457429

Red Hat. (2018, February). Intelligent process automation and the emergence of digital automation platforms. https://www.redhat.com/rhdc/managed-files/mi-451-research-intelligent-process-automation-analyst-paper-f11434-201802.pdf

Rivera, J. (2024, July 31). *How Design Thinking Transformed Airbnb from a Failing Startup to a Billion-Dollar Business*. Retrieved from https://review.firstround.com/how-design-thinking-transformed-airbnb-from-failing-startup-to-billion-dollar-business

Roberts, M. (2024). *Understanding legal design: A key transformation for the legal industry.* Korum Legal. https://www.korumlegal.com/blog/legal-design-im-convinced-thoughts-from-a-non-lawyer...-working-in-newlaw

Rodriguez, A., Gardey, J., Grigera, J., Rossi, G., & Garrido, A. (2022). UX debt in an agile development process: Evidence and characterization. *Research Square*. DOI: 10.21203/rs.3.rs-2190539/v1

Rodriguez, G., Soria, Á., & Campo, M. (2015). Virtual Scrum: A teaching aid to introduce undergraduate software engineering students to scrum. *Computer Applications in Engineering Education*, *23*(1), 147–156. DOI: 10.1002/cae.21588

Rokis, K., & Kirikova, M. (2023). Exploring low-code development: A comprehensive literature review. *Complex Systems Informatics and Modeling Quarterly*, *36*(36), 68–86. DOI: 10.7250/csimq.2023-36.04

Romero Viecco, I. (2022). *Legal design as a tool for developing solutions to make the law more efficient. Ámbito Jurídico*. Retrieved from https://www.ambitojuridico.com/noticias/en-ejercicio/el-legal-design-permite-construir-soluciones-para-hacer-el-derecho-mas

Scaled Agile, Inc. (2023, May 4). SAFe Lean-Agile principles. https://scaledagileframework.com/safe-lean-agile-principles/

Schroeder, A., Klarl, A., Mayer, P., & Kroiß, C. (2012). Teaching agile software development through lab courses. *Proceedings of the 2012 IEEE Global Engineering Education Conference (EDUCON)*, 1–10. DOI: 10.1109/EDUCON.2012.6201194

Schwaber, K., & Sutherland, J. (2020, November). *The Scrum Guide-The Definitive Guide to Scrum: The Rules of the Game*. Scrum.org.

Seufert, S. (2024). Impact of IT investments on a company: Towards an approach for managing the IT business value (Doctoral dissertation, Duisburg, Essen, Universität Duisburg-Essen, 2024).

Sherman, R. (2015). *Business intelligence guidebook*. Morgan Kaufmann.

Sibona, C., Pourreza, S., & Hill, S. (2018). Origami: An Active Learning Exercise for Scrum Project Management. *Journal of Information Systems Education*, *29*(2), 105–116.

Simon, H. A. (1996). *The sciences of the artificial*. MIT Press.

Sithipolvanichgul, J., Dhir, A., Talwar, S., Srivastava, P., & Kaur, P. (2024). Knowledge arbitrage: What are the risks, and do they matter? *Journal of Knowledge Management*, *28*(10), 2818–2842. DOI: 10.1108/JKM-05-2023-0411

Soegaard, M. (2024, November 29). What does a UX strategist do? Interaction Design Foundation. https://www.interaction-design.org/literature/article/what-does-a-ux-strategist-do

Solinski, A., & Petersen, K. (2016). Prioritizing agile benefits and limitations in relation to practice usage. *Software Quality Journal*, *24*(2), 447–482. DOI: 10.1007/s11219-014-9253-3

Spencer, J. R., Toshniwal, S., & Weiss, A. M. (2022). Human-centered design in software engineering: Methods and case studies. *IEEE Transactions on Software Engineering*, *48*(4), 1080–1094. DOI: 10.1109/TSE.2021.3112345

Sreenivasan, A., & Suresh, M. (2024). Design thinking and artificial intelligence: A systematic literature review exploring synergies. International Journal of Innovation Studies.

Srivastava, A., Bhardwaj, S., & Saraswat, S. (2017). SCRUM model for agile methodology. *2017 International Conference on Computing, Communication and Automation (ICCCA)*, 864–869. DOI: 10.1109/CCAA.2017.8229928

Stanford d.school. (n.d.). *An introduction to design thinking process guide*. Hasso Plattner Institute of Design at Stanford.

Stanford d.school. (n.d.). *What is Design Thinking?* Retrieved from https://dschool.stanford.edu/executive-education-resource-collections/keep-learning1

Stanford University Hasso Plattner Institute of Design. (2010, January 1). An introduction to design thinking: Process guide. https://web.stanford.edu/~mshanks/MichaelShanks/files/509554.pdf

Statista. (2024, November 26). Number of software developers worldwide in 2018 to 2024. https://www.statista.com/statistics/627312/worldwide-developer-population/

Statista. (2024, November 4). Number of internet and social media users worldwide as of October 2024. https://www.statista.com/statistics/617136/digital-population-worldwide/

Stickdorn, M., Hormess, M. E., Lawrence, A., & Schneider, J. (2018). *This Is Service Design Doing*. O'Reilly Media, Inc.

Stickdorn, M., & Schneider, J. (2011). *This is Service Design Thinking: Basics, Tools, Cases*. Wiley.

Suresh Babu, C. V., & Adhithya, S. (2023). ChatGPT and Other Generative AI Tools in Education: Transformative Potential and Ethical Considerations. In Keengwe, J. (Ed.), *Creative AI Tools and Ethical Implications in Teaching and Learning* (pp. 135–152). IGI Global., DOI: 10.4018/979-8-3693-0205-7.ch007

Sweeney, K. (2019). How Uber Uses Design Thinking to Keep Drivers and Riders Happy. *Forbes*.

Tang, M. C., Huang, C. H., & Chiang, F. H. (2022). Examining the development trajectory of IT outsourcing: A main path analysis. In *PACIS* (p. 76).

Tariq, M. U. (2024). Leveraging AI for Entrepreneurial Innovation in Healthcare. In Özsungur, F. (Ed.), *Generating Entrepreneurial Ideas With AI* (pp. 192–216). IGI Global., DOI: 10.4018/979-8-3693-3498-0.ch009

Tariq, M. U. (2024). Navigating the Personalization Pathway: Implementing Adaptive Learning Technologies in Higher Education. In Minh Tung, T. (Ed.), *Adaptive Learning Technologies for Higher Education* (pp. 265–291). IGI Global., DOI: 10.4018/979-8-3693-3641-0.ch012

Tariq, M. U. (2024). Streamlining Operations Insights and Innovations From the Gulf Cooperation Council (GCC). In Ayed, T., Ali, I., Abdelhamid, H., & Mohamed, A. (Eds.), *Utilizing Case Studies in Business Education* (pp. 188–216). IGI Global., DOI: 10.4018/979-8-3693-3779-0.ch010

Tariq, M. U. (2025). Breaking Boundaries: Computational Thinking in Educational Policy Leadership Management. In Agboola, B., & Thompson, C. (Eds.), *Navigating Leadership and Policy Management in Education* (pp. 77–102). IGI Global., DOI: 10.4018/979-8-3693-9215-7.ch003

Tariq, M. U. (2025). Empowering Learning Through Networked and Connected Education: Case Studies in Digital Engagement. In Gierhart, A. (Ed.), *Cases on Enhancing P-16 Student Engagement With Digital Technologies* (pp. 169–198). IGI Global Scientific Publishing., DOI: 10.4018/979-8-3693-5633-3.ch007

Tariq, M. U. (2025). Strategic Integration of Technological Advances in Modern Business Practices. In Sedky, A. (Ed.), *Building Business Knowledge for Complex Modern Business Environments* (pp. 95–120). IGI Global., DOI: 10.4018/979-8-3693-6447-5.ch004

Teo, Y. S., & Newhook, J. (2024, October 4). UX roles: The ultimate guide – Who does what and which one you should go for? Interaction Design Foundation. https://www.interaction-design.org/literature/article/ux-roles-ultimate-guide

Tetteh, S. G. (2024). Empirical Study of Agile Software Development Methodologies: A Comparative Analysis. *Asian Journal of Research in Computer Science*, *17*(5), 30–42. DOI: 10.9734/ajrcos/2024/v17i5436

Topping, K. (2003). Self and Peer Assessment in School and University: Reliability, Validity and Utility. In Segers, M., Dochy, F., & Cascallar, E. (Eds.), *Optimising New Modes of Assessment: In Search of Qualities and Standards* (pp. 55–87). Springer Netherlands. DOI: 10.1007/0-306-48125-1_4

Torka, S., & Albayrak, S. (2024). Optimizing AI-Assisted Code Generation. https://doi.org//arXiv.2412.10953DOI: 10.48550

Torres, J. F. (2020). *'Legal design' 2.0 (legal design) as a new academic discipline in law. Ámbito Jurídico*. Retrieved from https://www.ambitojuridico.com/noticias/columnista-impreso/tic/legal-design-20-diseno-legal-como-una-nueva-disciplina-academica

Trocin, C., Stige, Å., & Mikalef, P. (2023). *Machine Learning (ML) diffusion in the design process: A study of Norwegian design consultancies. Technological Forecasting and Social Change,* 194. *Technological Forecasting and Social Change*, *122724*, 122724. Advance online publication. DOI: 10.1016/j.techfore.2023.122724

Tufano, M., Watson, C., Pantiuchina, J., & Bavota, G. (2019). Empirical Study on the Use of Automated Refactoring Tools in Open Source Projects. *Proceedings of the ACM Joint European Software Engineering Conference and Symposium*, 612-623.

Ulrich, K. T., & Eppinger, S. D. (2015). *Product Design and Development* (5th ed.). McGraw-Hill Education.

Villarrubia, C., Vara, J. M., Granada, D., Gómez-Macías, C., & Pérez-Blanco, F. J. (2024). DesignScrum–An agility educational resource powered by creativity. *Software, Practice & Experience, 54*(6), 985–1009. DOI: 10.1002/spe.3308

Virnandes, S. R., Shen, J., & Vlahu-Gjorgievska, E. (2024). Shaping trust in public service: A convergent mixed-methods investigation of digital government transformation.

Von Wangenheim, C. G., Savi, R., & Borgatto, A. F. (2013). SCRUMIA—An educational game for teaching SCRUM in computing courses. *Journal of Systems and Software, 86*(10), 2675–2687. DOI: 10.1016/j.jss.2013.05.030

Wang, Y., Shi, J., & Qu, G. (2024). Research on collaborative innovation cooperation strategies of manufacturing digital ecosystem from the perspective of multiple stakeholders. *Computers & Industrial Engineering, 190*, 110003. DOI: 10.1016/j.cie.2024.110003

Weiss, T. R. (Sep 30, 2024). Exploring Docker for DevOps: What It Is and How It Works. Retrieved January 21, 2025, from https://www.docker.com/blog/docker-for-devops/

Werbach, K., & Hunter, D. (2012). *For the Win: How Game Thinking Can Revolutionize Your Business*. Wharton School Press.

Wohlin, C., Höst, M., & Henningsson, K. (2003). Empirical Research Methods in Software Engineering. In Conradi, R., & Wang, A. I. (Eds.), Lecture Notes in Computer Science: Vol. 2765. *Empirical Methods and Studies in Software Engineering* (pp. 7–23). Springer. DOI: 10.1007/978-3-540-45143-3_2

Wohlin, C., Runeson, P., Höst, M., Ohlsson, M. C., Regnell, B., & Wesslén, A. (2012). *Experimentation in software engineering* (Vol. 236). Springer. DOI: 10.1007/978-3-642-29044-2

World Wide Web Consortium. (W3C). (2018). *Web content accessibility guidelines (WCAG) 2.1*. Retrieved from https://www.w3.org/TR/WCAG21/

Yang, Z., Chang, J., Huang, L., & Mardani, A. (2023). Digital transformation solutions of entrepreneurial SMEs based on an information error-driven T-spherical fuzzy cloud algorithm. *International Journal of Information Management, 69*, 102384. DOI: 10.1016/j.ijinfomgt.2021.102384

Yawised, K., Apasrawirote, D., & Boonparn, C. (2022). From traditional business shifted towards transformation: The emerging business opportunities and challenges in the 'Metaverse' era. *Incbaa*, *162*, 175.

Zarsky, T. (2017). Incompatible: The GDPR in the age of big data. *Seton Hall Law Review*, *47*(4), 2. https://ssrn.com/abstract=3022646

Zimmerman, J., Stolterman, E., & Forlizzi, J. (2010). An analysis and critique of Research through Design: Towards a formalization of a research approach. In *Proceedings of the 8th ACM Conference on Designing Interactive Systems (DIS)* (pp. 310–319). ACM. DOI: 10.1145/1858171.1858228

About the Contributors

José Alfonso Aguilar-Calderón received his B.S. degree in Computer Systems Engineering and M.Sc. degree in Applied Informatics from the Universidad Autónoma de Sinaloa, Mexico, in 2005 and 2007, respectively. He earned his Ph.D. in Applications of Informatics from the Universidad de Alicante, Spain, in 2011. From 2006 to 2007, Dr. Aguilar-Calderón worked as a software developer at Empresaria and DpSoft. Subsequently, he joined the Computer Systems Department at Coppel S.A. de C.V., where he served in the Quality Assurance division from 2007 to 2009. More recently, he held the position of Project Manager at ARA Consultancy between 2018 and 2020. He is currently a full-time Research Professor and the Coordinator of the Master's Program in Computer Science at the Facultad de Informática Mazatlán, Universidad Autónoma de Sinaloa, in Mazatlán, Mexico. He also holds a professional certificate in Design Thinking. Dr. Aguilar-Calderón's research interests include Software Engineering, Web Engineering, Model-Driven Web Engineering, Smart Cities, Design Thinking. He has received the Best Demo and Poster Award at the 12th International Conference on Web Engineering (ICWE 2012) and the Best Paper Award at the 6th IEEE International Conference on Adaptive Science & Technology (ICAST 2014). He is a Level 1 member of the Mexican National System of Researchers (Sistema Nacional de Investigadores e Investigadoras – SNII, Secretaría de Ciencia, Humanidades, Tecnología e Innovación - SECIHTI). He is also a member of the IEEE Computer Society, the Association for Computing Machinery Special Interest Group on Software Engineering (ACM SIGSOFT), the Mexican Software Engineering Network (Red Mexicana de Ingeniería de Software – REDMIS), and the Mexican Academy of Computing (Academia Mexicana de Computación – AMEXCOMP).

Carolina Tripp-Barba received her undergraduate degree from the Facultad de Informática Mazatlán at the Universidad Autónoma de Sinaloa, Mexico, in 2006. She earned both her M.Sc. and Ph.D. degrees in Computer Science from the

Universitat Politècnica de Catalunya (UPC), Barcelona, Spain, in 2009 and 2013, respectively. She is currently a full-time Research Professor at the Facultad de Informática Mazatlán, Universidad Autónoma de Sinaloa. Her primary research interests include vehicular ad hoc networks (VANETs), the design and optimization of routing protocols, smart cities, and software engineering. Dr. Tripp-Barba is a Level 2 member of the Mexican National System of Researchers (Sistema Nacional de Investigadores e Investigadoras – SNII), under the Secretaría de Ciencia, Humanidades, Tecnología e Innovación (SECIHTI). She is also a professional member of the Association for Computing Machinery (ACM) and a member of the Mexican Academy of Computing (Academia Mexicana de Computación – AMEXCOMP).

***

SarmaA.D.N. is a leading IT Technology Consulting with over 20 years of experience in the IT industry. He received his M.Sc., M.S., and Ph.D degrees. With over 20 years of experience in the IT industry with research experience. His interesting research areas are AI, Business Intelligence, ML, Software Engineering, Data Mining and IT Operations.

Pablo Alfonso Aguilar-Calderón holds a Bachelor's degree in Law from the Facultad de Derecho Mazatlán at Universidad Autónoma de Sinaloa (Mazatlán, Mexico). He earned his Master's degree in Law in 2014 from the Graduate Studies Division of the Facultad de Derecho at the Universidad Nacional Autónoma de México (UNAM), and in 2017, he received a PhD in Law with Honorable Mention from the same institution. Since 2017, he has served as a research-professor at Facultad de Derecho Mazatlán at Universidad Autónoma de Sinaloa (Mazatlán, Mexico). His research areas focus on family law, procedural family law, technology legislation, and their interdisciplinary relationship. He is a core academic member of the Graduate Program in Law Sciences at Universidad Autónoma de Sinaloa (Mazatlán, Mexico), recognized by the Secretaría de Ciencia, Humanidades, Tecnología e Innovación (SECIHTI), and a member of the emerging research group "Law, Technology, and Innovation" (UAS-CA-320). He also serves on the Board of Doctors in Law at the Faculty of Law at UNAM. Among other recognitions, he is a Lead Science Communicator of the State Network of Science and Technology Communicators in Sinaloa. Member of the National System of Researchers Level 1 from SECIHTI, México.

David Granada, is an associate professor at the Universidad Rey Juan Carlos of Madrid, Spain, where he obtained his PhD on Computer Science. His research interests are focused on Model-Driven Engineering and Project Management. Contact him at david.granada@urjc.es.

Subhadip kowar is pursuing a PhD from UEM in Kolkata. He earned his MCA from Brainware University West Bengal, India, in 2023 and his BCA from Burdwan University, India, in 2021. He currently works as a Technical Assistant in the Department of Computer Science and Engineering (CSE CS & DS) at Brainware University in India. He has around 1.5 years of teaching experience. His research interests include Generative AI, machine learning for recommendation systems.

Dominik Salayandia Morales-Silva holds a Law Degree from the Facultad de Derecho Mazatlán at Universidad Autónoma de Sinaloa (Mazatlán, Mexico). She has completed her master's studies in Gender, Law, and Criminal Procedure at the Center for Postgraduate Studies of Mexico. Currently, she serves as a professor at the Facultad de Derecho Mazatlán at the Universidad Autónoma de Sinaloa. Her main research areas include gender, law, technology, and their interdisciplinary connections.

Oscar Manuel Peña-Bañuelos received the degree from the Facultad de Informática Mazatlán, Universidad Autónoma de Sinaloa, Mexico, in 2010, and the M.Sc. degree from Universidad DaVinci, México City, México, in 2016 and he is a PhD Candidate from the Centro de Estudios Superiores del Sur de Sinaloa, Mazatlán, México. He is a full-time Research Professor at the Facultad de Informática Mazatlán, Universidad Autónoma de Sinaloa (Mexico). His research interests include Artificial Intelligence in Graphic Design and Network Security. He is a member of the Research Group of the Latin American Society of Science and Technology (SOLACYT) and collaborator of the Center for Research in Mathematics, A.C. (CIMAT) Zacatecas Unit, Mexico.

Mala Rajasekhar is an aspiring technology professional currently pursuing a Bachelor of Technology in Information Technology at Hindustan Institute of Technology and Science (HITS), Chennai. With a strong academic foundation and a CGPA of 9.02, she has demonstrated a consistent commitment to excellence in both theoretical learning and practical applications. Driven by curiosity and innovation, Mala has worked on a diverse range of projects including smart automation systems, full-stack web applications, and data-driven solutions. Her notable projects include a Smart Dustbin using Arduino, a Lossless Image Compressor web application, and a voice-controlled assistant built with Python. She has gained hands-on industry experience through multiple certified internships in Data Analytics, Python with DSA, and Machine Learning via Internshala, where she applied her skills to solve real-world problems. Mala's technical expertise spans across programming languages like Python, C, and JavaScript, as well as tools such as MySQL, PHP, and Arduino IDE. In addition to her technical pursuits, Mala is a Cadet Captain in the NCC Naval Wing, where she has demonstrated exceptional leadership by guiding junior cadets and participating in prestigious national-level camps such as the Naval Technical Attachment and Sea Attachment Camps. She also holds both NCC 'B' and 'C' certificates, highlighting her discipline, commitment, and national service. With a goal to become a leading software developer and embedded systems engineer, Mala continuously pushes herself to learn, build, and lead. Her blend of technical skills, leadership qualities, and a proactive mindset make her a promising talent in the field of Information Technology.

Maaike Stoops is the Head of the Research and Development Department in LINKIT B.V. She is a strategic innovation leader focused on helping organizations navigate an unpredictable world by fostering relevance and adaptability. With a strong academic foundation from Delft University of Technology—including a Master's in Strategic Product Design (2012–2015), a Bachelor's in Industrial Design Engineering (2008–2011), and a Minor in Software Development (2010–2011)—she combines design thinking, technical acumen, and future-oriented strategy. With experience leading, software, customer experience and solution advisor teams in an IT context since 2016, Maaike drives forward-thinking transformation through vision-setting, trend research, and ecosystem analysis. She spearheads hands-on experimentation in the Innovation Lab, applying agile methodologies to anticipate future challenges and opportunities for clients, colleagues, and partners. Her work bridges strategic foresight with practical execution, ensuring that innovation is not only visionary but also actionable—equipping organizations to thrive in rapidly evolving landscapes. Maaike's expertise lies in translating complexity into clarity, helping businesses stay ahead by embedding adaptability into their core strategies while maintaining a relentless focus on what matters most in the long term.

C.V. Suresh Babu is a pioneer in content development. A true entrepreneur, he founded Anniyappa Publications, a company that is highly active in publishing books related to Computer Science and Management. Dr. C.V. Suresh Babu has also ventured into SB Institute, a center for knowledge transfer. He holds a Ph.D. in Engineering Education from the National Institute of Technical Teachers Training & Research in Chennai, along with seven master's degrees in various disciplines such as Engineering, Computer Applications, Management, Commerce, Economics, Psychology, Law, and Education. Additionally, he has UGC-NET/SET qualifications in the fields of Computer Science, Management, Commerce, and Education. Currently, Dr. C.V. Suresh Babu is a Professor in the Department of Information

Technology at the School of Computing Science, Hindustan Institute of Technology and Science (Hindustan University) in Padur, Chennai, Tamil Nadu, India.

Muhammad Usman Tariq has more than 16+ year's experience in industry and academia. He has authored more than 200+ research articles, 110+ case studies, 115+ book chapters and several books other than 4 patents. He is founder and CEO of The Case HQ, a unique repository for courses, narrative and video case studies. He has been working as a consultant and trainer for industries representing six sigma, quality, health and safety, environmental systems, project management, and information security standards. His work has encompassed sectors in aviation, manufacturing, food, hospitality, education, finance, research, software and transportation. He has diverse and significant experience working with accreditation agencies of ABET, ACBSP, AACSB, WASC, CAA, EFQM and NCEAC. Additionally, Dr. Tariq has operational experience in incubators, research labs, government research projects, private sector startups, program creation and management at various industrial and academic levels. He is Certified Higher Education Teacher from Harvard University, USA, Certified Online Educator from HMBSU, Certified Six Sigma Master Black Belt and has been awarded PFHEA, SFSEDA, SMIEEE, and CMBE.

Juan Manuel Vara, is a full professor at the Universidad Rey Juan Carlos of Madrid. His current research interests are focused on Model-Driven Engineering, Information Management and Agile Software Engineering. Contact him at juanmanuel.vara@urjc.es.

Carlos Villarrubia, is an assistant professor at the Universidad Rey Juan Carlos of Madrid, Spain, where he obtained his PhD on Computer Science. His current research interests are focused on agile methods, creativity and gamification in software development. Contact him at carlos.villarrubia@urjc.es.

Aníbal Zaldívar-Colado received the degree from the Faculty of Informatics, University of Sinaloa, Mexico, in 2000, and the M.Sc. and Ph.D. degrees from the University of Durango (UAD), Mexico, in 2000 and 2011, respectively. He is a full-time professor (researcher) at Facultad de Informática Mazatlán, Universidad Autónoma de Sinaloa, Mexico. His research interests include applied mathematical modeling, systems simulation, and educational technology. He is a National System of Researcher's level 2 member in the Secretaría de Ciencia, Humanidades, Tecnología e Innovación (SECIHTI) Mexico.

Index

www.ingramcontent.com/pod-product-compliance
Lightning Source LLC
LaVergne TN
LVHW081327300926
849161LV00008B/1900
9798369395318